CW00739813

Scuba Confidential

AN INSIDER'S GUIDE TO BECOMING A
BETTER DIVER

SIMON PRIDMORE

Sandsmedia Publishing

BALI, INDONESIA

Sandsmedia Publishing, Bali, Indonesia 80363

www.scubaconfidential.com

Book Layout ©2013 Createspace.com and Sandsmedia

Cover Image by Andrey Bizyukin

Scuba Confidential/Simon Pridmore. 1st ed.

ISBN 978-1491049242

For my three mermaids
Kayleigh, Savannah and Caroline

The Expert View

"If PADI's Open-Water manual is the Bible of scuba diving, consider this the New Testament. Scuba Confidential is the closest thing there is to a scuba diving self-help book and a must-read for any diver, new or old." **David Espinosa, Editor in Chief, Sport Diver magazines**

"What a welcome book! I have been instructing SCUBA for several decades now and this will be an excellent addition to the training books currently used. This is written by a diver who is up to date with the equipment on the market and knows how to configure it for clean and trimmed out divers. I would encourage all our clients to purchase this new publication. Well done, Simon! " **Evelyn Bartram Dudas NAUI #8672**

"Instead of writing another training manual, Simon has utilised a very unique approach to sharing his many years of experience underwater with those that may be thinking of becoming a diver or are already enjoying the wonders of the underwater world. Through the use of case histories Simon provides a black-box approach to avoiding some of diving's pitfalls and in doing so, he gives some great tips and insights on subjects important to divers at all levels that may not be found in other publications." **Terry Cummins OMA**

"A compelling page-turner packed full of thoughtful – and thought-provoking – information, tips, analyses and insights gleaned from more than thirty years as a widely-respected diving industry professional, Simon Pridmore's, 'Scuba Confidential: An Insider's Guide To Becoming A Better Diver', is required reading for all divers, regardless of experience level, whose minds remain open to the book's underlying message

that, "Learning to dive is easy; becoming a good diver is hard."
Deserving of a place on every thinking-diver's bookshelf, 'Scuba
Confidential' is much more than just another, 'How-To' diving
manual; it's a resource that, for those who heed its message,
will pave the way for exciting and enjoyable diving adventures
and discoveries." **David Strike, OZTeK Organiser**

TABLE OF CONTENTS

ACKNOWLEDGMENTS

Thank you to everyone who has supported this project:

Andrey Bizyukin, Jan Brown, Gennady Misan, Olga Kamensky, Victor Lyagushkin, Marcel Hagendijk, Jill Heinerth, Matthew Young, Matt Reed, Bill Bynum, Tamara Thomsen, Tracy Grogan, Peter Van Scoik, Brooks Jacobs, Dan Burton, Alan Wright, Mike Palmer, Kevin Davidson, Mike Veitch, Amberlee Gurr, Nic Alvarado, Elechang, Tom Collier, Houston Underwater Photographic Association, Baikal Tek, Dive Damai, Dive! Tutukaka, critters@lembeh, Maluku Divers Ambon, Evolution Diving Philippines, Scubapro-Uwatec, VR Technology, Ambient Pressure Diving, Dive Rite, Jetsam Technologies, IANTD, Analox and Ocean Management Systems.

Also Alberto Reija, Ian Thomas, Jane Gray, Margo Regas, Jeremy Stein, Bernie Chowdhury, Lady Dianne Strong, Deep Dave and Sue Hendricks, Tim and Geneva Gernold, Kim Sander Smith, Charles Yengel, John De Roo, Fiona Woodhouse, Al Chalabi, KC Wong, Mike Waterfield, Tina Brain, Graham Warren, Imelda O'Loughlin, Chieh Peng, Reuben Cahn, Alice Chu, Micaela Krumholz & Melanie Paul for valuable input in the early days.

And especially:

Dr Simon Mitchell for assistance with "The Black Gases":

Michael Menduno for advice on "Tekking It to the Extreme" and "Rebreathers – Is There One in Your Future?"

Tom Mount for checking I had remembered my lines correctly.

Tim Rock for companionship and mentoring

Roger Woodiwiss, Bill King, Ken Pratt, Rob Cason, Tom Mount, Billy Deans, Paul Neilsen and Kevin Gurr for making me a better diver

Garry Bevan and David Espinosa for making me write in the first place and the late Penny Glover for my first review.

And most of all …………

My wife Sofie for her unwavering support and extraordinary patience

FOREWORD

I have known Simon for many years and have been privileged to have had several diving 'experiences' with him.

His wealth of knowledge as a diving educator and experienced diver is evident within the content of this book. We are lucky that people like Simon take the time and effort to consolidate their knowledge and experiences into such texts not only for those of us that are still new to the underwater world but for those that wish to expand their horizons further into the part of our planet that so few of us get to see and bond with.

I especially like the 'Becoming a better diver' summaries with each chapter, which are obviously the thrust of the book. A wise diver should collect these into one document and study and understand them fully.

As Simon notes, it is tough to become a better diver, but it is something we should all strive for. It is even tougher to then write meaningful and concise guidance for others to share so that they can safely and enjoyably continue to expand their underwater horizons.

Kevin Gurr

IANTD IT #6, Author of Technical Diving From the Bottom Up, co-designer of the VR3 dive computer and Sentinel CCR

PREFACE

Why Scuba Confidential?

Why did I decide the world needed another book on how to scuba dive? It was not a decision reached quickly. I have been writing for dive magazines for the last decade or so and, over the years, a number of readers and editors have suggested I collect the articles in a book some day. This is not the "Best Of" compilation they were asking for, although the genesis for some of the chapters of Scuba Confidential does lie in those magazine pieces.

I have noticed over the years that as divers we all have a number of things in common. We make mistakes, are often plagued by insecurity, know we occasionally stray outside our comfort zone in the water and give thanks every time we get away with it. We are always eager to improve our knowledge. Many of us are aware of deficiencies in our skills and technique but are at a loss as to how to overcome these. A frequently asked question is, "where do you go to become a better diver if you have done the basic courses, logged a couple of hundred dives and do not want to take the faux-professional route to scuba slavery?"

I decided therefore to write a book offering an insight into the knowledge that top professionals in the world of scuba diving acquire from years of experience and that extreme technical divers learn through intensive training: knowledge that readers could use to develop their skills and become safer, more confident and more capable divers. The aim was to advise, educate and provoke thought, reinforcing essential truths about diving but also challenging common assumptions, presenting ideas in a readable and entertaining way, without preaching or adopting too didactic an approach; just plenty of common sense and straight talk.

A glance at the Table of Contents will give you a good idea of the range of topics on offer. For example, the top trends in scuba diving, liveaboards, rebreathers and muck, are covered in detail, as well as hotly debated issues such as etiquette, configuration, solo diving, decompression and accident analysis.

Why believe me?

How do I know what I am talking about? Scuba Confidential represents some of what I have learned from thirty years of diving and twenty years of teaching and writing about the sport. I have worked as a dive guide, divemaster, instructor, instructor trainer and instructor trainer-trainer, owned a dive centre, run a regional diver training agency, worked as international sales manager for a computer and rebreather manufacturer, organised dive tours all over the world and spoken at conferences on four continents. Being by nature an "early adopter" I have been fortunate to be involved at the cutting edge of the sport for a long time and am currently lucky enough to live in Indonesia where the present generation is the first to dive for fun. The enthusiasm for this "new" sport here is refreshing and inspirational.

Caveats

This is not a messianic pronouncement. The message of Scuba Confidential is not, "Dive Like Me!" All of us are different; we have different attitudes, needs, goals and intellectual and physical capabilities. How you choose to dive is for you to decide, based on as much research and advice as you can get. Scuba Confidential is designed to provide you with a short cut to that decision.

Some may criticize me for not covering basic information in the book, and it is true, I do assume that readers possess at least one diver certification card and have logged more than a few dives. In those chapters where I go back to the basics, I do so because I believe that insufficient emphasis is placed on the importance of these topics in early diver training. The concept of managing stress and cylinders and valves are cases in point.

Others may also accuse me of not covering subjects in adequate detail and, again, I plead guilty as charged. This is often deliberate. For instance, the Cave Diving and Ice Diving chapters do not teach you how to dive in caves or under ice. Reading this book is not a substitute for getting expert tuition and spending time in the water. However, the training chapters do endeavour to vicariously share with the reader some of the magic of the experience, so that he or she can decide whether a certain type of diving is something they think they would be interested in or thrilled by.

Some chapters, for example Solo Diving, deal with the more contentious and complex questions that face divers and, although I do attempt to be even-handed, I have often been unable to prevent my personal opinions from shining through and they will not be universally shared. Too bad: this is my book!

Learning to dive is easy; becoming a good diver is hard. It requires dedicated application. You may find on reading Scuba Confidential that you need to make changes to long-established habits, but you will find that even apparently minor things can make a world of difference to your comfort and confidence in the water. It is a good idea to opt for evolution rather than revolution and make changes or adopt new techniques one by one, as a step-by-step process is much easier to manage.

My main hopes are that you enjoy reading Scuba Confidential, that it causes you to review and reflect on how you dive, that it helps you progress, that you find it a useful reference to return to time and again and that you find that it does indeed succeed in making you a better diver!

Simon

August 2013

Safety

1. Mental Preparation for Scuba Diving

B ecoming a successful scuba diver is not just a matter of developing skills and getting the right equipment; it is vital that you also learn how to stay in control of what goes on in your head when you are underwater. Athletes call this 'mental conditioning' and it is an important factor that determines a competitor's level of performance in any sport. Scuba diving is no exception.

The skills we learn through diver training are designed to make sure that we know how to deal with anything that can happen to us underwater but to cope properly with any given situation simply being armed with the knowledge of what to do is not enough. You also need a clear head and a positive outlook to ensure that you function effectively and make the correct decisions. Your mental conditioning has a considerable effect on how much enjoyment you will derive from diving, directs how you will perform in an emergency and, perhaps most importantly, will help you to manage stress.

We all recognise that stress is a bad thing! Most of us have adopted mental conditioning strategies to avoid or reduce stress in our working and social lives but conventional scuba diver training does not really teach divers how to avoid or reduce stress underwater.

In chapters two and three I discuss how to identify and handle stress when it occurs and what to do when equipment problems strike. However, the primary aim must always be to do everything you can to try to prevent stress arising in the first place: to ensure that you are mentally prepared for the underwater world and always in the right state of mind to deal calmly with anything that happens. Here are a few tips and techniques to help you.

Focus on Your Skills

Your self-rescue skills need to be learned to the point where they can be performed automatically, so that when an emergency strikes you do not have to think about what to do, you just do it, instinctively. You can practice the skills on every dive you do. For example, it takes only a second or two as you are swimming along to switch from your primary regulator to your octopus and back again. Now and again, you can reach behind your neck to locate your cylinder valve so you know where to find it if you ever find yourself descending with your air switched off. When you are on your safety stops, practice sending up your surface marker buoy.

Build Water Confidence

Get as comfortable as you can in the water, not just by doing more diving, although that is always a good idea. Go snorkelling, do some free-diving, swim more often, spend more time at the beach or the pool!

Get Fit

You need to be both mentally and physically fit for diving. The better your fitness, the better you will deal with the rigors of swimming against a current or making a difficult shore exit in full-gear, things that could easily bring on high levels of stress.

Get Comfortable

You are more likely to panic on a dive if you are cold and uncomfortable. Think about your thermal protection, wear the right suit for the environment you are diving in and replace your wetsuit regularly. Frequent exposure to pressure crushes neoprene, reducing its efficiency, so resist the temptation to hang on to your old wetsuit until it gets thin, worn and loose. A new suit does not only make you look better, it keeps you warmer.

Don't Dive Drunk

Other factors that can predispose you to panic are fatigue and alcohol so, if last night went on a little later and was a little heavier than planned, sleep through the first dive of the day, get a little more rest and drink plenty of water when you eventually get up.

Learn to Breathe

Correct breathing can prevent the onset of stress and help you keep a clear head if a potentially stressful incident arises. Get in the habit of exhaling fully with each breath, contracting your stomach. Then take a long, slow deep breath in, pushing your stomach out to allow your lungs to expand as much as possible. Ideally, each breath in and out should last 7 seconds or so, giving you a 15 second breathing cycle and four breaths a minute. This is the perfect way for a scuba diver to breathe. It allows you to expel from your lungs as much tension-inducing carbon dioxide as possible and will even reduce your air consumption.

Visualize

Before a scuba dive, do as the technical divers do. Sit in a quiet place, (difficult sometimes aboard a busy dive boat, I know), and think about the dive ahead. Reflect on the dive master's briefing; review what you have researched about the site or what you remember from previous dives there. Think positive thoughts, think about what you are going to see and visualize a successful dive. Picture yourself early on in the descent, in control, checking all your gear is in place, relaxing your breathing rate maintaining good buoyancy, and staying in touch with your dive team. Then reflect on the dive itself, what you will be looking for and what you might find. Visualize yourself feeling comfortable and in control, checking your computer and high-pressure gauge frequently and regularly, then making a slow, safe and controlled ascent with a safety stop, finally establishing buoyancy on the surface and ending the dive with plenty of air.

Eliminate Apprehension

Visualization before a dive will usually remove any apprehension that you might have been sensing. Apprehension is best defined as a feeling of uncertainty about your ability to cope with a situation and the principal danger of embarking on a dive when you are in such a state of mind is that just a minor problem can turn the apprehension into full-blown panic.

By visualizing the dive you can build self-confidence and put yourself in a relaxed, positive, forward-looking frame of mind, the exact sort of attitude that you should have before any endeavour.

Follow Premonitions

There may be occasions when, no matter how well you visualize the dive, you just cannot shake off the feeling that something bad is going to happen. If you ever do feel this sort of premonition, don't ignore it. Cancel the dive and "sit one out" or change the plan.

Conduct an In Water Check

We all learn the pre-dive safety check during our beginners' course and this soon becomes something we do quickly and instinctively without realising we are doing it. Another very good habit to acquire is carrying out an in-water check at the start of your dive. The whole process of gearing up on a busy boat, entering the water and descending can be rushed and stressful and it can undo all the positive effects of your pre-dive visualization. So once you have left the surface and are a couple of metres under water, surrounded by the peace and quiet of the ocean, go through a quick in-water check. Take a few seconds to compose yourself, relax, get a long, slow, deep breathing cycle going, make sure all your equipment is intact, buckles are fastened, nothing is leaking and gauges are working then set off calmly for the depths.

Become a Better Diver by

Including mental preparation techniques in your dive routine

2. Detecting and Dealing with Stress

Stress is a potential risk on almost every dive we make. Some of the more obvious examples are time-pressure stress from having a limited air supply, task-loading stress from needing to do a number of things simultaneously and compound stress, which is what happens when a number of stressful factors coincide.

In scuba diving, stress is particularly unwelcome as, if it is not controlled, it can very quickly lead to panic and when we panic our untrained responses usually make the situation worse rather than better. Panic is always life threatening when it occurs under water and is the most common contributing factor to diving fatalities.

A classic example is the nervous diver who is worried that his regulator will not give him enough air. He gulps greedily when inhaling but only partially exhales before trying to take the next breath. Eventually, he finds it impossible to breathe in because his lungs are still full but, instead of breathing out, he concludes that his regulator has failed, tears it out of his mouth and bolts for the surface, holding his breath.

To deal with stress you must first recognize that it is present and to do this you need to be both aware of the signs and in tune with what your mind and body are doing.

Indicators of stress include clumsiness, delayed response, disorientation, fixation on gauges, an increased breathing rate, irritability, tension, unease, and unusual anxiety or apprehension. Be conscious of your mood and remain objective so that you interpret it correctly. For example, if you begin to find something your buddy is doing intensely annoying, it is far more likely that you, rather than your buddy, are the one with the problem.

Once you have identified that stress is present, your intuition will tell you that there must be a logical reason for it. That is to say, because you feel worried, you must therefore have something valid to worry about. This is, of course, not always the case. An increased breathing rate accompanied by a feeling of unease or apprehension can simply be a result of a build up of carbon dioxide in the bloodstream following a hard swim against a current.

The secret to coping with the onset of stress underwater is to clear your mind, analyse the situation and then act according to your training.

To clear your mind, stop all activity; grab a rock, (making sure first that it IS a rock,) and rest. Exhale slowly and completely, compressing your diaphragm to expel as much CO_2 laden air from your lungs as possible then inhale fully expanding your diaphragm. Do this a few times.

As your brain clears you will be able to work out what is going on. Do you have any valid reason to be worried? Is there any urgent need for action? Look at your pressure gauge and make sure you have plenty to breathe. Check your decompression status or no-decompression time remaining. Run a quick check over your dive gear to make sure everything is in place and working.

Then act. If you have plenty to breathe, are comfortable with what your computer is reading and all your equipment is functioning correctly then you may just choose to continue your dive, reducing your effort so the panic does not return.

If you are low on breathing gas and/or have exceeded your planned decompression status then your priority will be to make a controlled ascent to a shallower depth.

It is always wise to take a moment to gather your thoughts before you act to make sure that you are about to do the right thing. However, taking too long over this process when you are deep underwater can exacerbate your predicament due to the limits of your air supply. Therefore your thinking time is equally limited.

This is the main reason why it is important to practice emergency and self-rescue skills intensively to the point where your response to an emergency will be automatic, instinctive and appropriate.

Technical divers constantly practice gas sharing and switching between their primary and secondary regulators. Their responses are so conditioned that if a real-world emergency takes place and an out-of-air diver grabs the regulator they are breathing from, they will automatically switch to their back up regulator before they are intellectually conscious of what has happened. The emergency is over almost before it has begun.

Anticipation

The most effective way of dealing with stress is to anticipate it or spot it in the early stages so you can act decisively and nip it in the bud before it escalates into panic. Therefore you need to be constantly alert.

Professionals are not only required to monitor their own status but also learn how to identify the signs in others. This skill is sometimes acquired through bitter experience. At least once in our careers most of us have experienced that heart-stopping moment when a diver in our charge suddenly bolts for the surface. Yes, it is true that certified divers are ultimately responsible for their own safety whether a divemaster is present or not but nevertheless, we mentally kick ourselves for not having seen that the diver had a problem until it was too late.

In the following two case histories, the divers concerned recognized that they were suffering from stress but did not fully appreciate the potential consequences. Fortunately, both events took place in a training scenario so an instructor was there to over-ride their instincts and anticipate the threat on their behalf.

Case History #1 Anxious Andrew

"I was one of three students on a deep diving course. We had spent a long time discussing the dive plan and were all looking forward to it. We descended quickly down the reef wall but when we arrived at depth I felt uneasy. I was breathing more quickly than normal and I became anxious and disorientated. My instinct was to abort the dive but I didn't want to let down my instructor or the other guys in the class who had spent so much time preparing so I decided to tough it out and when the instructor signalled OK? I just responded OK. However, instead of moving on, he looked at me for few seconds with a quizzical expression in his eyes then collected us all together and signalled up with his thumb. "

"I felt an immense sense of relief but when we arrived back in the shallows at the top of the wall, my mind cleared, my

anxiety disappeared and I felt terribly guilty at having spoiled the dive. So I signalled to the instructor that I was happy to go back down again but he shook his head and we spent time in the shallows instead running through skills. The deep dive was rescheduled for the next day and everything went fine."

It is possible that had the group remained at depth on the original deep dive, the affected diver's mind would have cleared after a few minutes and the dive would have gone smoothly. However, once the instructor noticed that one of his students might be on the verge of panic, he assessed that, given the relative inexperience of the group, there was a high risk that keeping them at depth would cause the situation to escalate rapidly. His prompt action defused the situation immediately, ensured there was no escalation and completely eliminated the possibility of a host of adverse scenarios. The diver himself was aware that he was compromised and should abort the dive but decided to carry on and accept the additional risk in order not to disappoint the other members of the team. He was unaware that he was suffering from perceived peer-pressure stress as well as his other symptoms and this one additional factor could have led to disaster, had it not been for the instructor's intervention.

Case History #2: Bad News for Ruth

"I was at the dive centre with my buddy preparing our gear for the final dive in our TRIMIX course when one of the divemasters arrived with the news that a diver that we knew from another dive centre had died in the recompression chamber following an incident that had taken place the day before."

"On the boat, the news was playing on my mind but I told myself not to dwell on it as I had to concentrate on the forthcoming dive which would be our first to 90m (300ft.) On arrival at the dive site, we saw that a strong current was running and that it had carried the buoy, which was to be our ascent platform, underwater. I glanced at my buddy and he

looked concerned. It felt like everything was conspiring to prevent us doing this dive but it was the last day of our course and we would be flying out the following night so we were going to have to do the dive now, whatever the conditions."

"Our instructor came over as we were changing into our wetsuits and asked if we would mind postponing the dive to a future trip, given the circumstances. I almost cried as a strange combination of emotions flooded through me all at once, including grief for the diver who had died and also relief that we were not going to dive today. In the end, we rearranged our flights and enjoyed a perfect 90m (300ft) dive a couple of days later."

The instructor could not have known for sure how the news the students had received would work on their minds at depth. He did know, however, that the fact that they were undertaking a big dive would already be creating a certain level of anxiety, and that a strong current might lead to additional task-loading. Aborting the dive before they had even entered the water made absolutely sure that what seemed like a steadily cumulating series of stressors did not result in a tragedy. Even though the diver correctly identified a number of the indicators, the diver mistook the time stress created by their flight plans for the next day as a factor justifying additional risk. The diver would never consciously argue that a flight schedule is worth risking your life for but stress clouds the mind and leads to poor decision-making.

Breaking the Chain

In both these incidents, the instructor acted decisively to break the chain of events that might have been leading to disaster. Every accident has a chain of events that lead up to it but often the chain is only visible afterwards. You do not always see a chain before an accident takes place, but if you do see one or if you only think you see one, you need to have the courage to break it, even if this leads to your being criticised by others in your dive team.

Cave divers have a rule that eliminates peer pressure and fear of recrimination and saves lives. This rule is: -

"Any diver can abort any dive at any time for any reason without having to explain themselves to anyone."

When one of your team gives the up signal, (or turn signal in the case of cave diving,) the rest of the team acknowledges and complies immediately, no questions asked, either at the time or subsequently.

It does not matter if the threat to safety is genuine or not. For example, a diver may abort a dive simply as a result of misreading his pressure gauge. The important thing is that if one member of the team believes there is a threat, then that belief in itself is enough to put the team at risk if it continues.

Don't Let Your Baggage Get In The Way

A final point that goes back to the importance of mental preparation. Be aware that external factors can affect your concentration and add to your stress on a dive without you realising it. If your mind is occupied with problems elsewhere in your life such as money, girlfriends, boyfriends, family or work issues, these distractions can cloud your judgement in the event something goes wrong. So get into the habit of leaving worldly matters behind when you dip below the surface and immerse yourself In the peace of the ocean. Just go diving.

Become a Better Diver by

Knowing how to identify stress
Knowing how to manage stress when it appears

3. Trials and Tribulations

For the many dives we do which are uneventful, there is always the odd dive where something happens that reminds us of our vulnerability under water. We are terrestrial mammals, for goodness sake; we shouldn't even be there!

Contrary to what you may have been taught in your basic training, such events often involve the failure of a piece of equipment and many of us are guilty of not thinking too deeply about what to do if something goes wrong or how to prevent an incident occurring.

In this chapter I run through the things that you are most likely to encounter and discuss the precautions you can take and the drills you can practice to make sure that they remain annoying little problems and do not turn into major emergencies. Technical divers refer to this process as planning for the "What Ifs."

O-Ring Blowout

The regulator first stage to cylinder valve O-ring, which is found on the first stage of your regulator if you are using DIN, or on the valve itself if you are using an international yoke fitting, is a tiny but crucial link in the process of moving the air from the cylinder to your lungs. If this O-ring is missing or damaged a seal cannot be formed, the air will escape when the valve is opened and you will not be able to breathe properly from your regulator, if at all.

On land or on the boat, you know immediately when your O-ring is missing as there will be a loud high-pressure hiss when you open the cylinder valve. At which point you may go a little pink with embarrassment and make a mental note to check the O-ring before connecting your regulator next time.

Even if the O-ring is present it can be frayed or slightly torn, in which case it may pop suddenly and of course this will often happen at the most inconvenient time. As all instructors know, when you have a group of new students walking out through shallow water on a beach dive, there is an excellent chance that one of their cylinder valve O-rings will fail. This is why they will always keep a couple of spare O rings on their watchstrap or in their BCD.

You may choose to do the same so you have an O-ring easily to hand and so you don't have to ask for help at a time when everyone around you is getting their own gear together and has their own problems to solve.

Underwater, it is very unusual for the cylinder valve O-ring to fail, although I have seen it happen. If this O-ring does fail during a dive, the only way to stop the problem is to shut down the valve, which is possible if you are carrying another cylinder containing a breathable gas for the depth you are at. If you have just one cylinder, then obviously you are not going to shut it down. Your only option is to surface immediately and as quickly as safety permits, remembering that it is infinitely better to miss your safety stop than to run out of air underwater.

You will still be able to breathe through the regulator as you ascend but only for the short time it will take for all the air to rush out of your cylinder. This is a great reason to a) avoid going into deco when you only have one cylinder, and b) to practice air-sharing ascents with your buddies from time to time.

If you are planning a deep dive or a dive on which decompression is a planned event (or even just a possibility,) then you must carry an independent air source that you can switch to in an emergency. Ideally this should be a pony cylinder with a capacity of at least 3 litres (a 30 cu ft. cylinder in the Imperial world.) Then the failure of one tiny black rubber ring will cause only inconvenience and not tragedy.

Regulator Freeflow

Your regulator is designed with a downstream valve so that, if it fails, air will pour out of your scuba cylinder uncontrollably until it is empty. When you first learned to dive, your instructor described this as a good thing and you probably went along with that because at the time you were more worried about suddenly having no air to breathe rather than having too much.

Of course, this is not a good thing and the risk of a free-flowing regulator is yet another reason why you should always have a genuinely independent air source to turn to when diving deep.

In your beginners' course, you kneel on the bottom of the pool and breathe from a free-flowing regulator to give you the experience of breathing across a fast-flowing air stream. This is good training in one respect, in that, having had this experience in a controlled environment; you are less likely to panic when it happens for real. On the other hand, the training is flawed in that it might mislead you into thinking that you should remain stationary in the event of a regulator free-flow. In fact, unless you have an independent air source to switch to, a free-flowing regulator simply means that you are running out of air and running out of air fast so, rather than stay put, the thing to do is make a controlled move in the direction of the surface.

It seems to be obvious advice that you should keep your regulator well maintained, follow the manufacturer's service schedule and take it to a reputable service centre that uses new dedicated repair kits and rotates the contents of their o-ring drawers so the older ones are used up first. However, experience suggests that it is not a good idea to have a perfectly well functioning regulator serviced immediately prior to a big trip to a remote place or a course. Leave it alone. If it isn't broken, don't fix it!

Runaway Cylinder

You are swimming along and you suddenly feel unbalanced, the regulator in your mouth is pulling your head backwards and you know that your cylinder is slipping out of the BCD.

If you are close to the seabed, make sure the seabed is not covered with fragile marine life. Settle down on your knees, reach behind you with your right hand to support the cylinder, undo the BCD clip and Velcro at your waist and shrug off your BCD as if you were removing a jacket, left arm first, keeping your teeth tightly clamped on the regulator mouthpiece

Bring the whole set up round to the front of your body, keeping it very close to you, (especially if your weights are in the BCD!), and refit the cylinder strap calmly before donning the BCD again and resuming your dive.

Even if the seabed is not close, you will be surprised how, with a little practice, you can remove your BCD and cylinder and swim along with it in front of you while you fix whatever has gone wrong. This is something you can practice any time in a pool or shallow confined water. It will improve your buoyancy control as well as boosting your underwater confidence.

Of course, it is much better if the cylinder does not fall out in the first place! One way to reduce the likelihood of this happening is to soak the cam-strap with water before you lock it down onto the cylinder. Another way is simply to buy a BCD with twin cam-straps.

Mouthpiece Malfunction

The mouthpiece on your second stage can pose a couple of problems. The rubber can split and you can find yourself inhaling a fine mist of seawater with each breath or the cable-tie securing the mouthpiece can snap and cause the second stage to separate. Make a point of checking both the mouthpiece and the cable tie (that holds the mouthpiece on) as part of your pre-dive equipment check and carry spares of each in your Save-a-Dive kit.

Even a small split can be more than just an inconvenience; a diver once approached me and said that he loved the sport but was going to quit because after every dive he would get chest pains and flu symptoms for about 24 hours. I had heard of divers who liked using a certain brand of regulator famous for being "wet" who had experienced similar problems so we checked the mouthpiece on his regulator. Sure enough, there was a tiny split in it and once we changed it and he started checking it before each dive, he never encountered the problem again. During each dive, he had been inhaling sea water into his lungs with every breath and giving himself a form of bronchopneumonia!

If you ever find you are sipping water as you breathe or if the cable tie breaks and you lose your mouthpiece, no problem. You don't have to continue to suffer, just switch to your octopus and continue the dive. This is one of the many reasons why your octopus second stage should be just as good a regulator as your primary!

Broken Mask Strap

Do you remember having to do the mask flood and mask removal and replacement drills during your beginners' course? How could you ever forget, right? Do you remember hating them and thinking afterwards, "thank goodness that is over, I'll never have to do that again"? Or are you one of the fortunate ones who had all sorts of difficulty doing the drill and finally managed it one time only so that the busy instructor could tick off that box on his checklist and move the group on?

Well this message is especially for you! There was a serious purpose to those drills. They were not devised just to give you a hard time. On any dive your mask strap can snap or your buddy's wild fin kick can separate you from your face furniture with one blow. You might catch your mask as it flies off but the chances are it is gone. This in itself is not a serious problem; you will be visually impaired but you can still look around you, gather your thoughts, signal for assistance if you wish and see which way is up so that you can make a slow, careful ascent to the surface, breathing from your regulator as normal and remembering not to inhale through your nose which is now exposed to the water.

Losing your mask will not kill you but panicking when you lose your mask just might! Losing control of yourself when it happens and bolting to the surface could have tragic consequences. So you need to be certain you won't panic if you lose your mask. And how do you do that? Practice, practice, practice: in a pool or during a dive with a buddy in shallow water, remove your mask and then swim along for a few minutes, remaining calm. Can you see the readings on your watch, computer or depth and pressure gauges without your mask? Do you notice how the design of your regulator second stage diverts your bubbles away from your nose and eyes? See how easy this is?

If the possibility of losing your mask really bothers you, or if you do not want to allow the loss of your mask to interrupt a dive, do what many technical divers do to guard against the inconvenience of having to complete long decompressions without a mask. Invest in a frameless back up mask that will stow neatly in a pouch or BCD pocket. Make sure it is stored somewhere you can locate it and deploy it quickly in an emergency and practice fitting it and clearing it underwater until the action becomes instinctive.

Loose Weight-belt (leading to Lost Weight-belt)

There are two issues here. Your primary concern is making sure your weight belt does not fall off during a dive. Hold on to it at the buckle every time you enter the water and check that the buckle is still tight and the belt is correctly positioned around your waist before descending.

As you descend the increasing water pressure at depth will compress the neoprene in your wetsuit and your weight belt will become a little looser. So remember to reach down and tighten your weight belt once you arrive at depth. Of course, having done this you may find that the belt becomes a little tight when you return to the shallows. If so, just relax the buckle again.

The second issue is the risk of a runaway ascent in the event that your weight belt comes off. To minimise the danger that this presents, you can do three things.

First, buy a BCD with minimal integral buoyancy; that is, a BCD that will give you sufficient buoyancy on the surface when you inflate it but, when deflated, doesn't require a large amount of weight to get it underwater.

Second, practice dumping all the air from your BCD quickly in an emergency. Know where the dumps are and what body position you need to be in to make sure no air is trapped. Avoid complex jackets with huge wrap around air-cells.

Third, only carry as much weight as you need!

This last point is important because most people dive over-weighted. For instance, you are certainly diving over-weighted if you are still carrying the same amount of weight you used on your beginners' course. Your well-meaning instructor added extra weight to your belt to help you remain stable on the bottom as you went through your drills. But now you are a certified diver, your aim is to be neutrally buoyant on a dive, not planted in the sand.

BCD Failure

BCDs are highly reliable but they can fail in a couple of ways that you may not have considered.

The first of these is that your BCD can start auto-inflating. It is a great advantage to be able to add air to the BCD directly from the cylinder via the low-pressure inflator hose. But the valve at the BCD end of the hose can corrode and fail, allowing air to seep into the BCD and increase its (and your) positive buoyancy. A sign that this is happening is if you find yourself constantly having to dump air when you haven't added any.

You can keep the valve corrosion free by wiping it clean every now and then with a little white vinegar on a cotton bud. It's too late if the valve is already corroded but your local dive centre can fix it cheaply just by changing it out.

However, if you have not noticed the problem or you are using rented equipment and the valve suddenly fails explosively then you will need to have the presence of mind and the dexterity to disconnect the hose under water, dump the air and then inflate the BCD orally when you get to the surface. These skills are introduced in most beginners' courses and they should be practiced and maintained as they have real purpose.

Shocking as it may be to contemplate, you also need to be prepared for your BCD to stop functioning as a flotation device. The material BCDs are made of is tough and hard to pierce but it can wear or tear. The real potential failure points, however, are the dump valves, which are made of fairly brittle plastic that cracks easily. Scuba equipment is often handled roughly in transit and heavy cylinders fall on top of BCDs all the time. The cracks are often difficult to see and the first sign of a problem is usually bubbles escaping from the fitting. However, sometimes there is no warning: I have seen an apparently good shoulder dump valve shear off completely when the BCD was inflated underwater. If this happens, the BCD immediately becomes useless and the dive is over. Dump at least part of the weight you are carrying in order to swim to the surface and, once you get there, dump ALL your weight in order to stay buoyant.

Rolling Into the Deep Without Air

The history of diver training is based upon people assessing the causes of diving accidents and then designing courses to try to make sure the same thing does not happen again.

This is all very reassuring but this consistent approach also means that the writers of new course texts tend to add new techniques and new technologies to what has gone before but are very reluctant to omit the older material. This leaves us with some historical anomalies and one of these is the advice given to all new divers confronted with scuba gear for the first time that they should open the cylinder valve all the way and then twist it back a quarter or a half turn. This advice dates back to a time in the middle of the last century when our sport was in its infancy and it was feared that valves could be damaged if left open all the way. Today, once your cylinder valve has been opened the only thing you can achieve by twisting the valve back is to partially close it again.

Another culprit to blame for a number of incidents in which a diver has inadvertently entered the water with the cylinder valve closed or only a fraction open is the over-attentive diving partner with poor plumbing skills who misguidedly closes an open valve while performing a buddy check.

Here is how to make sure you never enter the water with your cylinder valve closed, even partially.

Forget what you were told in your training; turn your valve all the way on before you put your scuba gear on. Then do not let anyone else touch the valve after that, no matter how much your buddy insists or what exalted rank they hold in the dive industry.

Before you enter the water take four breaths from your

regulator and watch your high pressure gauge while you do so. If the needle moves when you breathe your valve is either fully closed or almost closed. Why four breaths? Because you might not be watching your gauge and if your valve has been opened then closed again, it will take you four breaths to clear the hose and that horrible empty sucking feeling will come on the back of the fourth breath.

Unless the dive site conditions demand it, never enter the water negatively buoyant. On the rare occasions that the dive site conditions require you to go in negative and plummet, know how to open your own cylinder valve if you suddenly find yourself with a vacuum in your regulator as you descend. The usual technique is to reach down and behind you with your left hand and push the base of your cylinder upwards. Then reach behind your neck with your right hand, grasp the valve firmly and turn it away from you.

Never enter the water with a cylinder that contains less than 50 Bar (750 psi). High pressure gauges can malfunction or they can just be plain misleading. Many have no actual zero reading; they just have a series of red dots below the 50 Bar (750 psi) mark that become smaller until they peter out. Often there is a registered trademark symbol (a circle with an R inside) below the point where the dots run out and you may think this is the zero. It isn't! Other gauges are just defective and the needle never actually points at zero. Look at your gauge when it is not attached to a cylinder and make sure you know where the needle will be when you have no air remaining!

Become a Better Diver by

Being prepared for things to go wrong
Practicing your skills
Knowing your equipment

4. Five Essential Strategies for Survival

Accounts of diving accidents hold a hypnotic fascination for us. We pore over the details looking for examples and lessons that we can learn from each incident to make us better divers and perhaps, by being forewarned and fore-armed, improve our chances of survival should we ever find ourselves in a similar situation.

Some common survival strategies include strength of character, determination, perseverance and a refusal to quit. However, not all survival strategies involve overcoming a predicament after it has become serious. Other strategies focus on preventing an incident from occurring in the first place or taking early action to avoid a situation escalating into an emergency.

The five stories told here each illustrate a specific preventative strategy. These are all true events; only the names of those involved have been changed.

Survival Story #1

Terry is an experienced rebreather instructor.

"I travelled out from the city on a Friday night for a weekend's wreck diving. I arrived around midnight and, although I was exhausted, I did not sleep well. I woke the next morning and did not feel at all like diving but the other guys were excited so I played along."

"Because I still had a bad feeling looming over me, I ran an extra-thorough check on the rebreather and thought to myself, "maybe I'll feel better when I get into the water." The dive started off just fine and I had shot some good video when I noticed that my oxygen sensors were reading high. "No problem," I thought, I'll flush the rebreather with air and that will take care of it. So I held the button down, injected fresh gas and took a few deep breaths. Then I suddenly realized that, unusually, I had my camera in my left hand instead of my right and, instead of air, I had just injected and breathed in a massive amount of pure oxygen at 30 m (100ft.)"

"I instinctively shut down my rebreather mouthpiece and switched to my open circuit air bailout so I would know for sure what gas I was breathing. At first I had no symptoms but somehow I knew it was going to come. I was not going to head for the surface, get an oxygen toxicity hit on the way up, drown and never be found. My buddy was only 3m (10ft) away and, although he had not noticed yet that anything was wrong, I was confident he would eventually."

"I wrapped the cord of my video camera around a rail post on the wreck, knelt down on the deck, leaned forward, grabbed hold of the regulator with my hand and wedged my lower arm against the railing. Basically, I did everything I could think of to keep my regulator in my mouth."

"And I waited. And it came. It felt like an electric current flowing through every muscle in my body, even my tongue, getting stronger as it continued. It did not hurt but every part of me was shaking. It gradually subsided. I have no idea how long it lasted. It could have been 10 seconds; it could have been 60."

"My buddy was by my side now, looking concerned. We exchanged signals, headed for the ascent line, did our deco and reached the surface with no further incident. I felt fine but a little weak."

"What did I learn? Don't dive when you feel bad. Always have the self-discipline to sit a dive out, even if it means disappointing your friends. I can't explain why I made the mistake. It just happened."

Comment

As NITROX divers know, if you breathe oxygen at a high partial pressure, you may experience convulsions. These are not fatal in themselves but if they occur underwater you lose control of your muscles, your regulator can fall from your mouth and therefore there is a high risk that you may drown. Terry's experience enabled him to react calmly and logically to the emergency and this, plus the reassuring presence of his buddy in close attendance, allowed him to survive. However, the incident could have been averted had he listened to his inner voice and just stayed in bed. As I discussed in Chapter 1 "Mental Preparation," if you don't feel like diving or have a feeling of foreboding about the dive, even if you cannot identify a reason for it, don't do it.

Survival strategy #1: Follow your feelings.

Survival Story #2

Alex was busy, successful and largely office-bound, not given to athletic pursuits but drawn by the lure of the ocean to become a diver. He bought a boat, took some training and started diving with friends at weekends. Diving did not come easily to him physically but, as an intelligent person, he stayed within his comfort zone, developed a good range of skills and fell in love with the sport.

One Monday, he walked into his local dive store to buy a weight belt and weights. In conversation with the owner, he explained that the previous day, he had ascended from a dive with his buddy. They had found themselves some distance from the boat, having been carried down current, and started to swim back to the boat. Surface conditions were choppy and Alex's buddy, a better swimmer, forged ahead of him and disappeared from view.

Alex soon became out of breath, took his regulator out of his mouth, took a couple of waves in the face and swallowed some sea water, causing him to choke. He sensed that he was on the verge of panic but in what he described as "a moment of clarity," he remembered learning in his initial diver training that, if he ever found himself in difficulty at the surface, he should drop his weight belt. This was something his instructor had made him practice over and over again. So he reached down, released the buckle and his weight belt fell away.

Immediately he found that he was floating higher in the water, his head now above the choppy waves, his mouth clear of the splashing foam. Free of the belt around his waist he found it easier to breathe. He could now see the boat and his buddy who had almost reached it. He lay back, took several deep breaths in and out and started to fin slowly but as powerfully as he could towards the boat.

Comment

A new weight belt and set of weights was a small price to pay for survival but the store owner was happy to give them to him free of charge on the understanding that he could use his story in a book some day. It is likely that Alex only thought to remove his weight belt because he had practiced doing it so many times that it had become deeply imbedded in his mind. Therefore, even when he was highly stressed, he still remembered his training.

Survival Strategy #2: Practice self-rescue skills so that they become instinctive.

Survival Story #3

Teresa was a relatively new diver at the time of the incident.

"The idea was to do a drift dive along a wall. I was a little worried as I had not been diving very long but I was with more experienced friends so I thought I would be OK. We all entered the water together but I had difficulty clearing my ears and as I descended I could not see the others; nor could I see the wall. I spun around a few times to get my bearings but it was getting darker and harder to see and I was still going down. I tried to add some air to my BCD but that did not seem to work so I started kicking hard to try to arrest my descent. I finally hit the bottom in a cloud of sand, my ears hurt, I was confused and the only thought in my mind was, "I'm all alone; I really do not like this. I'm getting out of here."

I remember looking up and the surface seemed a long way away but I reached for my BCD inflator and pushed myself off the sand desperate to get back to the boat and safety. But as I did so, I felt a hand on my shoulder, holding me down and then Sharon's face loomed in front of my mask, her eyes gazing at me gently and enquiringly. Her hand appeared, the fingers looped in an OK signal and I instinctively responded "OK," even though really I was feeling anything but alright. Her hand stayed on my shoulder and she just knelt there in front of me looking at me calmly. The panic gradually fell away and was immediately replaced by a feeling of horror at the realization of what I had been about to do before she arrived. I glanced at my gauge, plenty of air; looked at my computer, 33m (110 ft), and then noticed the rest of the group drifting around me, waiting. I gave Sharon another OK signal, a real one this time, and she relaxed her grip on my BCD. The rest of the dive was uneventful. I still find it almost incredible that panic set in so quickly and that it could induce me to contemplate doing something so amazingly stupid. "

Comment

Teresa did not know that descending quickly and losing control of yourself and your breathing under water can swiftly lead to panic. She did not expect the strength and speed of the emotion that overcame her and was completely incapable of responding logically. If she had been aware of the danger, she could have anticipated it and acted to calm herself, (see Chapter 2 "Detecting and Dealing with Stress") either before the panic took hold or when it was still in its early stages.

Survival strategy #3: Identify the potential for panic before it takes control of you.

Survival Story #4

Steve is a top divemaster. One day he was guiding a group at 20m (66ft) along a reef wall with the seabed over 90m (300ft) below. The plan involved ascending at the end of the dive through a Blue Hole in the reef. One of his divers had been a little nervous about the prospect of the ascent so Steve had instructed him to hold onto his harness when they reached the Blue Hole so he could help him maintain control of his buoyancy. Another of the group was an experienced diver using a NITROX 32 mix and Steve had reminded him beforehand to be careful of his buoyancy and make sure he did not drop below 40m (132ft) during the dive because of the risk of oxygen toxicity.

As the group arrived at the Hole and started to swim out over blue water and away from the wall, the nervous diver grabbed onto Steve's harness as planned. Seeing this, another of the group, having perhaps had second thoughts, approached and indicated that he would like to get similar support. Steve placed the diver's hand on his other shoulder strap and proceeded across the cavern with one person attached to each shoulder. He looked up and saw that the NITROX diver had begun a comfortable ascent but noticed that the last diver in the group was having difficulty maintaining his buoyancy across the void and had started to drop deeper than planned. Steve managed to attract his attention and indicated that the diver should add a little air to his BCD. The diver acknowledged the signal, picked up his inflator hose and released air instead of adding some. This of course led him to drop still further. When he did it again and fell away even more, apparently out of control, Steve felt he had no choice but to swim down to him to help.

He checked the grip of the two divers at his shoulders, both of whom seemed oblivious to what was going on, and then descended to deal with the third diver. He reached him, added a little air to the diver's BCD and managed to get the whole group neutrally buoyant. He now had three divers attached to him and a glance at his computer showed him they were all at a depth of 55m (181ft.) It was then that he noticed a movement out of the corner of his eye. It was the NITROX diver who had noticed what was happening and had come down to help! Steve used his free hand to signal in no uncertain terms that the NITROX diver, who was now a long way below his maximum permitted depth, should go up. He got the message and disappeared, leaving Steve to manage a slow and safe ascent for himself and the glassy-eyed divers holding onto him.

Once back on the boat, the three divers chattered excitedly on what a great dive they had had, while the only thing the NITROX diver had to say was, "you guys are not paid enough!" Steve made sure he brought a colleague along with him on future Blue Hole dives.

Comment

With experience comes confidence but the more experienced you become, the more you need to guard against overconfidence. Steve allowed his familiarity with his job and the dive site to persuade him that he could take these divers there on his own without help. As it turned out, when things started to go wrong, he was pushed to the limits of his ability to ensure the safety of the group. Only his refusal to panic, his calm determination and the fortunate fact that the oblivious divers also remained calm prevented a multiple tragedy.

Survival strategy #4: Know your limitations and dive well within your capabilities

Survival Story #5

Alan and Marty were completing a technical dive on an offshore shipwreck. They were at 4.5m (15ft) four minutes from the end of their final decompression stop when Marty suffered an oxygen convulsion, his regulator dropped from his mouth and he inhaled seawater. Alan took him to the surface unconscious, managed to get him into the boat with the help of the crew, began basic life support and almost at once Marty came to and began breathing. Thanks to the team's quick action, he survived the incident.

They had been using air as their "bottom" gas and NITROX 50 and 100% oxygen as decompression gases, carried in cylinders clipped to their harnesses, one on either side. The plan was to switch to NITROX 50 on their ascent at a depth of 20m (66 ft) then to switch to 100% oxygen at 6m (20 ft.) As they subsequently found out, Marty had mistakenly switched to the wrong gas and started breathing 100% oxygen at 20m (66 ft,) overloading himself with oxygen and eventually inducing the convulsion.

Marty had accomplished many such dives in the past and did everything right according to his training to ensure that he did not get his decompression cylinders mixed up. Yet he still made what was almost a fatal mistake. The irony is that there was no need for him to have been carrying two decompression gases. Either one would have been sufficient. Although on deep TRIMIX dives, the use of two decompression gases is recommended to reduce what could be very long ascent times, on a deep air dive such as this, carrying two decompression gases instead of one makes only a tiny difference to the required ascent time. The simple act of removing one of the decompression gases from the dive plan would have eliminated the risk and it would have been impossible for him to make the error that almost cost him his life.

Comment

Murphy's law states that if anything can go wrong, it will, and Murphy is certainly a diver. The lesson Marty learned is not just applicable to technical divers. It is related to the concept of anticipating the "What Ifs," a theme that is mentioned throughout this book. If something bad can happen and if the consequences are potentially fatal, then take every step you can to make sure it cannot possibly occur. This may be the best preventative survival strategy of all.

Survival strategy #5: Anticipate Mr Murphy

Become a Better Diver by

Following your feelings
Practicing self-rescue skills until they become instinctive
Identifying the potential for panic before it takes control
Knowing your limitations and diving well within your
capabilities

5. Why Divers Die

In 1979 cave diving pioneer Sheck Exley compiled a ground-breaking volume entitled Basic Cave Diving – a Blueprint for Survival. In this short book, he analysed cave diving accidents, breaking them down and concluding that there were common factors implicated in all of them.

As a result of these findings, he came up with: -

Ten Recommendations for Safe Cave Diving

1. Always use a single, continuous guideline from the entrance of the cave throughout the dive.

2. Always use the "Third Rule" in planning your air supply

3. Avoid deep diving in caves

4. Avoid panic by building up experience slowly and being prepared for emergencies

5. Always use at least three lights per diver

6. Always carry the safest possible scuba

7. Avoid stirring up silt

8. Practice emergency procedures with your partner before going diving and review them often

9. Always carry the equipment necessary for handling emergencies and know how to use it

10. Never permit overconfidence to allow you to rationalize violating recommended safety procedures

The echo of these recommendations resounds throughout the chapters of this book.

Thank Goodness All Divers Live

In his introduction to Basic Cave Diving, Exley stressed that the recommendations applied particularly to Florida but his preventative approach to diving accidents was highly influential in the wider cave diving community and the ten recommendations subsequently coalesced into five golden rules for safe cave diving namely, Training, Guideline, Air, Depth, Lights, remembered via the mnemonic Thank Goodness All Divers Live.

Training – dive within the limits of your training and gain experience slowly.

Guideline - maintain a continuous guideline to a point in open water outside the cave entrance.

Air – Always maintain a sufficient reserve of air.

Depth – Don't dive beyond the maximum operating depth of the gas mixture you are breathing.

Lights – Always carry 3 independent battery-powered lights.

The theory was that if you got these five things right, you were highly unlikely to die while scuba diving in caves and with the five rules incorporated into training programmes, the incidence of cave diver deaths did decrease. Perhaps just as importantly, the concept of actively evaluating incidents with a view to preventing future accidents began to play an important role in the continuing evolution of cave diving and this remains the case today.

Cave divers are relatively few in number and occupy a rarefied stratum in the scuba diving hierarchy but, as in so many aspects of scuba diving, it is they who lead the way for others and their analytical zero-tolerance approach to accident prevention is equally valid for the sport in general.

No matter how long you work in scuba diving, you never get used to the fact that every year you hear of people dying while engaged in this sport we love. If you are involved in technical diving, you know that the list of victims will include the names of a few friends. The most tragic thing is that the circumstances of the accidents and the events leading up to them are usually depressingly familiar.

In this chapter, I identify the major causes of general sport diver deaths and try to come up with a few recommendations of my own. Rather than focus on the specific symptoms, such as overweighting, panic, fast ascents or running out of air, I concentrate instead on the principal issues that lie at the root of diver fatalities.

Poor Watermanship

Some divers simply cannot swim. Aside from the issue of how on earth they managed to complete initial diver training without being able to swim, one would think that simple self-preservation instincts would drive them to learn to swim before learning to dive.

However, there are many other divers who, while able to swim, are not comfortable in the water and deprived of the crutches afforded by their BCD and fins, could easily get into difficulty on a surface swim.

Many accidents take place on the surface and involve panic, an understandable reaction when someone is placed in an environment where they are not comfortable. A diver's chances of surviving when something goes wrong are increased substantially if they are at home in the water.

Over the years, basic diver training has changed; today there are fewer watermanship tests and courses concentrate instead on handling (and selling) the equipment. Perhaps dive centres should offer watermanship classes as well, leaving the equipment behind and helping people become more at ease in the water?

Diving Beyond Your Level of Training

The concept of comfort is relevant here too. If you are diving in conditions and circumstances, which you have been trained to deal with and with which you are highly familiar, you are well placed to handle any problems you may encounter. Much cynicism surrounds the worth of the myriad course options available through training agencies but as I describe in "Picking your way through the Training Minefield," (Chapter 13,) there is a lot of value to be gained by doing certain courses, not for the card but for the skills you can acquire and for the opportunity to be criticised and advised by a professional. They can provide a faster track to becoming a better diver and this allows you to progress to more complex dives more safely.

Feeling that you are diving well within your comfort zone makes you relaxed and gives you confidence. Many divers report that a significant benefit of taking a cave diver or wreck diver class is the ease with which they can deploy in the open ocean the skills that they have spent time perfecting in an enclosed overhead environment.

One of the functions of diver training is to expand your comfort envelope in a supervised arena. Ideally the outer edges of this envelope are not a place you want to explore on your own. The key is to know your limits and be honest with yourself.

Failing to Anticipate Problems

Experience and good training gives you the knowledge to anticipate problems before they occur. Adopting a "what if" approach on every dive you do is a good tactic.

Imagining the problems that might occur and knowing in advance how you will deal with them enables you to respond quickly, correctly and without undue anxiety if something goes wrong. You never want to confront a situation and think, "I didn't expect this!" or, worse, "I was hoping that wouldn't happen!"

The "what if" approach is very useful in guarding against equipment failure in that you look at each item, imagine how it could fail and then figure out what you would do if it failed on the dive.

The same kind of mindset should be applied to planning the dive, anticipating obstacles, assessing dive conditions and identifying both a primary and back up ascent route.

Diving in Poor Health

The diving population in Europe and America is ageing and gaining weight. Heart attack is becoming an increasingly common cause of diver death and the victims of fatal diving incidents are often overweight. In a 2006 survey by the Divers Alert Network (DAN) a factor cited in 74% of the fatal cases reported was that the victims were overweight or obese.

Although it is true that our sport does not require that participants should be athletic and built like racing whippets, nevertheless a diver should be in good physiological and physical shape, particularly in order to survive when things go wrong.

All older divers should follow a basic fitness regime, get regular medical check ups and be aware enough of their limitations not to dive if they become ill, injured, incapacitated or after significant surgery. A history of heart disease or high blood pressure should give divers pause to consider whether they should continue diving, given the high number of fatalities where this is cited as a contributing factor.

If you feel unwell, don't dive. As we do more diving we gain in experience, but no matter how much we learn, the laws of nature still apply. As our bodies age they become weaker, we become more susceptible to ailments and our chances of dodging a physiological bullet decrease. To those who might argue that we all have every right to take risks with our own lives, I would point out that every diver not only has responsibility for themselves, they have a responsibility to the diving community whose reputation is damaged by every tragedy and, most of all, they are responsible to those who may be diving with them when the incident occurs and who may come to harm in trying to rescue them.

Poor Decision-Making/Failing to Use Common Sense

Diving is not for everyone. Some people have a fear of water; others feel claustrophobic when they don diving equipment. Some folk have nervous conditions that cause them to experience a high degree of anxiety when they put their heads underwater. Common sense should dictate to such people that diving is not for them and that they should pursue other activities instead. However, rather than heed the warning signs, some see their fears as challenges to be overcome.

Peer pressure also comes into play and there are many instances where someone will try to learn to dive despite their fears simply in order to please and spend more time with a diving spouse.

Diving is a wonderful sport but it is not worth risking your life for. If it is not for you, there are plenty of other things you can do which are just as rewarding.

We professionals are often implicated too. We are sometimes guilty of exhibiting poor judgement in encouraging divers to take training courses when they are not ready or continuing to teach people who obviously do not have the potential to become safe divers. This does not mean that we should only ever accept the "naturals" on diver courses. After all, there is nothing more rewarding for an instructor than to help someone discover his or her hidden potential. But it is wrong for us to be complicit in another person's self-deception.

Similarly, we should be careful of issuing certifications to those who have only been able to accomplish the skills as a consequence of their dependence on the instructor. It is always hard to withhold certification from someone who has paid for a course but the decision to unleash an incompetent diver onto the diving community should be much harder!

We are also sometimes guilty of agreeing to take divers we have never seen before to dive-sites that require advanced skills. One important reason divers are asked to provide evidence of certification and ideally show a logbook is that every professional falls at least once for a fictitious story and has to bear the consequences.

Deciding to dive when your decision-making processes are impaired by alcohol, marijuana or mind-altering drugs is obviously poor judgement but of course the flawed decision making processes themselves are often to blame. Slow response time and forgetting basic self-preservation skills are too often the result.

Coming Back Too Quickly / Getting Rusty

A disproportionate number of accidents occur to divers who have taken a few years away from the sport and then try to come back at the same level of diving they were doing before the break. When you are diving regularly and frequently good diving behaviour becomes automatic and correct responses become instinctive. However, these are often forgotten when you have not been in the water for a while. Spending time with an instructor to go through skills in a pool or shallow water before embarking on a few easy dives first is the ideal way to get yourself dive-fit again and back into the flow.

Even if you are diving regularly, you can prevent your skills from getting rusty by practicing them. There are often opportunities during a dive to practice clearing a flooded mask or air sharing with your buddy. Practice essential skills like removing your weights when you reach the surface until they become something you do without thinking. I choose this as an example because in the event of any problem at the surface, the first thing the diver should do instinctively is drop his weights. Once that is taken care of, the chances of the diver surviving the incident increase enormously. Ditching weights used to be drilled intensively in diver training; unfortunately this has become unfashionable in recent years. Nevertheless, the skill is just as important today as it used to be, as we saw in Alex's story in Chapter 5.

Booking a review session with an instructor can also benefit a regular diver. We all fall into bad habits and getting an expert to review your posture in the water, your fin technique, your weighting and other aspects of your diving behaviour can prove valuable.

Overconfidence

Experienced divers die each year and over familiarity with the sport can misguide some people into thinking that somehow the laws of physics do not apply to them any more and that they can cut corners and ignore the rules that they preach faithfully to others. Many instructors and divemasters go through this stage during their development and the lucky ones emerge unharmed on the other side. Some are not so fortunate. Common symptoms of overconfidence are making ultra deep bounce dives on air; wreck or cave penetrations without training or proper equipment and dives at the end of the day on partially full cylinders.

Failing to Break the Chain of Events

As we saw in previous chapters, most accidents are an accumulation of events that can lead a diver into an increasingly unmanageable situation. Maintaining a clear head and recognising the need to stop, think and act to break the chain of events can make the difference between a story and a tragedy. Experienced instructors and divemasters develop instincts and will terminate or abandon a dive when things start to go wrong even if the problems seem only minor. It is far better to plan to dive another day, rather than persevere when everything seems to be conspiring against you. Never be afraid to cancel a plan to dive if it just does not feel right or if you are having "one of those days."

Quitting

An apocryphal story told in technical diving circles is of a diver who, lost in a cave, spent valuable time and air writing a farewell note to his loved ones instead of using every minute he had left to try an find a way out. His mistake was to quit. Some divers are alive today having survived potentially fatal experiences not because of their superhuman qualities but because they simply chose not to give up. Confronted with apparently insurmountable circumstances, some inner force persuaded them to continue in spite of the odds stacked against them and, in doing so, they gave themselves the option of survival. When your equipment, your skills and the people around you are no longer sufficient to keep you alive, your mental strength and refusal to quit can enable you to survive.

Become a Better Diver by

Staying healthy
Improving your swimming skills
Diving regularly within the level of your training
Anticipating potential problems
Ensuring you are equipped to deal with them
Knowing your limits
Not being afraid to cancel a dive when things are not going well

6. Solo Diving

Your Buddy – An Indispensable Partner or a Complete Liability?

The shamelessly attention-seeking subtitle of this chapter suggests that this is a topic to which there is a black-or-white answer, or that towards the end I am going to deliver some sort of conclusive verdict on the buddy system, a mainstay of recreational diver training since people started going underwater for fun and a topic of much controversy for just as long. If you are expecting this, you will be disappointed. However, if you are looking for some thought-provoking discussion of the subject that might help you come up with your own verdict then you should keep reading!

People have the right to choose how they dive and with whom they dive but it is only a true choice if they take the time beforehand to make themselves aware of all the factors. Deliberately remaining in ignorance or only recognizing the validity of arguments that support beliefs you already hold leaves you just gambling on faith.

The Buddy System

The buddy system, as it was originally conceived, was a procedure whereby two confident divers would operate as independent members of a two-person team with their shared equipment and gas supply making the team stronger than its individual members acting alone.

The Perfect Buddy Team

A perfect buddy team share similar interests and have compatible aims for their diving. They double check each other's gear and stay together throughout every dive, maintaining a commonly agreed position relative to one another, staying in visual contact and adjusting their distance depending on the prevailing visibility and water conditions.

They discuss and practice what to do in the event of various emergencies, equip themselves accordingly and double-check each other's air supply and decompression status at preset waypoints during the dive. They accept full responsibility for the conduct of their own dive as well as the additional responsibility of helping out if their buddy runs into difficulty or suffers equipment failure. Perhaps most importantly of all, they agree that should either of them feel uncomfortable or ill at ease for any reason before or during a dive then they will abandon or immediately abort the dive together.

But Not Everyone Is Perfect!

It is hard to argue that this is not the safest way for people to dive. However, in reality buddy teams are rarely so perfectly in tune.

Sometimes buddies are thrust together by a dive operation's insistence that nobody should dive alone. Sometimes an individual who is nervous and feels they may not have sufficient skills to rescue themselves if they run into difficulty will choose a buddy who they believe they can depend upon to save them in an emergency. Sometimes two such people will choose each other, which is a well-cooked recipe for disaster!

Sometimes buddy teams form just because the two people are friends or spouses, not because they have mutually compatible diving interests. However, paradoxically, sometimes two people with similar aims will not make a good buddy team either. Imagine two keen photographers diving together!

Proponents of the buddy system argue that a diver is more likely to come to harm if they are alone than if they are with another diver. The statistics support this contention, showing that most divers who die diving, die alone. However, a closer examination of the reports shows that, in many cases, the diver did not start the dive on their own.

Sometimes a buddy team separates when one has a problem and the other leaves him to surface on his own. Or the buddy team ascends together but then one descends again to continue alone.

Inattention can also leave a diver isolated; for instance when one buddy leads from the front, forgets to look back from time to time and therefore does not notice when his buddy behind him has a problem.

There are plenty of instances too where subsequent analysis of what went wrong concludes that one member of a buddy team got into difficulty, the other tried to rescue them and this resulted in two fatalities instead of one.

The system would seem therefore to be flawed.

Inherent Flaws

The flaws in the buddy system derive primarily from the ambiguous way it is commonly taught and the counter-productive way it is often implemented and interpreted.

Rather than emphasising the original concept of mutual independence referred to above, the buddy system is instead often explained in such a way as to breed inter-dependence, encouraging both members of the dive team to abandon a degree of responsibility for the safe conclusion of the dive. The argument usually runs along the lines of reassuring each diver that they do not have to worry about what to do if an emergency strikes during a dive as long as their buddy is by their side.

Out of air drills are often taught with two divers kneeling facing each other. One signals to the other that they have run out of air. The donor passes their octopus regulator to the receiver; they establish a mutual grip and then start a timed swim sharing air before returning to where they began and repeating the exercise, exchanging roles.

The futility of this as a practical exercise is readily apparent. Instructors know how flawed it is but they have to complete basic diver training for a group of people in a relatively limited time frame and instructor insurance is usually restricted to certain tightly proscribed activities. Therefore it is difficult for instructors to introduce new drills or radically alter existing drills, even if they perceive the flaws in the ones they are required to teach.

First the exercise as described above presupposes an absurd scenario where two divers are side-by-side, arms-length apart and stationary when the emergency occurs. Second, it incorporates no element of stress management in what, in reality, would be a very stressful scenario, and third, the drill as conducted teaches the divers that, in the event that they find themselves sharing air, the right thing to do is remain at depth and go for a swim.

Of course, no one would suggest that this is actually the case and most good instructors would explain that the air-sharing swim is a simulated ascent but in a real situation the memory of something you have done is much more immediately accessible than the memory of something you have been told. Therefore, in a real-life emergency, it will probably not occur to trainees that two divers sharing one cylinder should immediately begin thinking about ascending before they both run out of air. They are more likely to assume that once they have established air sharing the emergency is over, whereas in fact all that has happened is that there are now two divers at risk instead of one. The emergency is not over until both divers have returned safely to the boat or the beach.

An Out of Air Emergency – What Really Happens!

On the two occasions that someone has genuinely run out of air and come to me for assistance, neither individual was part of the group I was supervising, both came at me from above and behind, both grabbed the regulator out of my mouth and both dragged my mask off as they took the regulator!

This is what typically happens. Someone who suddenly finds that they are out of air instinctively holds their breath and this causes them to float upwards. In the worst of cases, they panic and try and get to the surface as quickly as possible. As they go up, the expanding air in their lungs and BCD causes them to ascend faster and faster and the next thing that happens is that they explode through the surface like a breaching porpoise, probably with serious lung damage.

If they manage to retain enough self-control and awareness to resist making this sort of panicked runaway ascent, the first thing they do is look around desperately for anyone nearby who has air and swim as fast as they can to get to this person.

By the time they reach him, the original panic at finding themselves airless has been exacerbated by the build up of carbon dioxide and the effort of swimming, so they have only one over-riding priority, the desperate need to breathe. The thought of politely requesting assistance with a series of calm gestures could not be further from their mind. They grab at the most obviously functioning regulator, which is the one in the diver's mouth.

Because they are coming at the diver from above and behind they pull the regulator up and back and this drags off the unwitting donor's mask. The out-of-air diver exhales and then takes a huge breath in causing both divers to float up. The donor is temporarily shocked, blind and heading for the surface with nothing to breathe from.

"Real Life" Air Sharing Drills

Especially in basic diver training, (as new divers are far more likely to run out of air than experienced divers,) this sort of scenario can be avoided by teaching divers lifelike air-sharing drills.

In the past, sport diver training used to give students a chance to experience stress underwater and learn to handle it via a number of controlled scenarios. In recent years, the trend has been to eliminate such exercises from beginners' courses. This means that many divers only encounter exercises incorporating stress management when they begin technical diving.

This is a mistake. It is important that divers at all levels get some practice in resolving stress-inducing problems such as loss of air supply or equipment failure so that they have an experience to fall back on instinctively should anything similar ever happen during a dive. Achieving mastery of skills involving mental strength does wonders for a diver's confidence. There is no reason at all why such things should just be the province of technical divers, they should be for everyone. After this chapter I describe some out of air drills that you can practice with your buddy or dive team.

Implementation and Interpretation

Frequently in organized sport diving, the buddy system is enforced and this can generate passive resistance and a dangerously counter-productive set of circumstances.

Many divers object to being told that diving alone or as part of a loose group is not permitted. Forced to accept a buddy by the operator they are diving with and with the alternative of not being allowed to dive if they refuse, they will simply remain silent. However, they have no intention of taking any notice of their buddy once underwater. This produces one of two results; either the two divers go their own way or one diver follows the other around, unilaterally ensuring they stay together. This only serves to create resentment. There is absolutely no safety benefit at all. In fact, given that both divers would be in a much more relaxed frame of mind, they would actually be safer if the buddy system had never been mentioned.

Others abuse the system by choosing to interpret it as an opportunity to absolve themselves of responsibility for the dive and place this on the shoulders of their companion. Essentially they are entrusting the buddy with their safety. These are often people who have been poorly trained and have little confidence. Underwater, they constantly border on the verge of panic, relying on the supposed reassurance offered by the buddy system. Without it, they would probably not go in the water. Their companions are effectively diving solo.

If, as often happens, you have two people unwittingly diving together with this mindset, you actually have nobody taking responsibility for anyone's safety and again the two divers would be much better off diving alone and knowing that they are in charge of their own dive. If something goes wrong on a dive like this, the potential for a fatal accident is enormous as the stress of the event will be compounded by the realization that, far from having someone close by to rescue them, the diver is effectively alone with a buddy diver neither prepared nor competent to help.

When a Buddy Is Better

There are definite benefits, both tangible and intangible, to diving with someone else. We are human beings, after all, and we like to share our experiences. We also derive a great deal of emotional security from the company of others.

There are also occasions when having a buddy around can be of enormous practical assistance.

If you become entangled in fishing line or net, a buddy can see the situation much more clearly than you can and is better placed to extract you.

If you become confused or anxious, your buddy's mere presence and calm disposition can be reassuring. This is a good thing, unless of course your confusion is due to debilitating narcosis, in which case your buddy will be equally incapacitated and his relaxed demeanour may mean his brain's hard-drive has frozen!

If you get a serious marine life injury, you may need a buddy to get you safely to the surface and out of the water.

If your mask strap breaks and your mask is carried away by the current, your buddy's mask-assisted eyes can help you monitor depth, time and ascent rate. He might even be able to chase down and catch your errant mask!

Rebreather Diving – a Special Case

In the relatively short history of sport rebreather diving, so many of the fatalities have taken place when the diver was alone in the water that current wisdom dictates that no-one on a rebreather should be diving unaccompanied.

Two of the major hazards of rebreather diving are carbon dioxide poisoning (hypercapnia) (see Chapter 28 "The Black Gases",) and oxygen deprivation (hypoxia) and the potential risk that these can lead to a diver fatality is considerably amplified if the diver is operating alone.

Either of these conditions can cloud a diver's mind to such an extent that the diver will be completely unaware that there is anything wrong until it is too late, by which time he is no longer mentally capable of resolving the problem on his own or he passes out, loses his grip on his mouthpiece and drowns.

The cause of the problem is usually a malfunctioning piece of equipment or a rebreather that has been poorly set up and the reason why the presence of another diver can reduce the risk is that it is unlikely that the curse of a malfunctioning rebreather will strike at two rebreather divers in the same place, at the same time. It is easy to spot a rebreather diver suffering from the early stages of hypercapnia or hypoxia when you are not similarly afflicted and once you identify the issue, you can quickly take charge of the situation, get the diver off his rebreather onto an open circuit gas supply and ascend with him to safety and the surface.

However, there is not always "safety in numbers." To operate efficiently, a dive team has to be composed of equally capable, independently functioning components. I once witnessed an incident involving a group of four rebreather divers where the hypercapnia victim was the team leader. So deeply ingrained was the dependency of the other three divers, in the absence of direction from their incapacitated head, they did not respond and deal with the situation until it was almost too late. Their leader only survived thanks to some fortuitous positive buoyancy and a little quick thinking from the surface support personnel.

Taking Responsibility

Whatever your reason for diving with a buddy, you, and only you, are ultimately responsible for your safety on every dive. You should never put yourself in a position where you are not able to survive a dive by trusting your own knowledge, equipment and self-rescue skills, whatever happens. To borrow a maxim popularized by Tom Mount of the International Association of NITROX & Technical Divers (IANTD), "only you can think, breathe and swim for yourself."

The only time when you should hand over any part of this responsibility is when you take a training course teaching you how to dive in a new environment or with new equipment. In such circumstances you do not have the knowledge or experience to deal competently with every eventuality, (this is why you are taking the course,) and by accepting you on the course, your instructors also implicitly take on part of the burden of responsibility for your safety. That is part of what you pay them for.

What Is Solo?

Instructors effectively dive solo every day, even though there may be other people in the water with them. An instructor taking open water divers into the ocean without an assistant is on his own in the event that he has an equipment failure or other emergency. There is nobody who will be able to help him if he runs into difficulty. This is part of the job, however, and something that he should be prepared and equipped for.

Dive guides go solo all the time when they are setting the shot line on a wreck or guiding photographers for example. A young lady dive guide who used to work on Egyptian wreck safaris used to be besieged constantly by well-meaning male customers who would offer to accompany her when she went to set the shot line. The task involved huge concentration and not a little physical effort, as the boat would often drop the shot down current from the wreck. The last thing she wanted was to have a "buddy" to watch out for at the same time, so she would always politely refuse.

When Solo Is Safer

Diving on your own is certainly safer than taking a partner if you want to dive a plan that is beyond the experience level of your available buddies. For instance, if you are a Technical Wreck Diver and want to explore inside a shipwreck but none of your dive team has overhead environment training, it is far better to ask the team to provide support outside the wreck than to take one of them inside with you. They can be of much more assistance monitoring the line at the entry/exit point or helping with gear and gases during your decompression.

Generally speaking, any dive can be undertaken safely on your own as long as you have the knowledge and experience to anticipate potential problems and you equip yourself and plan your dive accordingly.

A key pre-requisite to successful solo diving is honest introspection. You need to be able to conduct an objective, truthful assessment of your abilities, state of mind and aims, free from ego and peer pressure. Here is a short checklist.

Dive solo if ALL the following circumstances apply

You are genuinely happy to do the dive on your own.

You have identified all the potential risks.

You are equipped to deal with anything that might happen.

You have practiced what you will do in the event of an emergency.

You have real-life experience of successfully handling stress underwater.

You have the discipline to stay within a dive plan.

You have the discipline NOT to change the plan on a narcosis-fuelled whim halfway through the dive.

AND you have the discipline to abort a dive as soon as something goes wrong or you feel ill at ease.

Here are three examples to illustrate what I mean by the discipline to abort.

Example #1: you are on a night dive when one of your two lights fails and you switch to your back-up light. You abort the dive at this point because you are now diving with one light and if that fails too, you have none.

Example #2: you are exiting a shipwreck recovering your reel and line when the line jams around the reel. You now have two problems, the reel and the decompression clock. Rather than sit at depth trying to unjam the line, you tie the reel off and follow the line out of the wreck keeping to your dive plan. You can always do another dive to recover the reel later when you do not have a decompression burden and such a limited gas supply.

Example #3: you are on a deep dive when you begin to develop a sensation that something is wrong although you cannot identify a specific problem. Rather than continue and hope the feeling goes away, you cut short your dive and concentrate even harder than usual on executing a perfect ascent.

Some training agencies now offer Solo Diving courses and these will certainly be valuable in helping you adopt the right mindset to diving on your own. When you think about it, however, there should really be no need to have a specific course: every diver course should be teaching self-sufficiency rather than dependency.

Larger Teams

A two-person team is the most efficient in terms of communication and choreography but many technical divers see three as the perfect number for a dive team because the collective pool of gas and equipment and 2 to 1 voting logic can be relied upon to deal with most incidents.

However, implementing this ethic requires training and practice. In a standard sport diving scenario, choosing a three-person dive team can lead to confusion over roles and responsibility. In many cases, a three person team is actually a two-person team who are watching out for each other and a third person who is essentially diving on their own but unaware of it.

A final word: whatever the size of the dive team; always dive well within the comfort zone of the least capable or least experienced member.

Become a Better Diver by

Understanding that
The buddy system is only effective when it is deployed properly
There are many reasons why it is safer to dive with someone else
A fellow diver is not always a buddy, and
There are times when you are definitely better diving alone

Out of Air Drills

Phase 1:

To be practiced in a swimming pool or calm, shallow, protected body of water

You and your buddy position yourselves 10m (33ft) apart. Your buddy "runs out of air" and swims towards you without breathing.

When you see him signal that he needs air, prepare whichever of your second stage regulators is on the longer hose and give this to him when he arrives. Begin air sharing then ascend slowly together. On arrival at the surface you auto-inflate your BCD while supporting your buddy as he orally inflates his BCD.

Repeat the drill, alternating roles and increasing the distance between you until the person who is out of air starts experiencing significant stress towards the end of his non-breathing swim.

Then add a new level of difficulty. Turn your back so you cannot see your buddy coming and do not prepare a response until he arrives and spins you round.

Finally practice the drill while you are both swimming, one following the other, so your buddy is in the realistic position of having to catch up with a moving target in order to share air.

Each time do not end the drill until both divers are positively buoyant on the surface.

Phase 2:

To be practiced during ocean dives

Begin phase 2 only when you are both comfortable with the phase 1 drills.

Once in a while, particularly at the beginning of a dive season, agree that one or other of you will initiate the drill at some point during a normal dive in open water. Advise anyone else diving with you that this is what you intend to do, just so they do not mistake it for a real emergency and try to intervene.

Then practice the drill as you did in the pool, first when you are swimming close together in the shallows then extending the distance and depth as you become more accomplished.

Always follow an out-of-air swim with an ascent and establishment of surface buoyancy so the sequence is burned into your minds and become automatic.

Finally, to test yourselves in a realistic scenario, involve a third person to act as the trigger for the drill. Ask this third person to pick a time in the dive when it looks like you or your buddy has become distracted or when you have drifted a little further apart from each other than usual, then signal to one of you that you are out of air. This initiates the drill, which should by now have become instinctive.

Skills

7. Acquiring Perfect Buoyancy

Perfect buoyancy: this is the holy grail for many divers, a lifetime quest for a nirvana where they will eventually attain the gift of remaining completely motionless in the ocean in any position, mastering the art of immobility, relaxed, effortlessly neutral, a passive observer instead of a harbinger of doom for the marine life around them; no longer constantly inflating, deflating, rocking and rolling.

Here are five tips to help you on your way to neutral nirvana.

Lose that Weight

The main reason many people find it difficult to attain perfect buoyancy is that they dive over-weighted and have to compensate for this by adding more air than necessary to their BCD. The excess air moves around within the cell as they swim and change position in the water and this makes it very hard for them to maintain their balance.

It also means they cannot become horizontal in the water as the weight around the waist carries their legs down while the air in their BCDs settles around their shoulders and lifts their head up. It is this phenomenon that gives new divers that less-than-attractive seahorse posture.

How do you know if you are carrying too much weight? At the end of a dive when you have 50 Bar (750 psi) or so in your cylinder, position yourself at safety stop depth, 3m to 5m (10ft to 15ft), remove all the air from your BCD and try to remain neutrally buoyant. If you find yourself sinking you are carrying too much weight so get rid of it. If you find yourself tending to float to the surface then you are not carrying enough weight. Easy!

If you have a lot of weight attached to your belt and you worry that if it ever slipped off you would be at risk of a runaway ascent, spread the weight about. Put a kilo or two, (3 or 4 pounds,) on your cylinder cam strap, add small weight pouches to your harness or get a BCD with integral weight pockets. You might even contemplate buying a harness with a stainless steel backplate. But be wary of putting too much weight in places where it can't be dumped. In the event of a BCD failure you always need to be able to drop enough of your weight to enable you to keep yourself comfortably afloat at the surface.

Get to Know Your BCD

Once you are weighted correctly you will only need to make minor adjustments to your BCD from time to time during a dive, primarily to compensate for the effect of changing depth and pressure on your wetsuit. But this fine-tuning is an advanced skill in itself and requires that you know your BCD well.

Chapter 21 "Taking Control of your BCD" has a number of tips on how you can get better acquainted. The key points are these.

Spend time studying it and imagine where the air will sit when you are in various positions under water. It will always gravitate to whichever part of your BCD is closest to the surface.

Ask yourself which way you would need to turn your body to release air in a variety of situations

Learn where the controls are and practice using them

Master the skill of venting your BCD completely; you would be surprised how many divers fail to do this and consequently add unnecessary extra weight in order to descend.

Learn to Breathe

Adopting a long, slow, steady breathing pattern when you dive will benefit you in many ways. It will help to prevent the onset of stress and ensure you have a clear head if a potentially stressful incident arises. It can even substantially reduce your air consumption. It will also help you develop the ability to ultra-fine tune your buoyancy by lung control, exhaling just a little more completely in order to drop a few centimetres to examine something on the reef or inhaling fully in order to rise slightly in the water to swim over an obstacle. See Chapter 9, "The Art of Conservation" for detailed advice on how to execute the perfect diving breath.

Change the Way You Move

When you are diving, only move when you need to go somewhere. If you are not going anywhere keep your fins still. This is harder than you may think; many divers are unaware that once underwater they flap continuously. Your fins are for propulsion and occasionally for balance; they are not secondary buoyancy control devices.

Practice remaining completely motionless in mid water and take full advantage of the three dimensions you can move in. If you find yourself slowly moving in an unplanned direction, roll with it then turn your body gradually until you are back on equilibrium. You will feel an almost uncontrollable urge to kick: resist it! Instead, change your position in the water by dipping a shoulder or using breath control to make yourself more or less buoyant.

Keep your arms tucked in and hands still. These are not designed for buoyancy control either. As a diver you move your arms only to signal. The closer your arms are to your body the easier it is to maintain perfect buoyancy and balance. This is the reason why many experienced divers adopt the classic crossed arms posture.

Stay Focussed

Finally, be aware at all times of where you are in the water. Get into the habit of glancing quickly and frequently at your computer to check your depth. This is much easier if it is mounted on your wrist where your watch normally is. The underwater environment is disorientating even when visibility is good and the deeper you are the less you will sense changes in depth by the change in pressure in your ears.

Become a Better Diver by

Reducing the amount of weight you carry
Getting to know your equipment
Learning to breathe like a diver
Knowing when to move and when to stay still

8. Improving Navigation Skills

Do you, like many divers, harbour a guilty secret desire? Do you want to jump off a dive boat and, without relying on an instructor or divemaster, always know exactly where you are during the dive and how to get back to your starting point without having to pop up embarrassingly in mid ocean to recover your bearings?

Knowing how to find your way underwater is one of the main things that mark out the experienced diver from the neophyte. In the industry, we are required to do it all the time when leading customers or students, even when we are diving in new or unfamiliar locations. What is the secret? How is it done?

The good news is that becoming a capable underwater navigator is well within your grasp. It just takes five key steps: basic dive skills, concentration, some technical expertise with a compass, pre-dive preparation and, most importantly, the exercise of your powers of observation. With a little perseverance, confidence and faith in your abilities you will be able to navigate like a professional!

Step 1: Get Some Dive Time In

When you start diving your brain's RAM is fully occupied with the business of controlling your breathing rate, checking your air supply, maintaining buoyancy and achieving that delicate compromise of getting close enough to observe the marine life but staying far enough away to avoid disturbing or molesting it.

There is so much to think about and, to make things even more difficult, at depth you have to deal with narcosis clouding your short-term memory.

Once you have mastered the key skills, when breathing correctly and buoyancy control have become second nature, you will find you have more time to devote to finding your way. So the first step is to get more diving under your weight belt!

Step 2: Concentrate

There is a lot going on down there. The ocean is entertaining and distracting and it is easy to let your mind drift away. However, if you watch your instructors and dive guides closely, you will notice that, no matter how much fun they are having, they are always focussed on looking for cool things, keeping the group together, taking note of their surroundings and monitoring their computer and gauges. If you are going to assume charge of your own dive, you need to concentrate similarly.

Step 3: Learn

Add a compass to your dive gear and learn how to use it. The navigation dive on your Advanced Diver Course will have taught you the basics and, from there it is just a matter of practice. Trust your compass. If it ever seems to disagree with your memory, instincts or common sense, believe your compass. It is far more likely to be correct than you are!

Step 4: Prepare

Before the dive, when you are looking out at the patch of water where you will be diving, try to visualize the underwater scenery. Look for rocks or sandbars breaking the surface. Notice how and where the colour of the water changes with depth. If you are diving close to shore, remember that the underwater landscape often mirrors the contours and features of the coastline. For example, a cliff line or a rock fall is likely to continue below the water.

Again, still while on the boat or the beach, use your compass to plan your outbound and return compass headings and note these on a slate. Memorize the position of the sun; the best natural reference there is, as long as the water is clear.

When diving wrecks, (which are often made of steel so your compass is not a reliable tool), do a little research in advance on the shape and features of the wreck, then make a drawing on your slate and remember to take the slate with you.

Step 5: Observe

You did not learn to dive just so you could spend the whole time staring at a compass underwater. Your powers of observation can help you navigate naturally. Here are a few tips on natural navigation.

On a boat dive, as you descend, look up and note what the boat looks like as you are descending; see the shape of the shadow it makes and the depth you need to be at to see this. On a shore dive find a prominent feature close to your entry point and note its depth.

After you descend and before you set off, check your depth, look around you and memorize features. Throughout the dive be alert for significant landmarks and waypoints and, after you have passed a good waypoint, turn round and see what it will look like on the way back.

Contrary to popular opinion, you can sometimes use marine life as waypoints. The underwater landscape does not remain the same and you will notice that certain fish congregate in fixed places and do not move too far from home.

When returning in sandy areas, where there may be fewer good waypoints, look for silt trails created by your fins on the way out. Sand ripples are a great navigation aid as they normally run parallel to the shore and the more pronounced the ripple, the closer you are to the beach.

Combining compass use with natural navigation can be vey effective. Knowing the direction you want to go, you can look across the compass and identify waypoints ahead of you, then use them to guide your way before referring back to your compass and repeating the process.

Returning to Base

To know how far you are away from your starting point and when you need to start looking up for the boat or returning to the shallows on a shore dive, you need to know how far you have come. The best way of measuring distance underwater for navigation purposes is by keeping track of time.

If there is no current and the pace of the dive remains the same then the time it takes you to get to the point when you turn to come back will be the same time it takes you to return to the boat. However, a dive is rarely that straightforward.

The strength and the direction of any prevailing current will have an impact on how long it will take you to get back. Spend a moment before you head out to assess what current is present and which way it is heading. When the professionals plan a dive where they need to return to a fixed point such as a pier or an anchored boat, they will normally start the dive against the current so that the return journey, when legs are tired, is easier and takes less time. If there is a strong current then the only practical way to do the dive is with a mobile chase boat to follow you.

To be sure you will make it back safely to your starting point with plenty of air left in your cylinder then a good procedure is to copy what cave divers do. They call it the "Rule of Thirds." You look at how much air you have at the beginning of the dive, say 200 Bar or 3000 psi, then calculate how what your cylinder pressure will be when you have used a third of this, (133 Bar or 2000 psi.) This is your agreed "turn pressure." The first diver in the team to reach this pressure remaining turns the dive. In general terms, they will then use the same amount of air on the return leg and get back to "base" with 67 Bar or 1000 psi remaining. This means you will always have a little extra air in case you need to deal with a current that picks up suddenly or in the event that you need to share air with a buddy.

There are more accurate ways of measuring distance than using time and air supply but they are not really practical. Counting fin kicks and arm-spans are useful techniques if you are involved in a search and recovery mission but they require far too much concentration and it is highly unlikely that you will ever persevere with them on a fun dive.

Low Visibility Navigation

When diving in very low visibility, there is no substitute for a reel and line. Tie off at your point of descent and run line out as you go so you can always find your way back. This is an excellent technique to deploy if you have dropped a descent line at a wreck site and missed it. You can run the reel out and back in various directions until you find the wreck then tie it off to give you a continuous path back to the surface.

Cavern diver, cave diver and wreck diver courses are a great opportunity to learn how to run a reel and line correctly. When laying line, it is important to wrap it or secure it regularly as you go. You want the line to be taut so it does not float around in the water where it can get you or others all tangled up. Running the reel and laying the line are best done as a two-man task with your buddy checking the wraps and placements on the way out and unwrapping them on the way back as you reel the line in. Practice on land, in the woods or around the house.

For advice on buying a reel see Chapter 26 "Accessorize Wisely" and, to get an idea of what it is like to do a cave diving course see Chapter 19 "Learning Your Lines."

Become a Better Diver by

Doing more diving
Learning how to use a compass
Using your powers of observation
Keeping track of time and air supply
Acquiring and practicing reel and line skills

9. The Art of Conservation

No matter how experienced you are or what sort of shape or size you are, you can always get more out of your diving by reducing your air consumption. The tips in this chapter will not only help you enjoy longer dives, they will also ensure you dive with less stress and, as an added bonus, make you look even better in the water than you do now, more relaxed, more comfortable and more professional. If that is not enough, you will also find you are much more aware of what is going on around you and become better at spotting marine life.

Get in the Mood

Spend a little time preparing yourself mentally following the procedures set out in Chapter 1. Find a quiet space where you can be alone and focus on the dive ahead. Slow your heartbeat, establish a deep breathing rhythm, close your eyes or gaze out on to the ocean. Get yourself into a nice peaceful zone. Put away any thoughts circling around your mind concerning other aspects of your life, particularly areas where there is something negative going on. You are going diving; there is nothing you can do about anything that is happening in your surface existence while you are underwater.

Learn to Execute the Perfect Diving Breath

Take that nice slow, deep breathing pattern with you underwater. Establish it early on in the dive and maintain it.

The most effective way for a diver to breathe is from the diaphragm, rather than the chest, so that when you inhale your stomach distends to allow your lungs to expand and draw as much air in as possible. Push your tummy out; (don't worry, no one's watching!) Ideally, take 5 to 7 seconds to breathe in; the air in your cylinder is to be sipped like wine, not guzzled like beer. When you exhale, compress your stomach muscles to reduce your lung volume to a minimum and breathe out for at least 7 seconds. This will give you a breathing cycle of around 15 seconds and a rate of about 4 breaths per minute.

The extended exhalation will ensure that you expel from your lungs as much as possible of the carbon dioxide that your body has generated via the metabolic process. A build up of carbon dioxide will cause you to breathe faster and become anxious.

Make this long, deep and slow breathing cycle an instinctive part of your diving behaviour. This will help you keep it going if something goes wrong or a current picks up. Controlling your breathing in such circumstances means you don't use up more air and helps you stay calm and think clearly.

Breathing from the diaphragm does take a little practice but you will be impressed at how calm it makes you feel. However, it is something you can practice any time, anywhere, while you are riding the bus, sitting in your car in a traffic jam or watching TV. A good exercise is to lie on the floor, put a dive weight on your stomach and focus on moving it up and down by breathing in and out. Try not to move your chest during the breathing cycle.

Get Fit

As I mentioned in Chapter 2 "Detecting and Dealing with Stress," diving is a sport for almost everyone but it is still a sport and the fitter you are the better you will dive and the less air you will use. Start a programme of progressive aerobic training and increase the level of your training as a dive trip approaches. This will enhance your stamina and help you keep a slow, steady breathing rate even when you are expending effort.

Don't Move Unless You Are Going Somewhere

When you are underwater, only move when you need to go somewhere. If you are not going anywhere, stay completely still. After all, as you sit here now, reading this book, you are unlikely to be moving your feet or flapping your arms around.

A diver's hands and arms are for communicating and holding lights and cameras. They are no use at all in the medium of water for regaining balance, maintaining buoyancy or changing direction.

Keeping your arms close to your body helps you move more smoothly through the water as it makes you more streamlined. This in turn makes it easier to swim against a current. The less effort you exert, the less air you will use up.

If you want to change direction dip your shoulder as if you are riding a motorbike and use your fins like the rudder on a boat. If you lose your balance, go with the flow at first and let yourself move with the water column. Then adjust your body position by shifting your shoulders and torso to regain your equilibrium and use breath control to make yourself more or less buoyant.

In the water, concentrate especially on what your fins are doing. Experienced guides and instructors know that the degree of a diver's mental agitation is reflected in the movement of his feet, especially when he is at the surface. Much of this movement is completely unconscious but, of course, the more the diver flaps his fins, the more energy he is expending and the more air he consumes.

The corollary is true also. Keep your feet and fins still and you will be more relaxed and you will not waste air.

Remove Weight

It is worth repeating the point that many divers carry too much weight, a hangover from their early training. This means they need to inflate their BCDs at depth excessively. The main effect of this is to give them the head up tail down posture of a seahorse. Moving through water with a profile like this takes much more effort and uses up more air than if they are horizontal and streamlined. So trim your weight down to the minimum and wear your weight-belt higher on your waist to bring your feet up and give you a horizontal swimming profile. Remember to adjust your weight belt during the dive, as it will slip when the neoprene of your wetsuit is crushed at depth.

Being over-weighted and compensating by air injection will also make it harder for you to maintain your balance underwater as the excess air moves around in your BCD every time you change your position in the water. Constantly struggling to adjust your position will cause you to get agitated and lose control of your breathing. Take off the excess lead and the balance issue will disappear too.

Know Your True Starting Pressure

The cylinder pressure you see when you check your gauge on a sunny boat deck can be misleading, and lead you to think you are starting the dive with more air than you actually have. The pressure reading will change dramatically with the drop in temperature when you enter the cool water. The underwater reading is your true starting pressure.

It is a good idea to make a pressure check part of your in water checklist as you descend at the beginning of a dive.

Carry Out an In-Water Check Early in Your Dive

In Chapter 1 "Mental Preparation" I mentioned a procedure called an "In Water Check" that is very useful for putting you in the right frame of mind for the dive that you are about to do. It involves stopping briefly just below the surface before you begin your descent to check your gear and recover your spiritual equilibrium after the turmoil and chaos of gearing up and entering the water. The In Water Check also gives you a great opportunity to get a good, long, slow, deep breathing cycle going right at the start of the dive.

Learn Different Kicks

As well as improving your air consumption, different methods of propulsion can minimise the disruption you cause to the environment through which you are swimming. There are a number of different ways of finning other than the classic wide full-legged flutter power kick. Before your next trip, go to the beach or the pool and practice doing the kind of frog kicks a breaststroke swimmer uses or a modified flutter kick with knees bent and feet up. You will find these take less energy and can be maintained for a long time with little effort.

A useful trick to avoid having to push yourself away from a coral-covered reef wall or to back your head out of a hole is to learn to fin backwards by adopting frog kicking in reverse, changing the power element of the kick from the inward to the outward stroke.

Practice with a buddy as you will need an extra pair of eyes to see what your fins are doing behind you, get advice from a local instructor or, during a trip, watch closely how your dive guides swim and copy them.

Always Know How Much Air You Have

Of course, you always know how much air you have. That is what your high pressure gauge is for. However, the gauge doesn't tell you how long your air is going to last. There are air-integrated computers on the market that will give you this information but the best computer to use is the one that's in your head.

It just takes a bit of mental arithmetic, as follows.

For those who operate metrically: as you descend, make a note of your air pressure. Let's say this is 200 Bar. After five minutes at depth, look again. Maybe you now have 180 Bar. This means you have used 20 Bar. Assuming you are diving the deepest part of your dive first, you now know that you will use at most 20 Bar every five minutes and therefore, if you want to surface with 40 Bar, you have 140 Bar left to use. So a simple calculation (140 / 20) x 5 tells you that you have AT LEAST 35 minutes of air left.

For the imperially challenged, as you descend, make a note of your air pressure. Let's say this is 3000 psi. After five minutes at depth, look again. Maybe you now have 2700 psi. This means you have used 300 psi. Assuming you are diving the deepest part of your dive first, you now know that you will use at most 300 psi every five minutes. If you want to surface with 600 psi, you have 2100 psi left to use. So a simple calculation (2100/300) x 5) tells you that you have AT LEAST 35 minutes of air left.

A DM's Trick

This trick is similar to a little technique that divemasters use when they have a group. They will draw the group's attention to something cool early on in the dive and while the divers are all distracted, they will slyly look around to see which of their divers has used most air so far. That person is then the one they watch a little more closely, knowing that the other divers will always have comparatively more air left. Of course, a good divemaster is also always on the alert for changes in breathing patterns. A lazy, out of shape diver with good buoyancy going with the flow and sipping his air may suddenly become a panting, gas-guzzling monster if the current picks up or shifts direction!

Become a Better Diver by

Perfecting your breathing technique
Improving your shape in the water
Avoiding unnecessary movement
Doing a little mental arithmetic

10. Demythologising Deco

The mantra "No decompression diving!" is right up there with "Never hold your breath!" and "Never dive alone!" in the list of well-meaning but inadequate aphorisms parroted at you during your initial diver training. You will have seen it again and again in the agreements you are asked to sign before going out diving and you will have read the phrase over and over again in the instruction manual for your dive computer.

But what does it really mean? After all, the dictionary definition of decompression reads, "the returning of a subject experiencing increased pressure, e.g. a scuba diver, to atmospheric pressure, usually in a controlled manner." Therefore, you might think, every dive is a decompression dive, no matter how deep you go or how long you stay down. And you would be absolutely right!

What your dive instructors, dive guides and computer manuals are trying to say is that you should always keep your dive depth and time to what are termed "no stop" limits, that is, the limits within which, our current knowledge of decompression science tells us, it is safe to make a slow direct ascent to the surface without having to make decompression stops.

So what they should be warning you about is no decompression STOP diving! But doing a little decompression never hurt anyone. In fact, the problem lies rather in NOT doing the decompression or failing to understand what it is. Deco needs to be demythologized.

Why Do We Have Decompression Stops?

Decompression stops are an artificial concept. The people who modelled the first decompression tables invented them to simplify the ascent from a dive where direct access to the surface is impossible.

What the mathematical models actually require is that divers make a really, really slow ascent according to a virtual ceiling which moves upwards as the reduced pressure of the gas in their bloodstream allows their body tissues to release the excess nitrogen. On a time/depth (pressure) graph the line follows a smooth curve.

This virtual ceiling ascends even more slowly as divers approach the surface, so to follow it gradually would be a very difficult thing to do, especially when the water around you is moving and the pressure sensors in dive computers are not minutely accurate.

So the modellers came up with the concept of decompression stops. They divided the water column into 3m (10 ft) slices. Wherever the mathematical model decided your virtual ceiling was when you began your ascent, based on the amount of nitrogen your body had absorbed during the dive, your decompression table directed you to stop at the boundary of the 3m (10 ft) slice below that ceiling and wait there until your virtual ceiling had moved up beyond the next shallower 3m (10 ft) slice. Then you could swim up to the boundary of that slice and wait until the ceiling moved up the next 3m (10 ft) and so on.

This was such a clever concept that even today our sophisticated dive computers and desktop decompression programmes use decompression stops to guide a diver's ascent.

What to Do with the Deco?

So what happens if you go beyond no-decompression-stop limits accidentally? You may not be surprised to hear that this happens to scuba divers every day because they are having fun, they are only human and they tend to get distracted by all the cool stuff they are seeing down there! If it has not yet happened to you, it certainly will, so it is useful to know what to do when it does!

Strangely, many divers are unaware of this. Many is the time I have seen divers suddenly panic when they inadvertently "go into deco". Worse, I have had divers approach me on the boat after a dive complaining about a broken computer which, on examination, turns out to be a perfectly functioning computer flashing a warning about a missed decompression stop!

The first thing you will notice when you "go into deco", is that your computer screen looks a little different. Instead of the no stop time you are used to seeing you will see a depth and a time on the display. The depth shown will usually be 3m (10 ft) or 6m (20 ft), although some computers give intermediate stops. Check your computer manual to see exactly what the screen will look like. Remember, the computer is NOT telling you to ascend immediately to the depth shown. It is just telling you not to go shallower than this depth. This is known as your decompression ceiling. On a no-decompression dive your ceiling is the surface.

So what do you do? First, look at your pressure gauge. Do you have plenty of air left? If so, relax; you have nothing at all to worry about. However, the longer you spend at the depth you are at, the more decompression stop time you will accumulate and if you have not planned your air supply to allow for decompression time there is a risk you will run low. The situation you want to avoid at all costs is to run out of air when you still have a decompression obligation.

So finish what you were doing or looking at, then ascend gradually, keeping a close eye on your computer. If the required decompression stop time keeps increasing then slowly move shallower still until the figure starts to fall away. Continue your dive at that depth, air supply permitting, but do NOT go deeper again, as neither your computer nor your body will like that! What you will find is that eventually your deco-stop time will disappear and you will once again have no-decompression minutes showing. This will happen quite quickly if you are at a depth of 10m (33 ft) or shallower.

One important thing to be aware of is that, while you are still deeper than the required stop depth, the decompression minutes remaining on the computer will take longer to elapse than "real" clock minutes.

At the end of any dive where you have inadvertently gone into decompression, remember to extend your safety stop time to eight or ten minutes, air permitting. Make sure you have enough air left. A good rule of thumb is to arrive at your safety stop with at least 50 bar (750 psi) remaining. Even a new diver needs no more than 30 bar (450 psi) in a normal dive cylinder to float a few metres below the surface for 10 minutes.

Deco Myths

There are a couple of myths about decompression that we should debunk right now.

Myth 1: some people associate decompression stops with decompression sickness and think that if they have a deco stop to do, they will get bent! Quite the opposite, it is only if you do not complete the decompression stops required that you risk decompression sickness. And if this ever happens, then again, there is no need to panic. Monitor yourself for symptoms of the bends, most commonly pain or a rash, and if these do present themselves, breathe 100% oxygen and seek medical assistance as soon as you can.

Myth 2: many also misunderstand that decompression is all about stopping at exact depths during your ascent. This is not the case. Deco-stops are just a convenient means of slowing a diver's ascent, an artificially created concept devised by the programmers of decompression software designed to help divers manage a slow ascent more easily by stopping at convenient 3m (10ft) intervals. The perfect decompression schedule would be a smooth curve, or an infinite schedule of tiny stops following a virtual ceiling that becomes ever shallower with time. In fact, it is a good idea to make sure you do not inadvertently breach the ceiling by staying a little below the required stop depth. This will allow for variations in buoyancy and the accuracy of your computer's pressure sensor.

A Word on Safety Stops

The designation of 3m, 4.5m, 5m, 6m, (10ft, 15ft or 20ft), (depending on your training agency and nationality,) as the depth at which you do your safety stop is purely arbitrary. If you have remained within no decompression limits throughout your dive, then it is an excellent idea to pause for three to five minutes at between 3m (10ft) and 6m (20ft) before surfacing as long as you have enough air and water conditions allow you to do this safely.

Sometimes there is no need to make a safety stop. For instance, if you have spent the last twenty minutes of the dive at 6m (20ft) cruising over a shallow reef top, then your safety stop requirements have already been fully met and, when you are ready to end the dive, you just need to make a slow direct ascent to the surface.

Ascent Advice

The key word here is "slow." Whether you have done a safety stop or not, as you are making your final ascent to the surface at the end of your dive, move slowly. Remember, the closer you get to the surface the greater is the pressure change as you ascend, so this is the part of the water column where the speed of your ascent is most crucial.

How fast does this final ascent from your safety stop usually take you? About ten seconds? Count out ten seconds to yourself. That feels pretty slow, right? Unfortunately, it is nowhere near slow enough. Going from 4.5m (15ft) to the surface in 10 seconds means you are moving at a speed of 27m (90ft) per minute!

The commonly accepted recommended maximum ascent rate for sport divers is 9m (30ft) per minute, so an ascent from 15ft (4.5m) to the surface should take you a MINIMUM of 30 seconds.

Yet it is very common to see divers assiduously carrying out their safety stops for several minutes then undoing all the benefits of this and heading fast for the surface.

Do this: mark out 4.5m (15ft) on the floor then walk the distance in 30 seconds and see just how slowly you have to move. That is the maximum ascent speed you should be aiming at as 30 seconds is the minimum time you should take to go from your safety stop to the surface. In practice it is a good idea to take even longer.

It is Not Always Safer to Stop!

There are also occasions when carrying out a safety stop just adds risk to your dive. Imagine, for example, that while you have been underwater a storm has come up and as you ascend you look up and see that the ocean has become very choppy, your descent line is jerking up and down reflecting the pitch and roll of the boat and from 6m (20ft) to the surface the moving water will make it difficult to maintain a constant depth. Technical divers learn procedures for decompressing in such conditions. On a no-decompression dive, however, where a stop is a luxury rather than an absolute requirement, in such circumstances the safest procedure for everyone is for you to omit your safety stop, continue your slow ascent to the surface and get back on board quickly. This will allow the crew to move the boat to a calmer and more secure location.

A Good Way to Dive (Or What Works, Works!)

Descend slowly to the deepest point of the dive and swim with the current, if there is one, ascending to an intermediate level when your computer shows a single digit no-decompression time remaining. Stay at this new level until again the no decompression time remaining drops to a single digit and then ascend again, always staying well ahead of your decompression curve. As your air supply falls below 70 bar (1000 psi) or so, move up to a depth shallower than 9m (30ft) for a while before spending the last few minutes of the dive watching the action on top of the wall at around 4.5 to 6m (15ft to 20ft.) Finally, slowly ascend to the surface when your air runs low or you are ready for a surface break.

In the dive industry, we know from experience that typical tropical reef dive profiles like this one work well and produce an extremely low incidence of decompression sickness.

Assuming that you have smooth conditions and plenty of air to breathe you can create a similar profile when you ascend from a dive with no shallow section, such as a mid ocean shipwreck, by pausing for a few minutes at a couple of intermediate depths as you come up.

Planned Decompression Diving

If you want to dive deeper and longer, you need to take training courses to learn how to plan for decompression, work out your air consumption rate and calculate the amount of air you will need including a healthy reserve supply. Ideally you will also carry a second gas with a higher percentage of oxygen to switch to on ascent to reduce your decompression burden.

You will also be taught how to use alternative self-rescue and team rescue procedures and equipment. These are different to those you are taught in beginners' recreational diving courses because when you are "in deco" the surface is no longer an avenue of escape in the event of equipment failure. You will learn valuable skills that develop both your ability as a diver and your self-confidence.

Become a Better Diver by

Not worrying about a little deco
Understanding what is happening
Making sure you always leave yourself enough air for an extended safety stop

When A Safety Stop Is Not Safe!

Some folk really do not understand the concept of safety stops and perhaps training agencies need to review the way the topic is taught and ask if perhaps too much emphasis is placed on the necessity of performing one on <u>every</u> dive.

They are a really good idea if you are coming up to the surface from a no-decompression dive, the conditions are calm and you have plenty of air left. But, as I mention elsewhere in this chapter, missing a safety stop when you have plenty of remaining no-decompression time showing on your computer is not going to hurt you.

I once had a diver in my group who used her air up quickly so I took her and her buddy to the surface and escorted them back to the boat before rejoining the rest of the group. When I brought everyone else back to the boat a few minutes later, I noticed that the couple that had come up early were nowhere to be seen. I eventually found them under the boat hanging on to the anchor rope at 5m (15ft)!

When, later, I calmly (not really!) asked them what they had been thinking, they replied that after getting back on the boat they realized they had not done a safety stop on the initial ascent with me, so they put their gear back on and went back into the water to do it!

11. Ten Things Tech Diving Teaches Us

F ar from being the mythical daredevils of diving legend, technical divers are actually thoughtful, careful individuals who are attentive to detail and constantly looking out for ways of improving the way they dive. Over the past twenty five years the technical community has proven to be a crucible of creativity from which several equipment and procedural innovations have emerged that have had an enormous impact on the sport. There are also a number of ways that their more carefully considered approach can serve as an example to divers who may not be engaged in such extreme diving but are keen to improve their skills and build confidence.

Here are five things technical divers do that we should ALL do.

1. Configuration

A technical diver constantly evaluates and re-evaluates the purpose of the equipment he carries with him under water and the way he puts it all together.

Among other things, he makes sure that everything has a

function to perform on the specific dive he is planning, each item is secured and easily accessible and anything that is essential for the safe conclusion of the dive is backed up .

He also checks that his equipment is balanced and as streamlined as possible and nothing is loose or hanging down.

This process is discussed at length in Chapter 25 "The Concept of Configuration." If your equipment is currently set up exactly as it was when you learned to dive, a review may be well overdue!

2. The What Ifs

All but a very tiny percentage of diving accidents involve an event that was predictable and could have been avoided or handled comfortably if the diver had anticipated it and planned and practiced what he would do if and when it happened. This is the basic premise behind a process that technical divers refer to as "Assessing The What-Ifs."

They assess all the things that could go wrong on a dive and make sure they have the knowledge, skills and back up equipment they will need to deploy to survive such an event. In corporate terminology, they are implementing a risk management action plan.

They list all the variables that could create stress or lead to an emergency, formulate a plan to combat each eventuality and then practice the correct response until it becomes instinctive.

Although it may not have been explained as such, this was the concept behind the skills that you learned in your diver-training course right from the start. Your instructor was not just harassing you for his own entertainment when he made you remove and replace your mask or scuba gear. He was teaching you what to do in the event of a broken mask strap or if your cylinder were ever to slip out of the BCD cam-band.

The chapters in this book, particularly those in the Safety Section, cover many of the things that can go wrong. They analyse the action you need to take and the equipment you need to carry in order to prevent an emergency or deal with one when it occurs. You may find the chapters useful in compiling your own "What If" checklist but do not assume that I have thought of everything! This book is not a substitute for independent thought! The important thing is to adopt a "What If" mindset. Your checklist is an individual thing and particular to you. It can vary depending on the sort of diving you do, where it takes place, the equipment and gases available, the number of people in your dive team and the skills and preferences of each member. It should also be considered as a work in progress, always capable of being improved.

3. Gas Calculation

The way to calculate how much air you breathe is something that all divers should learn from the start but it is rarely taught. A technical diver knows his breathing rate as well as he knows his blood group but few recreational divers are aware of this vital statistic. Non-divers might find this unusual!

Once you know your breathing rate, you can easily calculate how much air you are likely to breathe during a given time at depth and can relate that to the volume of air in your cylinder. This knowledge makes you more aware of your status in the water, helps alleviate anxiety and instils a great deal of confidence.

It is a simple thing to do. Descend to a depth of 10 m (33ft) and record your cylinder pressure on a slate. Swim normally at 10 m (33ft) for ten minutes then stop and record your new cylinder pressure.

Let's say you used 20 bar during your swim and you were using a 12-litre cylinder. That means you used 240 litres in 10 minutes or 24 litres per minute at a depth of 10 metres (2 atmospheres absolute (ata)), which equates to 12 litres per minute at the surface.

Armed with this figure, you now know that you will use 36 litres per minute at a depth of 20 metres (3 ata) and 60 litres per minute at 40 metres (5 ata.) Isn't that good knowledge to have in the back of your mind?

In imperial terms, say you used 300 psi during your swim and the cylinder you were using is rated at 77.4 cu ft when filled to 3000 psi. 300 psi in this cylinder is therefore the equivalent of 77.4 /(3000/300) = 7.74 cu ft. You breathed this volume of air in 10 minutes so that means you used 0.774 cu ft of air per minute at a depth of 33 ft (2 ata,) which equates to 0.387 cu ft per minute at the surface.

You can now calculate that you will use around 1.2 cu ft of air per minute at a depth of 66 ft (3 ata) and around 2 cu ft per minute at 132 ft (5 ata.)

It is a good idea to repeat the exercise a number of times and take an average. Also, try it a couple of times swimming fast and see what that does to your consumption rate!

4. Reels and Lines

A technical diver will carry a reel and line on every dive. If using a reel is an integral part of the dive plan, such as when entering a wreck, cavern or cave, he will carry at least two. Deploying a reel requires a little tuition and a great deal of practice as line in water can take on a life of its own and seem wilfully to conspire against you. However, perseverance carries the reward of being armed with a tool that you can use in a variety of situations. For example, your reel can help you find your way in poor visibility; create an emergency ascent platform or tie yourself in and float free of a bouncing anchor or shot line.

5. Ascents

In recreational no decompression stop diving, the majority of any planning that occurs usually revolves around the "bottom" portion of the dive. It is understandable therefore that divers tend to get into the habit of switching off once they begin their ascent and focus their attention instead on the tea and biscuits (or beer and hotdogs) waiting for them on shore. This is a tendency that instructors have to work hard to change when introducing sport divers to the technical world.

In technical diving, the marker of a successful dive is a safe ascent and decompression rather than the accomplishment of any specific mission. If you did not achieve all your aims on a dive, you can always try again later. A failed ascent could be life threatening.

As with the "What Ifs," it is a question of mindset. Recreational divers may not have the decompression burden that technical divers have but planning in advance for where and how you will make your ascent is conducive to a successful dive, no matter what the parameters are. After all, in scuba diving, going down and staying down are not the difficult bits, (a brick can do that.) Coming up again is the part that requires skill.

Technical divers ascend slowly, even at the beginning of the ascent. In fact, they will often make short stops in the depths far below the decompression stops required by their computer or dive table. These are called Pyle stops (or deep stops) and are named after Hawaii-based ichthyologist Richard Pyle, who noticed that after deep dives when he caught fish, he felt much better and less tired than when he had not caught any fish. He concluded that this was nothing to do with his happiness quotient; it was all to do with the different profile he had to follow on an ascent with fish in his net when he would stop every few metres to depressurize their swim bladders and make sure they did not explode on the way to the surface. Although we still do not know for sure why these deeper stops are physiologically beneficial, nevertheless the technical community has a saying, "What works, works!" and Pyle stops or similar procedures are now a feature of some more advanced computers and decompression algorithms.

On ascent, technical divers will also switch away from their bottom gas as soon as it is safe to do so, and start breathing from a supply with a lower inert gas content and higher oxygen content in order to accelerate elimination of inert gas from their tissues. This is done to reduce decompression time and improve physiological well-being. This is something that recreational divers could also consider, not to the extent of carrying an additional cylinder containing a higher NITROX mix with them on the dive, as technical divers do, but perhaps the boat's hang tank at safety stop depth could be a NITROX 50 mix instead of air and have a number of second stages attached to it instead of just one?

In recent years, cave divers, wreck divers and technical divers in general have been responsible for a number of innovations in scuba equipment, diver training and diving practice which have been passed on to the sport diving community at large and which are now universally accepted. Here are some examples.

6. Alternative Diving Gases

It may be hard to believe now but there was a time, not so long ago, when many of scuba's most influential organizations and periodicals forecast that to introduce NITROX to the recreational diving community would lead to disaster. They dubbed it the "Devil Gas" and forbade all exhibitors at Dive Shows from advertising anything to do with NITROX. One major tourist destination, the Cayman Islands, initially issued an edict banning NITROX diving from its waters completely.

However, technical divers had been using higher oxygen mixes to extend bottom time and conduct safer decompressions for years and, in a demonstration of people power, divers as a whole all over the world decided that they would ignore the warnings of the entrenched conservative scuba establishment and flocked in their thousands to the technical training agencies to see for themselves what NITROX was all about. This forced a dramatic about-turn from the mainstream organizations who now of course espouse NITROX wholeheartedly and even offer it as an option on beginner diver courses. Today it is everywhere and, whereas in the early 1990s a diver with a NITROX tank on his back raised hackles, now the sight of the green and yellow band does not even raise an eyebrow.

Now there are signs of helium-based diving gases entering the mainstream. The use of breathing mixtures such as TRIMIX, HELIOX and HELIAIR has long been the province only of ultra-deep divers, who use them as a bottom gas to avoid oxygen toxicity and reduce narcosis, (see Chapter 30 "The Folly of Deep Air and the Joy of Mix.") Over the last few years, however, technical divers have also been successfully using helium-based mixtures with a high oxygen content for decompression and this has led some training agencies to introduce single cylinder, no-decompression, recreational TRIMIX courses for divers wanting to offset the effects of narcosis even on comparatively shallow dives.

There are still very few TRIMIX capable dive computers around but decompression tables are now available for mixes such as TRIMIX 32/15 (32% oxygen and 15% helium), which offers similar no decompression times to NITROX 32. If you get a chance, "Try MIX". The difference from diving on air is astonishing. You are more alert, you notice more, you are a more attentive dive partner and you remember more about the dive afterwards.

7. Longer Regulator Hoses

For decades divers carried only one second stage regulator and learned to "buddy breathe" in an out of air emergency, with two people sharing a single second stage. However, cave divers trying to exit together following an air supply crisis found it very difficult to buddy breathe through narrow sections of a cave, (known as restrictions), and solved this problem by adding another second stage attached to a hose long enough to permit two divers following each other to breathe from the same cylinder. Eventually this practice found its way out of the caves via the wreck diving community and now an octopus regulator is part of a diver's standard equipment.

Unfortunately, as discussed in detail in Chapter 20 "Running the Rule over Regulators", the original purpose seems to have been lost in the way many recreational divers choose to set up their alternate second stage on ever shorter hoses.

Unless the hose on the regulator extended to an out-of-air diver is long enough to permit both divers freedom of movement an air-sharing ascent is likely to be hard to accomplish without difficulty.

8. Clips and D Rings

It was diver demand that led equipment manufacturers to start selling clips and attaching D-rings to BCDs. This is a relatively recent innovation as you can see if you look back in time at old diver training videos and TV shows like the Cousteau series or Sea Hunt, which show that keeping control of "danglies" was not always a priority.

Again, the idea came from technical divers. A key feature of the configuration process is deciding where and how to stow equipment. Using clips and D rings allows accessories and hoses to be attached closely and securely and makes them much more accessible than if they are stowed away in a pouch with a variety of other items. At depth, time is critical: gas supplies diminish fast and narcosis slows a diver's speed of thought. For example, taking extra time to locate and deploy a cutting tool in order to extricate a diver from an emergency might make the difference between survival and failure. Other advantages are that a streamlined diver moves more quickly, wastes less energy and consumes less air and a dangling hose or accessory can snag on a wreck or a coral head, causing damage to both equipment and environment.

Divers saw the practical value; manufacturers took note and D rings and clips started sprouting everywhere. Not all the products that appeared were an unqualified success, however. Some of the manufactures just did not get the concept. Some added D rings to loose chest straps that just swung free below a horizontal diver. Others decided to economise and paint plastic D-rings silver instead of using stainless steel. A range of plastic hose retaining clips also appeared that seemed to work well when the diver was standing up but just allowed the hoses to slip through and dangle free as soon as the diver started swimming. Nevertheless, the overall trend was positive and divers were now able to buy accessories that allowed them much more flexibility in setting up their equipment.

9. Surface Marker Buoys

Initially developed by technical divers as an aid to maintaining control of their depth during long drifting decompressions and to enable a boat to follow the dive team over a distance, the idea of inflating a surface marker buoy to identify the location of divers on a safety stop has become a common practice among divemasters all over the world.

10. Harness and Wing Systems

Harness and wing BCD systems were another innovation that was initially greeted with disdain by the mainstream dive industry. The objections came thick and fast, "they throw you on to your front"; "it is difficult to vent air from them." Of course, all that was required was a little training in the use of a back-mounted air cell and divers could benefit from a design that held a divers head higher on the surface, was easier to control than a wrap-around BCD and did not squeeze the diver's ribcage and inhibit breathing when inflated. People liked the lack of encumbrance and freedom of movement permitted by having just a harness instead of an inflatable jacket around their torso and voted with their wallets. Now most BCD manufacturers have back-mounted options.

Become a Better Diver by

Copying some of the things technical divers do
Keeping an open mind
Always being alert for ways in which you can improve the way you dive

12. Don't Always Copy The Pros

The Mythology

Your first dive instructor is always a golden god or goddess of the sea! He or she has the answers to all the questions, sees everything that goes on, is always around to offer help when you need it and, most impressive of all, can move around underwater effortlessly like a fish while you flail around awkwardly. Nothing is ever a problem; life is fun and full of high fives.

As you gain more experience, you realise that the tanned, blond deities that greet you off the plane may have only been there a few weeks and could have fewer dives logged than you do.

This is of course all part of the scuba diving industry. We sell a certain relaxed, carefree lifestyle. The advertising for scuba instructor courses sells the job with images of gorgeous coral reefs (the office), cool dudes and chicks in sunglasses (your colleagues) with the wind blowing in their hair as their speedboat carries them off to the next dive site (meeting.)

The Reality

The reality, of course, is very different. After the customers have returned to their hotels, the real work begins: filling cylinders, washing and fixing equipment, doing the paperwork, preparing for the next day's classes and dives, nursing aches and pains and reviewing the day's work to see where mistakes were made or what could have been improved. Believe it or not, it is work!

We do not tend to show the work that goes into preparing for a dive because that is not what the customers want to see. The perfect dive operation can be compared to a duck, serene and effortless on the surface, with lots of unseen paddling going on beneath. This misleads many into believing that when you become expert you do not have to prepare so assiduously or take so many precautions. The truth, as professionals often learn by bitter experience is that the more familiar you are with a procedure, the more instinctive it becomes but the more careful you have to be to guard against complacency and carelessness.

Preaching and Practising

You will see many examples where professionals say one thing and then do exactly the opposite. For instance, an instructor will tell his beginner students about the inherent risk in diving a yo-yo profile with frequent ascents and descents and then on dive four of their course he will escort all six of them individually as they practice emergency out-of-air ascents to the surface from 6m (20ft), going up and down several times, (yes, like a yo-yo,) in that part of the water column where the pressure change, and therefore the risk, is greatest.

Similarly, no diving manual would ever condone the practice of doing a deep bounce dive incorporating substantial physical stress followed a few minutes later by a longer dive to the same depth but this is something that divemasters in some areas do, several times a day, as they set the shot line into a wreck and then ascend in order to pick up the group and guide them around the site.

The fact that contradictions exist between what we preach and what we practice does not mean that our advice is flawed and that the practices are safe. Nor does it imply that we are indeed mythological "dive gods" and that somehow the laws of physics and physiology do not apply to us.

It is true that, when they dive twenty to thirty times a week, every week, professionals develop a high level of dive fitness. They are also aware of the risks involved in some of the work they are required to do and mitigate the risks wherever possible, for instance, by ensuring the key elements of their equipment are in perfect shape and keeping themselves well rested and hydrated before and after each dive.

However, it is also the case that the risks sometimes carry painful rewards and, unfortunately, although this is certainly not something that the scuba diving industry advertises widely, professionals are more frequent visitors to the recompression chambers than their amateur counterparts. Most long-term dive instructors have chronic aches and pains accumulated over years of submitting their bodies to constant pressure changes.

The Paradise Conundrum

A beach on a remote tropical island may seem like paradise when you visit for a couple of weeks but, limited entertainment opportunities, overconfidence and the temptation of believing their own propaganda can often induce those who have to live and work in paradise for months on end to do some pretty dumb things.

Many instructors and divemasters go through this "adolescent" stage at some point during their development. Some common symptoms of the syndrome are listed at the end of this chapter. Do not try any of these things at home!

"Intro" and "Trust Me" Dives

This is a good place to discuss introductory dives and "Trust Me" dives.

If you are diving in a new environment for the first time, in a shipwreck or a cave system or under ice for example, you do not have the knowledge or experience to anticipate what could go wrong or even to identify potential dangers early enough to deal with them. So, when you pay to take a course with an instructor you implicitly hand over to them a certain amount of the responsibility for your safety.

Professionals accept that responsibility because our knowledge and experience in the environment enable us to anticipate and deal with problems on your behalf and we are comfortable enough within the parameters of the dive to be able to concentrate our attention fully on you, the student. If this is not the case, then we should not be teaching the course.

We do hundreds of dives a year in a variety of conditions. This gives us an instinctive familiarity with the processes of scuba diving. We acquire a sixth sense of when something is going wrong or about to go wrong and, like an experienced tennis player who is in position for the shot before it arrives, we develop an uncanny ability to anticipate problems and be in the right place at the right time to deal with them.

These are the primary skills that enable us to take on responsibility for our students' safety and why we can be trusted with this burden.

No matter how good a diver you are, unless you are involved in teaching and looking after divers full-time, you will not develop these instincts. Therefore, never get yourself persuaded into a situation where others are depending on you for their safety. Experienced divers are often tempted by their own egos or persuasive friends and colleagues to take them on "trust me" dives, to show them what it is like to go deep, dive inside a shipwreck or use TRIMIX. No matter how capable an experienced individual is at conducting such dives on his own or with a dive team that has similar training, he does not have the knowledge or instincts to take care of someone else.

It is best, therefore, to leave such things to the professionals. This advice applies even more strongly to introductory dives.

There are many instructors whose daily task it is to take non-divers out and introduce them to the underwater world on a scuba experience. These professionals do not have the most glamorous jobs in the industry; they generally work in the same place every day, they never get to dive deep or in currents or see new animals, but they do develop superb dive management and control skills.

In their situation, they are completely and utterly responsible for the safety of their customers, who, although they may have been introduced to a couple of basic skills in a pool or confined water, are certainly not able to rescue themselves if left alone.

Although economic considerations sometimes intrude, the smart dive centres pick their best instructors to run introductory dives. This is similar to skydiving, where only the top trainers are licensed to carry out tandem jumps. The dive centres do not only do this on safety grounds, they also know that if a non-diver has a great time on their Discover Scuba Diving experience, they are more likely to sign up for a course!

So if your friends ask you to show them what it is like to dive, resist the temptation to stroke your ego. Take them down to your local dive centre and ask a professional to do it.

Become a Better Diver by

Not falling for the mythology
Leaving the teaching to the teachers

Dumb Things Dive Pros Do

Making a forward roll entry from the deck or dock in full scuba gear. Do not attempt this unless you want to practice sewing stitches in your own cracked skull.

Putting their scuba gear on by placing it in front of them, tucking their arms through the shoulder straps and throwing it over their head, and possibly straight into anyone walking or sitting behind them at the time.

Doing an ultra deep single tank bounce dive on air.

Strapping on a used cylinder at the end of the day to "use up the air" or to "pop" down and free the boat anchor. Air fills are cheap: use a full cylinder, always!

Stroking or feeding marine animals with large teeth, spines or stings. The animal may not completely understand that it is expected to play only a passive role in this entertainment.

Holding free-diving depth competitions between dives. (See section on Shallow Water Blackout in Chapter 28 "The Black Gases.")

Training

13. The Training Minefield

Diver training agencies are in the business of teaching. The more courses a diver takes, the more money the agencies make. They have therefore created what can often seem to be a bewildering array of programmes and promote these very effectively via their network of dive centres and instructors who, at times, can seem to be encouraging card accumulation rather than offering education.

Some specialty courses are well worthwhile and will make you a better diver. Some are absolutely essential if you have specific diving ambitions to achieve. Other courses may probably not develop your skills sufficiently to warrant the expense. The programmes discussed below are not an exhaustive list; for instance, I have not included courses that purport to teach sport divers commercial diving skills; but I have endeavoured to cover all the usual offerings.

A couple of points: first, a major benefit of signing up for further training, quite apart from what you learn, is that you get to spend plenty of quality time in the water with someone who is paid and perfectly placed to give you constructive criticism on all aspects of your diving. A good instructor will not confine himself rigidly to the specifics of the course he is teaching, he will also be open to questions and attentive for ways in which that he can help you improve your general skills. So, to a certain degree, in the right hands, there is no such thing as a wasted course.

Second: some of the wording and descriptions below may suggest that my comments are directed at the programmes of specific training agencies. This is not the case. Any coincidence of terminology is entirely accidental.

Advanced Training

Most beginner scuba diving courses involve four or five dives, after which you are certified to go diving without supervision in the company of a similarly experienced person. It is rare that a new diver is genuinely equipped to do this safely. Primarily for this reason, it is a good idea to sign up for an advanced course directly on completion of the beginners' programme.

The course gives you five or six further dives under an instructor's supervision, all of them in different conditions or circumstances, and this widens your experience considerably. It does not turn you into an expert overnight but it does prepare you much better to become a well-functioning, independent diver.

Another reason to take an advanced course early is that, whether it is right or wrong to do so, many dive operations require evidence of advanced certification before they will take you below 18m (60 ft.)

A good advanced course will include a deep dive, a night dive, an underwater navigation dive and a couple of other specialty dives that give you the maximum amount of in-water time possible.

Rescue Training

Many divers find this the most rewarding of all training courses and, in the right hands, this can be a watershed course that transforms a diver who has been completely fixated on events in his own mind during his diving to date into a considerate team member who is confident, watches what is going on around him and is ready to help another diver if required.

Buoyancy Skills

With the knowledge and basic skills acquired during Beginners and Advanced training most divers can usually develop competence by observation and simply doing more diving. A specific Buoyancy Skills course would only usually be necessary to fix inadequate initial training.

Planned Decompression Diving

Most people spend their entire diving lives only flirting casually with decompression. However, if you intend to deepen the relationship it is essential that you take courses so you are fully informed of the risks and obtain the knowledge and equipment required to undertake decompression dives safely. The training path is outlined in Chapter 17 "To the Extreme."

Deep

A Deep specialty course is highly recommended for divers who have plenty of dives under their weight belt, are comfortable with their basic skills and are starting to dive deeper, albeit briefly. It should teach you how to use a genuine alternate air source such as a pony bottle, how to calculate your air consumption, how to handle narcosis, what to do if you accidentally find yourself with an unplanned decompression burden and how to deploy an SMB.

Drift

This is a good type of dive to include as an elective during an advanced open water course or similar but most of the necessary skills can be picked up by observation and experience.

Equipment (Drysuits, DPVs)

If you buy equipment that requires particular skills to operate, such as a drysuit or a diver propulsion vehicle (DPV) then a fast track to familiarity is to seek instruction in its use, rather than waste time figuring it all out for yourself. Although both drysuits and DPVs offer enormous benefits to divers, both add a degree of difficulty to your diving and there are a number of tips and tricks you can learn to reduce the risks and take maximum advantage of the opportunities they offer.

Ice

See Chapter 16 "Under Frozen Seas" for a good idea of what to expect from an Ice Diving course.

Naturalist

This is an excellent course to take if you have been out of the water for a while and need to get in some dive time with an instructor around. The course will involve marine life identification but should also teach you techniques to enable you to get closer to the animals without disturbing their environment such as non-silting fin kicks and finely-tuned positioning skills.

This is also a very good way of getting acquainted with diving in a new part of the world or an unfamiliar environment. There is every reason, in fact, to do several naturalist courses during your diving career. A course run in Newfoundland, for example, would be very different from one conducted in Indonesia.

Navigation

An underwater navigation specialty course will give you confidence and improve your awareness. It should teach you a mixture of natural and compass navigation techniques as well as ways to calculate distance underwater and how to make sure you can always return to your starting point. This is a good course to take early in your career, especially if you do a lot of diving without a guide.

Night

The night dive on your advanced course should teach you all you need to know about night diving. It is difficult to imagine who would really need an entire course dedicated to diving in the dark.

NITROX

This is another course to do early on in your diving career especially as NITROX is increasingly available in resorts and on liveaboards where it often governs group dive profiles and time at depth. If you are on air and your fellow divers are on NITROX, they will be spending most of the dive cruising comfortably along several metres below you with plenty of no-decompression time remaining while you are glancing anxiously at your computer and planning your ascent.

Overhead Environment Diving / Wreck/ Cavern / Cave

Once you have mastered the open ocean, the final skill frontier in recreational scuba is diving in an overhead environment, which requires exceptional comfort in the water and physical control. Many divers love to explore inside shipwrecks and cave diving is the most demanding and most rewarding of all disciplines. Divers frequently ask if they should do a wreck diver course or a cave diver course in order to obtain the skills to dive in an overhead environment and the answer is usually, "both!"

There are wreck diving courses available that will give you some minimal experience in an overhead environment and practice running a line and reel. These have some value as a starting point but wreck diving and cave diving are really technical diving programmes and should be undertaken only after you have had some decompression diver training.

On a wreck diving course you will learn about shipwrecks and acquire superb control and penetration techniques but the distances you can cover will be limited by the size of the wreck. A cave diver course is the ultimate skill challenge. The best place in the world to do one is in the cave systems around Florida's Lake City. Why? Because the instructors in that area pretty much invented the sport and were responsible for developing many of the techniques and some of the equipment that all scuba divers use today, such as octopus regulators and BCDs.

The Florida systems are deep enough and extensive enough to give you the kind of lengthy swim time and decompression time you need to complete during a good cave course; 600 minutes in-water time is the usual standard. They are also varied enough to give you experience of many of the conditions that you will face in a cave career and to show you why people become obsessed with this exotic niche of the sport.

This is an environment that makes adjectives like spectacular, gorgeous and humbling come tumbling through your mind at every turn of the tunnel. A cave course in Florida has proved to be a life-changing experience for more than a few divers: you will develop hitherto unimagined levels of skill. See Chapter 19 "Learn Your Lines" later in this section for one person's account of his experience.

Photography

This course can help you avoid making expensive mistakes and provide a useful shortcut to taking good images. Wait until you are completely comfortable with your buoyancy skills before thinking about taking a camera underwater and wait until you have taken the course before you buy a camera system. Start small and be patient.

Choosing the Right Instructor.

It is common for divers to follow further training with the instructor who taught them to dive in the first place. A bond has been forged, a friendship has been developed and there is a degree of comfort in extending your skills and the range of your diving with someone you know and trust.

However, this relationship can also involve an element of dependency, which can inhibit your growth as a diver. Choosing a different instructor for a new training course may take you out of the comfort zone you have established with your original instructor and force you to be more self-reliant.

It may also expose you to a different approach to diving as everyone has their own style and no two instructors will approach the sport in exactly the same way. Another factor to consider is that some instructors are specialists in certain fields, such as Underwater Photography or Wreck Diving, and they may have more to offer than a "general practitioner" whose skill set covers a wider area but who is not so expert in one specific subject.

It is unlikely that you were the one who chose your initial instructor but if you did, you probably made the decision based on a suggestion from a friend. To ask for recommendations from people who have already done the course and whose opinions you trust is still a good first move when looking for a new instructor.

However, as you are now a certified diver, you are better armed with the knowledge and experience to conduct more in-depth research and reach a more informed decision.

Talk to the instructors directly, either by phone or in person. Ask all the questions you can think of and assess the enthusiasm of their response. If they don't have time for you before you've paid, then you cannot expect to receive the attention you need after they've pocketed your money!

Observe at first hand the instructor's attitude to training and personal dive skills. Go out on a boat trip with your buddy when the instructor is teaching or guiding dives. Is he sufficiently comfortable with his own skills to devote 100% of his underwater attention to the divers? Do you find his personality and approach to work sympathetic? After all, these are crucial qualities to look for in someone to whom you will be handing a considerable degree of responsibility for your safety.

Do not choose an instructor simply on the basis of experience. Of course, experience is important but be aware that, as in all professional fields, a person who has been doing something for a long time can become jaded and set in their ways or they might just be too busy and successful to devote all their attention to you. Newer instructors are often more enthusiastic, attentive to detail, open to new methods and ready to put in extra time. After all, time is a very important element in any course: not only time to practice skills or acquire knowledge, but also time to review and reflect on what you are learning.

Never choose your instructor on the basis of price alone. You always get what you pay for. A cheap course will invariably mean rushed lectures, short dives, a tight schedule and little time for questions, individual assessment or remedial work. If the course is cheap, the instructor will cut corners or you'll find yourself incurring extra fees during the course. Beware of incomplete courses or phrases such as, "ah, you already know this stuff!" that are the hallmark of the lazy instructor. All the agencies publish "Standards and Procedures," which list the required elements of every training course. Ask to see these; a good instructor will give you a copy before you ask!

Become a Better Diver by

Always being ready to learn
Doing further training
Working with different instructors

14. Beneath Dark Waters - Night Diving

After a day's diving, many people choose to head for happy -hour to mull over the events of the day and exchange notes with other divers. If you postpone the aperitifs for a couple of hours, however, and do a night dive instead, you will find you have a whole lot more to talk about!

When the sun goes down, even a patch of nondescript seabed that seemed boring in the daytime can turn into an underwater wonderland. It's a little like Las Vegas – a dull desert town by day and a fantasyland after dark. The marine world is transformed by the many nocturnal fish and animals that come out to play: and everyone gets dressed up for the party!

Daylight denizens of the reef such as triggerfish lock themselves into crevices with their dorsal spines; parrotfish surround themselves in a mucus bubble and the bizarre creatures of the night come out to patrol the seabed. Nudibranchs, crabs, lobsters, octopus, brittle stars, urchins and other weird forms of life hunt, mate and feed all over the place! Coral polyps spread their glorious tentacles and plankton erupts in incandescent bioluminescence illuminating the scene.

To participate in this bacchanalian orgy you just need to plunge in, take it easy and take it slowly, but some tips and tricks will come in useful as well, which is where this chapter comes in.

Making All The Right Night Moves

Keep It Simple.

Don't carry a camera until you have mastered the key night-diving skill combination of using a torch while maintaining neutral buoyancy and keeping track of where you are. Dive the site during the day first. It will make natural navigation much easier.

Choose Your Partners

Dive with your regular buddies. Make sure you agree on plans for the dive in advance. Stay close and keep the beam of your buddy's lights in your peripheral vision or look up and check frequently.

Move Slowly, Look Closely

Night diving is not an exercise in swimming great distances or moving quickly. Restrain your ambitions. It is all about staying still, concentrating on a small area and observing carefully.

Leave Word

Tell someone where you are going and when you'll be back. Then stick to the plan no matter how good a time you are having to avoid creating undue anxiety or causing them to activate the emergency services needlessly.

Feet First

To avoid disorientation, use a down-line if you can and descend slowly feet first, facing the other members of your team. Shine your light downwards and keep fins still so you avoid touching and disturbing the seabed below. Pause at a pre-determined depth, check your buoyancy, and then get yourself nice and horizontal before moving off. At the end of the dive ascend via a line or up a wall so you always have a reference.

Stay Still

Good buoyancy control and minimal finning are crucial ingredients for a good night dive. If you are one of those divers whose feet move when the rest of your body is still, work hard on the under-rated skill of remaining motionless.

Relax

During the dive, relax. Adopt a long breathing pattern, taking slow deep breaths.

But Remain Alert

Check your computer and pressure gauge a little more often than you would on a day dive.

Carry Back Up

Take three lights with you on every night dive: a primary, a secondary and a marker light.

Lights

Your main and brightest light is called your primary light. To get the most from night dives, it is worth investing in a good torch. Choose one with rechargeable batteries, as these are both more cost effective and provide a more consistent beam throughout the dive. Many good lights have variable settings so you can adjust the level of brightness. If your light is too bright you will spook the animals you are trying to approach.

Look for a floodlight rather than a spotlight. Most of the time, you will want to bathe a large area in a smooth, featureless pool of light without filament or reflector shadows. Make sure the burn time is more than adequate for the length of your dive plus a few minutes before and after.

Lights with a one-finger on/off switch are much easier to use than those that are activated by twisting the lens cover, as you may not always have two hands free. Make sure the light has a wrist lanyard as most lights are negatively buoyant and you do not want to lose it if you find you need your light hand for something else in an emergency.

Your primary light should also have a metal clip so you can attach it to a D-ring on your BCD in the event that you need to switch to your secondary.

Your secondary light is not a luxury. Sooner or later, your primary will fail during a night dive, and when it does, your secondary light has to provide the illumination required for you to terminate the dive, ascend, and leave the water safely.

As with the primary light, you want a good quality secondary that is dependable. It should be smaller than the primary as it needs to be stored on or in your BCD. A great idea is to use the torch you normally carry on daytime dives to look inside holes and under overhangs as your secondary as you are far more likely to keep it charged and will instinctively know immediately where to find it if you need it.

You wear a marker light not so you can see but so that you can be seen both on the surface and underwater and from all directions at all times. Tie it to your cylinder valve or attach to the shoulder harness of your BCD. Switch it on before you enter the water and leave it on until you are back on the beach or boat.

Chemical light sticks are the most popular choice of marker light. They are cheap and disposable but even though the latest models contain reef-friendly liquid they still need to be disposed of responsibly. Battery-powered marker lights are more expensive but they are reusable and the best of these also have a strobe mode in which you can set optional flashing sequence, which conserve battery power and make you more visible to searchers if you are drifting at night.

Light Tips and Tricks

When getting ready for your dive, use a normal land torch. Your dive light has a limited battery life so it is better not to waste it on the surface.

Always switch your light on BEFORE entering the water, but not for long. Be aware that some dive lights burn so hot that their reflectors and lenses will melt if switched on at the surface for more than a few minutes.

If entering the water via a giant stride or backward roll from a boat, protect your light to keep the impact to a minimum. Once you are in the water, check the light is working before descending.

Once you have your light deployed and spot something cool, use the edge of the pool of light (not the centre of the beam), to illuminate it so you do not scare it or blind it.

During the dive, snuff your light out occasionally by turning it to your chest and let your eyes adjust to the ambient light. If you are in shallow water on a clear night – with the illumination given by the moon and stars – it may not be as dark as you expected and often you will find that you are surrounded by bioluminescence, tiny sparks of light emitted by plankton and other animals.

Don't turn your light off and back on underwater. This just increases the likelihood that it will fail.

Finally, if your primary fails and you have switched to your secondary, terminate the dive and return to the ascent/exit point immediately as you no longer have a back-up light and will be completely in the dark if your secondary fails too.

Communicating in the Dark

Before setting out on the dive, go over light signals. Avoid any signal that calls for turning the light on and off. If you want to pass your buddy a message shine your light onto your free hand and illuminate the same hand signals you would use in daytime diving.

The most effective way to attract the attention of your partner on a night dive is to shine the beam of your dive light into the pool of light thrown by their light. That is most probably where they are looking. Move your light in a slow circle to ask "OK?" or move the light swiftly from side to side if there is a problem or if you want to draw attention to something. Once you get your buddy's attention, all you need to do is move your light to where you want them to look.

Resist the temptation to shine your light on a diver's face! You may not get the friendliest of responses from your buddy as he struggles with having been temporarily blinded! On surfacing, avoid pointing your light directly at the boat. The crew needs their night vision to look for divers who may have surfaced without a functioning light.

Dive Control Marker Lights

If boat diving, make sure there are marker lights positioned both on the boat, and at the top and bottom of any descent line. The lights should be on before the dive begins and left on until every diver has successfully returned and been accounted for.

If diving from the beach, shore lights are valuable reorientation tools. They should be visible from all directions and of sufficient brightness that they can be seen from the sea even if rain or mist comes up during the dive. Two or more shore marker lights can be used, one above and behind the other, so that divers returning on the surface can navigate back to their starting point by aligning the two lights.

Become a Better Diver by

Embracing night diving
Developing your skills
Getting the right lights

15. Going All the Way In – Wreck Diving

The divers peered down the long dark steel corridor ahead of them, noticing how it seemed to become ever narrower as it stretched away beyond the limits of their vision. Illuminated in the beam of the powerful light mounted on the back of each diver's hand was what looked like a smooth soft pile carpet on the corridor floor but they knew that this apparently smooth and solid covering was in fact a thick layer of potentially deadly silt laid over the bare metal by the passage of water and time.

They were entering a place where delicate forces were in fragile balance and, fully aware of this, they proceeded cautiously using techniques honed over hundreds of similar dives. Fin movement was restricted to the bare minimum necessary for forward momentum, buoyancy had to be inch perfect and body trim exact. Nevertheless, the divers' very presence was introducing chaotic elements into the environment and water was being shifted in unusual patterns by the slightest movement. Small eddies of silt formed around them, discharging rusty particles into the hitherto clear water.

Bubbles rose towards the surface but were trapped by the ceiling and burst, producing small explosions of corroded metal. The occasional brush of a cylinder against a hanging cable caused objects that were previously motionless to swing gently back and forth. A gloved finger placed against a bulkhead for balance produced a small hole, revealing that the apparently solid metal was now treacherously wafer-thin.

The divers moved along the corridor, the leader running a thin, strong line down the side of the wall, tying it off occasionally to keep it taut. The line was positioned to be accessible but not to intrude into the narrow space through which they were swimming. The second diver's job was to assist the leader, providing additional light for him to work by, double checking the line placements and fixing them as necessary. The third diver merely observed his surroundings and the line's location and held himself ready to assist if required. The team could only communicate by light signals projected onto the corridor floor, as turning to each other without disturbing the silt layer catastrophically would be impossible. The team passed doorways, some fully open, others partly blocked, but no portholes adorned this internal passage, no glimmer of exterior light could be seen.

Later the divers would report that they had heard no tearing of steel, no crashing of debris. Nothing had been audible behind the slow, reliable, confidence-building, steady rhythm of their breathing, a long inhalation, a short pause, then a longer exhalation. But all this breathing was sending stream after stream of exhaled gas up against a steel beam that was being maintained in precarious balance by a heavily rusted joint. It only needed an eruption of bubbles around the joint to shatter the rust and the beam was released from its grasp.

The beam fell through the void and crashed into Diver 3's

cylinders, propelling him downwards through the silt layer onto the metal floor of the corridor. His instincts took over; he did not struggle. He lay in the dark with what felt like an enormous weight on his back. His chest felt tight and he heard a roaring, pulsating noise growing ever faster and louder like an approaching train. He felt panic rise within him but had the presence of mind to try to force it down. He held his breath briefly; the noise stopped; he exhaled slowly and fully and his anxiety began to dissipate. He fought to control his breathing and gradually his head cleared and he began to analyse what had happened and what he had to do.

The lead diver paused, sensing something was wrong, perhaps alerted by the absence of light movement from behind him. He craned his neck downwards to peer back towards where he had last seen the rest of his team. But all he saw sweeping up the corridor towards him was a turbulent, roiling wall of silt. He glanced instinctively down, saw a protruding hook below him and quickly tied off his line and reel as the silt engulfed him. It was as if night had fallen; his powerful dive torch was now only a pinprick of light.

His thoughts now turned to the new job in hand. The mission had changed. Any thought of progressing further was gone; the only task now was to ensure the safe extraction of the dive team from the wreck. As the reel man he had been at the front of the team; there was no one further down the corridor so he had only one direction to go, back along the line.

He checked his line tie to make sure it was secure and made a circle around the line with the thumb and forefinger of his left hand, his right hand extended in front of him. In seconds his fingers encountered the previous tie off he had made and he negotiated it carefully ensuring that contact with the line was not lost. Visibility was still zero but he reasoned that he should shortly encounter Diver 2.

The silt cloud engulfed Diver 2 before he was conscious that anything had happened. He had no time to swim for the line before it and everything else around him disappeared. He reached out for an object, any object, to steady himself and found himself grasping a pipe. Tugging at it first to test its strength and judging that it was secure, he removed a small reel from a clip on his harness and tied the end of its line to the pipe. Holding on to the reel he deployed it slowly, moving away from the pipe with his free arm outstretched searching for the line his team leader had run into the wreck, a line that he knew led to sanctuary. He was highly conscious that a wild and untethered search might just succeed in taking him through any one of the doorways they had seen and possibly deeper still into the wreck. With his reel attached to the pipe he could at least wind himself back to his starting point if necessary and commence a new search for the line in another direction.

As Diver 2's arm brushed against the main line, he felt a hand on his head as the lead diver made contact with him. Diver 2 circled the line with his thumb and forefinger, let his own reel fall away and with the lead diver gripping his upper arm and pushing him in the direction of the exit he moved slowly along the line hoping to find Diver 3 waiting patiently a few metres further on.

Diver 3 was nowhere near the line but he was calm. He had a good idea of what had happened and knew he had plenty of time to find a solution to his predicament now that he was in control of his breathing. They had all started the dive with double the amount of air they needed for the penetration element of the dive. He cautiously released a little air from the rear mounted wing-like cell on his harness and felt the pressure on his chest ease. He released a little more air.

Evidently the beam was not only lying on him but had come to rest on another object that was partially supporting the weight, and as Diver 3 deflated his wing further he found he could move enough to squirm out from the trap.

Just as Diver 2 had done, he used his own reel and line to initiate a search for the main line, found It and emerged from the corridor into clearer water to find his two colleagues waiting for him.

All three then followed their line back through the wreck, emerging onto the deck where they had placed their initial tie off and made an incident-free ascent.

Their dive-logs show no more than an aborted dive, but the outcome could have been very different. They only survived because they responded instinctively, calmly and correctly to the emergency. Their training, their equipment and their experience turned what could have been a fatal tragedy into a minor inconvenience.

The Wonder of Shipwrecks

If a friend called and suggested you go for a walk in the woods with him to look at some rusty old abandoned cars, you might raise an eyebrow or two. But if your buddy came by and proposed that you go out next weekend to do some wreck diving, you would probably jump at the chance!

Shipwrecks are all about history and the romance of the sea; they offer excitement, adventure and a lot of fun. They even appeal to the fish fanatics among us as they provide an excellent gathering point for marine life. It is not surprising that many divers get a little obsessed with this aspect of our sport.

However, as the above story illustrates, wreck diving is not to be entered into lightly. It is an endeavour that places considerable demands on a diver. The adventure of visiting places and seeing things beyond the reach of others is a major draw. But with the rewards come risks and achieving wreck diving goals requires the acquisition of extraordinary skill levels to mitigate the dangers. A sunken ship is an environment that raises some unique considerations.

A Question of Time

Time is the main problem when diving in any overhead environment because of your limited air supply. If you were to get lost during your walk in the woods, this would not be potentially fatal. You would have plenty of time to find your way out because your air supply is limitless.

The more you have to breathe, the more time you have and the more you reduce your risk. Having said this, carrying several large cylinders into a confined space would impede your ability to swim efficiently and negotiate tight spaces so you need to compromise.

Wreck divers always plan their dives in detail and work out in advance how much air they will use. They then make sure they have a healthy reserve supply and carry a minimum of two cylinders with independent regulators so they can still get access to all their air even if one of the regulators fails.

Some divers also like to place spare air supplies on or inside the wreck in case of an emergency but unless it is absolutely certain that you will exit the wreck at the same place you entered it, you should always carry your primary reserve and any decompression gas with you.

It is essential that you have the discipline to remain calm when something goes wrong and the training to know how to respond instinctively and immediately because delay, panic or losing control of your breathing will all eat up precious time.

A Fragile Environment

Every shipwreck is a disintegrating environment and you should always be aware that your movements and bubbles could disrupt the fragile balance of a man-made object and the natural forces at work on its eventual destruction.

Water Movement

If there is little or no water movement in a section of the wreck, silt will build up. Silt is not just sand, it is lighter, has a less solid consistency and most significantly, when it is disturbed it stays suspended in the water column for a long time, creating a phenomenon called a "silt-out." In such a situation, you lose all visibility, no matter how powerful your lights are.

The presence of heavy current or surge within a sunken ship can produce different problems. The moving water can make it difficult to swim along narrow corridors and stairways and can bring you and your equipment into contact with the sharp bits of metal and hanging cables that are a feature of almost every wreck.

Finding Your Way

It is essential to know for sure that you can always find your way out of the wreck, even if your lights fail or you find yourself blinded by a silt-out. Divers use two very different techniques for this. Some, like the team in the story, copy cave divers and use reels and lines to make sure they have a continuous path to their entry point.

Others believe this is not safe as lines can easily get cut on metal edges, leaving the team without a guideline. They also worry that by introducing a potential source of entanglement into a confined area, you unnecessarily add further risk to the dive.

These divers use an alternative strategy called progressive penetration, whereby they explore the shipwreck little by little, memorizing each section before moving on to the next one. By doing this and practicing visualization they can make their way through the wreck even with their eyes closed, operating just on their memory of the environment, just as you would be able to move around your home at night without bumping into anything.

Training

To wreck dive safely you need to acquire advanced skills, but the fun, adventure and excitement on offer make all the effort worthwhile. Most of the training agencies teach limited range diving in and around shipwrecks and, if you want to find out if wreck diving is for you, it is a good idea to enrol in one of these courses first.

If you then want to take your exploration further you can sign up for a class in wreck penetration with one of the technical diving agencies. Do a little research and ensure you choose an instructor who genuinely has a lot of wreck diving experience.

Become a Better Diver by

Following the rules for safe wreck diving

Rules for Safe Wreck Diving

Use a single continuous guideline from OUTSIDE the point of entry.

Use AT LEAST the Rule of Thirds in planning your gas supply.

Use TRIMIX when diving deep.

Build up experience slowly.

Before the dive, analyse EVERYTHING that could go wrong and make contingency arrangements.

Carry everything you need to handle emergencies and know where it is.

Make sure you can reach it in a tight squeeze and know how to use it

Always take at least three lights per diver.

Avoid stirring up silt.

Practice emergency procedures with your dive team and review them often.

Never permit overconfidence to allow you to ignore common sense.

REMEMBER: The visibility going in will be much better than the visibility coming out!

16. Below Frozen Seas – Ice Diving

You are perched on the edge of a triangular hole cut through thick ice in the middle of a jagged, white wilderness, one leg crossed over the other, pulling your fins on with thick gloves. Flecks of ice picked up and carried by the invisible, incessant wind as it crosses the glacier sting your cheeks. Your surface tender knots the thick umbilical line around your waist and you extend a buddy line to your dive partner seated on the other side of the hole, legs dangling in the dark water.

You take a deep breath, signal to both tender and buddy and drop into the deep, green ocean below, regulator in hand. Once beneath the surface you shift a little to the side, wedging yourself under the ice shelf while you place the regulator in your mouth and exhale. If you had done this above water where the temperature is holding steady at around minus 30 the moisture in your exhaled breath could have frozen in the regulator, causing it to free flow uncontrollably. This is why the tender has a flask of boiling water on the ice next to him.

Even here under the ice, where the temperature is only minus 2, there is still considerable risk of a free flow, which would discharge all the air in your cylinder uselessly into the water. It could also cause chunks of ice in your mouthpiece to break off and force their way into your throat provoking life-threatening laryngeal spasms. Understandably therefore, you breathe with caution using your tongue as an ice guard.

You run a detailed personal leak check of your dive gear and drysuit while your buddy does the same and after a swift exchange of hand signals and a few mutually reassuring tugs on the umbilical with your tender, you push yourself away from the ice and set off. You are part of a three-person team diving in one of the most harsh and unforgiving environments imaginable.

You are submerged beneath an impenetrable ceiling in a disorientating world from which the only possible escape is via the small hole through which you entered, a hole which needs constant attention to prevent the ice reforming and sealing you in a green translucent tomb. Around you the ice has contorted itself into fantastic sculptures and the green water is crystal clear in the beam of your light. This is inner space, the final frontier.

Many professionals find their love for the sport is invigorated by new experiences. If you want to improve your dive skills and are up for a challenge that is both mental and physical, think about an ice diving course. Diving in an overhead environment is not for the claustrophobic, it requires better water skills than tropical fun diving and it is often hard work, just getting ready for a dive can be physically taxing. However, you may well find learning to ice-dive one of the most fulfilling and rewarding diving experiences you could ever hope for.

Ice Diving Russian-style

Just as the Florida cave diving community can justifiably claim to be pre-eminent in its field, so can the Russians pride themselves on knowing more about ice diving than most. From February to April each year, ice diving opportunities abound: from the northwest beyond the Arctic Circle in Russia's White Sea, just south of the old Soviet nuclear submarine pens in Murmansk to Siberia's Lake Baikal and the Pacific ice floes off the Kamchatka Peninsula in the Far East.

The journey every day to the dive sites can be an adventure by itself! In the White Sea you travel in a snow train, consisting of hand-built wooden sleigh boxes pulled by snowmobiles, which transports both people and gear across the ice floe and then up over the hills to neighbouring bays via a narrow track lined with pine trees flecked with the previous night's snow. On Lake Baikal, you speed across ice several metres thick in four-wheel-drive vehicles with snow tyres.

A typical dive site is marked by a collection of huts on skis parked next to a series of triangular man-made holes in the ice called maina. You change in and out of your dive gear in these huts, each of which has its own gas heater maintaining the temperature at a comfortable 20 degrees C. When it's your turn to go diving you squeeze yourself out of the doorway fully dressed carrying your fins and mask and head for the nearest hole where your instructor/guide is waiting.

You always use cylinders equipped with dual outlet valves, so you need to have two separate regulators, each with its own high pressure gauge too. It is good practice to have your BCD inflator attached to one regulator and your drysuit inflator to the other, to make sure you have a means of inflation should you need to shut down one of the valve outlets.

A drysuit with an ice-hood and dry-gloves are essential. Do not even contemplate doing ice diving in a wetsuit; no matter how many millimetres of neoprene you are enveloped in.

Having a line and good surface support solves the problem of getting lost under the ice. During the dive you maintain constant contact with the line, which you hold up and away from the body to avoid entanglement and you frequently check behind to see that your line does not become chafed or trapped and also to ensure that the right tension is being maintained. A loose line could mean that something has happened to your tender and that you are all alone. Some operations use two tenders, as these guys are so important to the success of the dive.

The tenders hold your line and enable you to communicate with your surface. They ensure that the maina does not freeze solid while you are down there and they are the ones who are going to pull your freezing butt out of the water if you have a serious problem and need to make an urgent ascent. They may not be under water but they face their own challenges. They start their day hacking through the ice to set up your dive site and have to withstand surface air temperatures considerably below those you are experiencing, while accepting a share of the responsibility for your safety whatever foolish things you may decide to do.

It is easy to get carried away. Ice diving is not deep diving so narcosis is not a major concern but the extra-planetary environment and unexpected beauty of the experience can prove distracting. The main attractions are the beauty of the semi-transparent, sculpted ice formations and the marine life that flits among them. These twisted compressed contortions of frozen water rarely extend below 12 m (40 ft) although, particularly in Lake Baikal, the bottom may lie over 1000m

(3300ft) away in the darkness. At the surface, the sunlight turns the ice shades of blue, yellow or green and refracted rays illuminate the shadows of the shallows.

Strangely, rather than the obstacle you may have initially perceived it to be, you may find yourself, like the Russians, embracing the cold as an integral part of an experience that infuses you with a sense of rude natural health and well-being. The sting of the freezing water on your cheeks and lips is invigorating and the after-effects of a dive under ice are similar to those experienced following a day's skiing. You feel energised, bursting with life and vigour and ready to go again!

Amid the excitement, however, you are sometimes confronted with a sober reminder of the dangers involved. As you swim, you occasionally pass beneath maina used for earlier dives. Although you can clearly see blue sky through the holes, when you tap your fist against the thin layer of ice that has covered them since they were made, you realise that you could never punch your way through in an emergency. They could never be an escape route; they could only serve as your final window on the surface world.

Après Dive

To borrow again from a skiing metaphor, in Russia the après dive can be as memorable as the diving itself. The culture of Banya is an integral aspect of Russian life and the end of an ice diving day will often feature a steam bath, a little whipping with birch twigs by your fellow divers and a semi-naked plunge into a snowdrift. This is all entirely optional, of course, but what a great after-dinner story it makes!

Once you have joined the very select group of people that have viewed the solid cold surface of the waters of this planet from below, you will see that ice diving is much more than just another specialty to tick off on your list, it is a magical, mind-expanding experience.

Become a Better Diver by

Adding ice to the cocktail of your dive experiences

17. To the Extreme - Technical Diving

After almost three hours underwater, the divers surface silently behind the boat and slowly fin to the ladder where the crew is waiting to relieve them of the torpedo-like propulsion vehicles they are towing. They unclip unused cylinders slung to their harness and hand them up carefully.

Back on deck they close the mouthpieces integral to their full-face masks and check the twin monitoring devices strapped to their forearms before shucking off their shell-clad electronic life-support devices and laying them down gently.

They methodically shut down and stow away their equipment piece by piece. The atmosphere is calm; the divers concentrating on each task, following a mental list burned into their minds by experience.

If you were to glance at the plan charted on the curved wrist slates they carry you would see that for a large part of the dive they have been cruising undetected at depths greater than 50 metres (165 ft) beneath the South China Sea.

However, although they have just accomplished the sort of dive that would have been impossible a decade ago, there is no whooping, hollering or backslapping. Tomorrow they will carry out a similar but deeper dive, then on Monday they will be back sitting behind desks wearing a different kind of dark suit. These are not professionals, military divers or explorers; they are just two guys out of the city on a long weekend break indulging themselves in their hobby.

Their chosen sport is technical diving; extreme scuba diving performed with a high degree of preparation and precision.

A Little History

The term "technical diving" was coined in 1991 by Aquacorps Magazine founder Michael Menduno to bring under one banner the activities of a number of groups of divers up and down the east coast of the USA. They were all using technology, ideas, equipment and decompression tables which had formerly been the province only of professional military or commercial divers to safely go beyond the bounds of normal sport diving to explore caves and deep shipwrecks.

A community was formed, procedures were debated, information was shared and news eventually spread beyond the USA. This brought people flocking from all over the world to acquire the skills and knowledge that would enable them safely to exceed the sport's commonly accepted limits.

The diving industry establishment was outraged, many forecast disaster and there were campaigns to ban this 'dangerous' new trend. But the lure of hitherto unimagined opportunities was too strong and divers continued to queue up to acquire the necessary equipment and training.

Another aspect of the appeal was that technical diving offered experienced divers an alternative path towards mastery of their chosen sport. Previously, having progressed through their initial courses and decided that diving was to be a significant part of their life, divers who wanted to learn more about scuba diving only had the option of moving on to the leadership levels, divemaster and instructor, even though they had no ambition to work professionally in the industry.

Eventually, of course, the industry gave in to popular demand and the introduction in 2011 of a range of closed circuit rebreather courses by PADI, the world's dominant sport diver training agency, completed the journey taken by technical diving out of its original specialist niche and into the mainstream.

If you are reading this because technical diving beckons you, how do you know if you are the sort of person who would make a good technical diver? How do you choose a course, what equipment do you need and what other things should you consider?

A Technical Mindset

The popular (and erroneous) image of a technical diver is an adrenaline crazed individual, dressed head to toe in black, foolhardily festooned with the contents of a small dive shop, launching himself into the depths without a thought for his own safety.

This image is reinforced by the common practice of defining technical diving in terms of the nature of the dive or the equipment used: a dive deeper than 40m (132ft), using gases other than air, inside an overhead environment such as a cave or shipwreck, using multiple cylinders or rebreathers. However, when a diver armed with standard scuba gear plummets below

40m (132 ft) or swims down the corridor of a ship that does not make his dive "technical." When a diver uses a rebreather, he does not immediately become a technical diver.

The true definition of technical diving owes far more to the attitude and state of mind of the diver than the particulars of the dive. A technical approach to a dive involves analysis of the risks involved, the amount of gas required and the best equipment and gases to use. It also involves consideration of potentially life-threatening events that might occur on the dive and an assessment of the skills and back up equipment that the diver may need to deploy to survive any such event. This assessment involves a considerable degree of accident analysis, a process I covered in detail in Chapter 4 and which is a central tenet of technical diving.

Accident Analysis

Despite the care that technical divers take and the safety procedures that have evolved, there is still a much higher death rate in technical diving than in standard recreational scuba diving which has far more participants and where divers take much less care and give far less thought to their dives.

The main reasons for this are human error and complacency. The more extreme the dive, the more likely it is that a mistake will be fatal rather than inconvenient. Of course, this is exactly why technical divers place so much emphasis on preparation and back up equipment. Complacency is often the counterbalance to experience; the history of technical diving fatalities includes just as many experts as neophytes.

When a technical diver dies diving, news travels fast through the community, which, though widespread geographically, is closely linked online. As well as grieving for the loss of one who shared their passion, divers pore over the details of the incident, not out of morbid curiosity but to see if there is any lesson to be learned, any element in the cause of the accident that might suggest that a commonly adopted procedure might be flawed in some way.

Occasionally a flaw is found and when it is, things move quickly, word passes around, training standards are amended and equipment is modified.

Motivation

The discipline required of technical divers means that in most cases they are thoughtful people who are attentive to detail, sometimes to an obsessive degree.

Most of the early proponents were explorers driven to go further: set records, visit virgin shipwrecks, solve maritime mysteries, penetrate flooded cave systems, learn more about the sea and record and research marine life.

Some of those that have followed them share similar ambitions but there are also many who are simply motivated by knowledge and skill development, a desire to improve their level of performance, to master their sport, to become a better diver.

It is interesting that, contrary to common misconception, very few people are brought into technical diving by the quest for a thrill or adrenaline rush. After all, rather than court danger, the whole ethos of the sport is to counter risk by the application of planning, training and technology.

As technical diving becomes more popular and accessible many more people will become attracted to an area of the sport that has hitherto been the province of relatively few. But is it for you? Would you make a good technical diver? It is not always wise to generalize but there would seem to be some essential pre-requisites.

Experience

It's not the card you hold but the nature of the diving you've done that counts. Also, the quality of your diving is more important than the number of dives. Ideally, you need to have experienced a variety of environments and water conditions.

Self-Reliance

If most of your dives have been done under the supervision of an instructor or divemaster, then making the transition to the technical world, where divers perform as independent parts of a mutually supporting team can be difficult.

Competence

You need have mastered basic scuba diving skills before progressing to this level. You should be able to control your buoyancy instinctively and maintain a stationary position in the water column while you execute drills. Air-sharing exercises, emergency self-rescue procedures and lending assistance to a team member in difficulty are important elements in every course. A conceptual grasp of decompression tables and theory is a useful asset.

Self-Discipline

You must be able to adopt a disciplined approach to your diving and stick to a plan. As trainees soon discover, while standard no-decompression single cylinder diving offers guidelines to follow, technical diving has rules based on physiological and physical limits, rules upon which your life depends!

Meticulousness

If you are the type of diver who regularly jumps in without securing your BCD to the cylinder or turning your air on, then technical diving may not be for you. Ask your buddies; do they privately think that you are an accident waiting to happen? Technical diving, by its nature, involves a higher level of risk. You have a responsibility not only to yourself but to your friends and family. Do they accept the risk too?

Fitness

You should be fit. Technical divers carry more gear, swim further and stay underwater longer. A key skill to be mastered is the maintenance of a normal gas consumption rate under stress, something that requires both mental and physical fitness.

Financial Health

The last pre-requisite is plenty of disposable income. Technical diving requires a substantial investment in training, equipment and travel; there are no short cuts. Cheap training at this level is likely to be inadequate training.

What's Involved?

Generally speaking, the first training level will be a single course or combination of courses introducing you to decompression diving within a 40m (132 ft) depth limit starting on single oxygen/nitrogen (NITROX) gas, and moving to the use of a second NITROX containing a greater oxygen percentage to optimize decompression. There's plenty to learn, so beware of initial courses that rush you quickly into the use of oxygen and very high NITROX mixtures. The use of these is best left until the second level of training, by which time you will have already mastered the basic skills.

The second level will take you below 50m (165 ft), either using air or a light helium/oxygen/nitrogen gas mixture (TRIMIX), and again one decompression gas. By then you will be well into the realm of technical diving, and will know if you want to take things deeper and further using custom TRIMIX and multiple decompression gases, or perhaps branch out into cave diving or wreck penetratlon.

Equipment Matters

No matter how well equipped you are, you're going to have to buy more gear: two good regulators for your back gas, an oxygen clean regulator for your decompression gas, a harness and wing style BCD, submersible marker buoys, reels, cutting tools, slates, waterproof tables and a dive timer or multi gas capable computer. Don't buy without advice! Consult your instructor before the course begins.

Gear configuration is an important part of the initial course in particular, and should be covered in detail before you go in the water. There are key basic tenets to follow and you should be prepared to adopt new concepts very different from those you mastered when you originally learnt to dive.

If you do the training alone, the chances are that when the course is finished you won't have anyone to practice your new skills with! It is far better to do your technical diver training with a friend or group of friends who have a similar level of experience and similar ideas of what they want to achieve.

A Final Word

Technical diving is a challenging and rewarding sport and it can take you to places on our planet seen first hand by very few. However, whatever motivation drives you to take up the sport, there is one caveat worth remembering with a little humility.

We who dive today are no more skilled or courageous than our predecessors. It is only thanks to the invention of others that we are able to go beyond the limits that held our predecessors back. This is a privilege and one we should respect!

Become a Better Diver by

Expanding your horizons

18. Current Events – Drift Diving

This isn't diving, it's flying!" were the first words out of her mouth as she removed her regulator, eyes still wide and heart still pumping after an adrenaline-fuelled ride along a kilometre or more of Bali's north-eastern coastline where she was carried along across a sea bed teeming with life by the waters of the Indonesian Throughflow flooding the Lombok Strait on their way from the Pacific to the Indian Ocean.

This is drift diving, letting the prevailing ocean current take command of the direction and speed of your dive. The prospect of diving when a current is running is often a major source of diver anxiety before a dive. This concern is well placed as a current puts the ocean firmly in charge and many of us feel uncomfortable when we are not in control of what is happening to us, but with good planning, good surface support and good skills, dives when a current is running can be the best of your life.

Where and Why?

The places where you will typically encounter current while

scuba diving include reef walls parallel to the shore, exposed and submerged seamounts, channels between islands and passages through fringing reefs.

Quite apart from the excitement, the main reason we choose to dive in such places when there is current is the fish! If you want to see big pelagic animals and enormous schools of fish, a current-strewn reef is definitely where you want to be, as moving water brings everything in from the blue.

On a reef wall, look out especially for points, peaks and outcrops in the topography. The flow is usually higher there and these tend to be the places where the fish gather in greatest number. A fine example is Blue Corner in Palau.

Large volumes of water passing through narrow channels and reef passages can create enormous congregations of marine life and mid-ocean pinnacles that are quiet and relatively life-less when the water is calm can turn into phenomenal action-filled aquatic circuses when a current picks up, as huge schools cling together close to the rock for shelter and predators come in to feed.

How to Spot a Current

From the surface, the major tell tale signs are whirlpools and floating debris. A wavy line of calm water running parallel to the coast can be a sign of a current along the shoreline.

Underwater, it is pretty easy to know when you are diving in a current. If your bubbles are streaming out horizontally rather than heading straight up to the surface or if finning is suddenly very hard or very easy, then you know you have a current running.

In the tropics, a good indication that currents are common at specific sites is the presence of gorgonian fans, black coral and sea whips. The more water that moves past them and brings them nourishment the larger they grow and if these large corals are permanently bent like trees in a high wind you know that strong current is a common feature. Off the coast of North-east Bali, even enormous 2m (6 ft) tall barrel sponges are inclined at 45 degrees.

To get the best idea of how the current is running look at the fish. After all, they are the experts.

When there is no current, the fish, large and small, will be milling around in every direction all over the reef and up and down in the water column. In a mild current they will all be facing the same way, into the current, and the stronger the current becomes the closer to the reef they will go.

As the current increases in strength the little fish, anthias and the like, will be spread out flat as close to the coral as they can get and waving their tails like crazy to stay in position, but when it is really strong they will be down in and among the coral structures and even the big fish will be hovering very close to the reef or will have found a calm place out of the action.

If you want to take a break from the current yourself during a drift dive, use these big fish as a guide. You will find them behind large rocks or outcrops where they can hide in the lee, out of the current. You may also see groups of fish gathered closely together up on the wall where they have found a calm place, out of the main flow.

Tips for Diving In Currents

On a drift dive, the best advice is to go with the flow, resist the instinctive urge to use your fins for anything more than balance, tuck your arms in and enjoy the ride.

The ability to anticipate, quick reactions and good control of your buoyancy and positioning in the water are useful qualities if you want to stay on course and avoid damaging either yourself or the reef. A good drift diver needs to be something of a slalom skier and know how to adjust speed and turn smoothly.

Make yourself as streamlined as possible as you will be moving fast close to an uneven surface and you do not want to get caught up as you pass. A clean profile also helps you move more easily against the current if that should become necessary.

This means your shape in the water has to be horizontal. If you tend to dive head up, fins down, (ask your buddy,) move your weight belt further up your middle to bring your legs up and make a mental note to tighten it once you are at depth as it will slip down when your wetsuit compresses with depth and increased pressure.

Wear a full-length wetsuit with neoprene on your arms and legs. Currents often carry tiny waterborne stinging cells called nematocysts and although these are not going to cause you other than temporary discomfort it is better to be protected.

Always keep plenty of air in reserve and avoid going into decompression. As mentioned below, current dives often have to end with a blue water ascent in moving water and these are not circumstances where you want to be burdened with required decompression stops.

Reef Hooks

Reef hooks are becoming increasingly common tools for divers wanting to hang out in a current to watch the action without wasting energy finning to stay in position or lying prone on the reef and damaging fragile marine life.

They normally consist of a length of cord passed through the eye of a large fishing hook. The point of the hook is blunted to reduce the risk of it puncturing a BCD air cell if it is tucked away in a pocket. The idea is that the diver hooks onto a rock and hangs on to the loose end, floating neutral in the current.

This means, however, that one of the diver's hands is not free, a major disadvantage for a photographer, and if the diver attaches the cord to his BCD instead, it can be difficult to balance on a single point of contact with the current rushing past. Also, a fishing hook is not the perfect shape to wedge into crevices.

Against the Flow

Nobody enjoys swimming against a current. It saps your energy, increases your breathing rate, generates stress and is an experience best avoided. However, sometimes you find yourself having to do it, at least in short bursts, as marine topography is not all straight lines and smooth curves. The reef line is made up of outcroppings, ridges and canyons that can deflect and re-direct the current to produce back eddies or contraflows, upwellings and downdraughts.

There are techniques to make swimming against a current a little easier when it has to be done. Use the contours to shelter you from the main thrust of the current. On a rocky seabed, you can use a cave diving technique called "pull and glide' reaching forward from stone to stone using a single fin-kick to power each move. Over sand, you can use a similar technique called finger walking to help you sustain momentum and stop you going backwards.

Descent Strategy

To get the timing right for current diving you need to have the advice of an expert with good local knowledge of tide tables and moon phases. The timing is critical if the site is to be enjoyed at its best. A difference of just a few minutes can make the difference between a good dive and a great one. Safety is also a factor as some sites can be unpredictable if caught at the wrong time.

You also need to know the site well, so you can predict exactly where the big fish will gather when the current starts running and make sure you begin the dive in the right place. This is especially important when diving a seamount or pinnacle as getting it wrong could cause you to miss the site completely and find yourself floating in the blue.

One common tactic is for the dive boat to position itself directly above the dive site and have all the divers enter the water together, negatively buoyant, and fin straight down, equalizing furiously as they go. This often results in some divers getting to the site just fine, others arriving panting and confused, a few missing the site completely, having delayed their descent and one or two discovering an equipment problem as they go down and aborting the dive immediately. The team is separated from the start and it is already certain that during the next hour or so the pick up crew are going to be picking up divers scattered over a wide area.

A less stressful and far more effective method in terms of communication, control and safety is what is called a "rolling" entry. You choose a point on the surface from which with a normal descent rate the current will carry the dive team to the dive site. Ideally you mark this with a buoy and then drop all the divers in the water upstream from the descent point. As the divers drift on the surface they can unite with their buddies, give their equipment a quick, final check and then, as they approach the buoy and on a signal, start their descent together.

Ascent Strategy

Current dives, especially on pinnacles and sea mounts, often require "blue water' ascents where there is no reference.

The boat crew will have a general idea of where you will be ascending as they have been watching your bubbles and know which way the current is running. To help them find you more quickly, to keep the team together and to give everyone a reference, a useful technique is to send up a Surface Marker Buoy (SMB) from depth. You only need to send up one SMB per dive team although every diver should carry one in case the team gets separated.

One diver takes charge of sending up the SMB while his buddy stays close ready to assist if necessary and makes sure he stays neutrally buoyant in the diver's line of sight to give the diver a depth reference.

The team then stays close to the SMB line, ascends and completes their safety stop together before surfacing all in the same place, making them easier to spot and facilitating an efficient pick up.

Once on the surface stay calm even if you cannot see the pick up boat. It may be busy picking up other divers, so keep the group together, inflate your SMB so it is standing as tall as possible and have your signal mirrors and sonic devices handy just in case the crew need extra help in finding you.

Downdraughts and Upwellings

Just the mention of a downcurrent is enough to inspire fear in many divers as they visualize themselves getting caught by an irresistible force that drags them into the abyss with no opportunity for escape.

The natural response when confronted with a situation like this where you feel out of control is to panic but there is no need. Normally, downdraughts or downcurrents are localized phenomena that occur along reef walls: think of them as waterfalls in the sea.

When you encounter one, the first thing to do is get out of the flow by moving closer in to the wall so that the contours offer you shelter. Once out of the stream, relax, exhale, take a few deep full breaths, check your air supply, depth and decompression status, look around you and plan. Look to see where the big fish are hiding or if there is a place where the sea whips are not waving around.

It is not a good idea to fight a downcurrent. It is a struggle you cannot win. The oft-quoted tactic of inflating your BCD to counteract its efforts to carry you down is potentially dangerous as the current might suddenly release you from its hold and you will find yourself on a runaway ascent to the surface, which will do you much more harm than the current could do.

Unless you have spotted a place further along the wall that seems calm, usually the best advice is to swim laterally out away from the reef towards the blue. If you find yourself being carried a little deeper initially, stay calm and keep swimming, you will emerge from the pull of the downcurrent before long or its effect will weaken and allow you to begin your ascent and return to the wall.

Think of upwellings as reverse down currents. The same advice applies. First move into the wall out of the flow, relax, think, observe and act calmly.

Rip Currents

Finally, a few words on rip currents, which have been implicated in a number of diving accidents over the years. A rip occurs where water flows over the top of the reef towards the shore and returns through gaps in the reef. The gaps offer tempting access for shore divers to get out onto the back of the reef but when they try to return, the water flow can sometimes be too strong so they either fight the current to the point of exhaustion or try to exit over the reef where the waves are crashing. Both options carry the potential for disaster.

The simple advice is never to swim out through gaps in a reef when the water is breaking over the top.

Become a Better Diver by

Embracing the opportunities offered by a current
Being prepared and staying calm
Making sure you drift dive with an expert boat crew
Choosing gentle drift dives first to develop your skills and give you confidence

19. Learning Your Lines - Cave Diving

Safely managing long dives through extensive, complex, flooded cave systems requires special techniques and a high degree of expertise. A training program to learn how to perform and survive in such a demanding environment is something that all advanced divers might consider.

This chapter consists of notes taken from the dive log of an experienced sport diving instructor who decided to take a cave diving course hoping that it would challenge him, improve his skills and reinvigorate his love for the sport after fifteen years of doing the same thing every day.

The course took place in the limestone solution caves of Central Florida. It lasted six days and consisted of 12 dives and a total of over 14 hours (883 minutes) of in-water time. The deepest depth reached was 33m (110ft) and the longest single dive lasted 127 minutes. The air temperature was around 5 degrees C (41F), the water temperature a consistent 20 degrees C (68F.) The author of the notes was accompanied by fellow students Peter and Geoff; the instructor's name was

Roger. All divers were using double back-mounted steel 15 litre cylinders with an isolation manifold and stainless steel bands; a steel 7litre cylinder for decompression gas and a double wing and harness BC system. They each carried three lights and three reels (one primary, one search, one jump) and were wearing 7mm wetsuits and (on Roger's instructions,) no gloves.

If some of the cave diving terminology is new to you, there is a glossary at the end of this chapter.

Diver's Log: Cave Day One

Today was land-based with line drills, lectures and a long equipment configuration session.

Diver's Log: Cave Day Two

Two cave dives today, each preceded by a separate open water skills practice dive in the shallow river above the caves, where we rehearsed valve shutdowns, light deployment and signalling, leak testing, finning techniques, gas sharing drills and reel and line use.

The first of the cave dives was Devil's Ear in Ginnie Springs. I was instructed to lead the way in followed by Peter and Geoff. My first task was to lay line with my primary reel from outside the cave through the entrance and tie it off onto the permanent (Gold) line inside the cave so that on return we would have a continuous guideline to the exit and beyond.

We entered via a narrow entrance, dragging ourselves along the limestone walls and finning as hard as we could to make progress against a strong outward flow. Once through the restriction, we aimed for a shelf on the left of the cave to get out of the flow, recover our composure, acclimatize to the darkness, check air and adjust buoyancy.

Setting off again we passed two further restrictions at "The Lips" and "Keyhole," practiced buoyancy and different fin techniques above the thick layer of silt and eventually turned the dive on gas-matched Thirds about 150 m (500ft) into the cave.

As Roger pointed out in an extended debrief, I did not do well. As leader, I was far too focussed on myself, (I remember feeling great throughout the dive but worrying continuously if claustrophobia was suddenly going to strike.) In the rocky sections I did not pull and glide against the current aggressively enough and, in the silty sections, I mistakenly stayed low in the middle of the cave where the current was at its strongest. I went too slowly and failed to keep contact with the other members of the team, missing light signals frequently, so fixated I was on my own introspection. Not a great start!

On the second dive in Devil's Ear, Peter was leading and started off like a train but the strain of fighting the current slowed him down and the more we swam, the more comfortable I felt that we were acting as a team, communicating successfully and much more aware of our environment. We got to "Maple" before turning the dive on Thirds at 400m (1300ft) into the cave. At the turn, I made the first of two mistakes, getting caught up on the permanent line and unconsciously kicking up the silt as I worked to free myself. Roger's expression as he thrust his face into my mask space suggested it might be wise if I never did that again! The second error was failing to anticipate the impact of a reduction in visibility ahead, the result of silting by another team of divers in the cave. We all had to be told to make contact with the permanent line just in case we lost sight of it. On a positive note, on the way back, we remembered to recover the jump reel we had set on the way out without being reminded and that earned us a compliment (our first) in the debriefing.

Diver's Log: Cave Day Three

Our start at Peacock Springs this morning was substantially delayed as Roger turned up late due to traffic issues and we were all afflicted by numerous equipment problems. By the time we were ready to dive, moods were fragile.

I laid the primary line into "Olsen," entering the cave via a funnel onto the permanent line without too much difficulty. I stayed near the roof of the cave to avoid the very deep silt on the bottom but found it difficult initially to establish an effective finning rhythm. Geoff was having serious balance and buoyancy issues as he had not tightened his harness straps sufficiently and his cylinders were shifting about on his back. As he was struggling to keep his equilibrium, Roger threw him an "out of gas" drill, whereby he had to simulate a catastrophic gas loss, remove his regulator and swim to the nearest diver, Peter, to share. This additional task caused him to lose control completely and he dropped towards the silt, kicking frantically. Roger intervened instantly, cancelled the drill, got Geoff onto an even keel, tightened his harness and, evidently exasperated, signalled to us all that we should turn the dive. We emerged from the cave without further incident but when I eventually surfaced last, having been left on my own to recover the primary reel, the black looks all round told me that harsh words had been exchanged.

Later, over lunch, Roger pointed out that the morning's experience had been a good lesson for all of us, including him. As he said, when it looks like the diving Gods do not want you to make a dive, it is best to take notice of what they are telling you.

In the afternoon, good moods restored, we returned to the cave and this time the preparations went smoothly. I led into "Peanut"; Peter led on the way out. Our collective technique was much improved this time. We swam up to the "Big Room" before turning the dive and executed two "out of gas" drills and a "lost diver" exercise on the return leg.

Diver's Log: Cave Day Four

This was an exhilarating day, starting with a skills intensive dive in "Peacock" along the "Peanut" tunnel. Peter laid the primary reel with me assisting, and in the run we were given a "lights out, gas sharing" drill. Paul then laid a jump line into the tunnel at "Olsen." As always, after turning the dive, we came out in reverse order. Roger signalled that we were to assume that Peter's primary light had failed. He switched to his secondary light and I moved him from the back into the middle of the team so that Geoff was now leading and I was bringing up the rear. Before picking up the primary reel and leaving the cave, we each practiced finding the permanent line in complete darkness, with all lights switched off. We tied off our search reels to a rock and then ran line out to where we thought the permanent line, (and our pathway to the surface and safety,) might be, then followed our line back to the reel if we were unsuccessful and tried again. It took us all a few attempts and the exercise was quite chaotic. The blackness of the cave is hard to describe: it is total, absolute and darker than screwing up your eyes and covering your face with your hands. You see nothing at all and the exercise dramatically reinforces the importance of having multiple lights, multiple reels and a guideline to the exit.

For the second dive of the day we moved to "Little River" Springs, a deeper cave system consisting of contorted, winding pathways through wintry-white limestone formations.

Metaphors we came up with post-dive included "rock cathedral" and "Swiss cheese." We pulled and glided against the slight outward flow, having entered via a steep shaft in the bed of the Suwannee River. The surface of the river was tannin-red and almost opaque but from 4m (12ft) down it was crystal clear. We hit a good pace and, although we were constantly on the alert for simulated emergencies, Roger just let us enjoy the dive and, for the first time on the course, I felt relaxed, competent, able to really observe what was around me and appreciate the enormous privilege of being able to visit a place where comparatively few have been.

Diver's Log: Cave Day Five

Another amazing day: the first dive was back at "Peacock," Geoff laid the primary line and I laid a jump line at "Pothole" on the way to "Olsen" sink. We paused there to look at the tunnel to "Challenge" then returned to the crossover to "Peanut," where Peter laid a second jump line. After turning the dive, we came back on to the "Olsen" line where I let Peter get a little too far ahead of me. This did not go unnoticed by Roger, who immediately indicated that I was "out of gas." It took me a hard 20m (70ft) to 30m (100ft) swim without breathing to catch up with Peter and ask him to share gas and, although I made it, this was yet another good lesson learned.

It was a very long dive but highly enjoyable. With the technical progress I am making and with our improved performance as a team, I find I have time to look around me, and not just at the Gold line and the silt layer. "Peacock" is another complex, beautiful cave system with high domes and a myriad maze of passageways.

Our second dive followed a long drive to "Little River" so we were late going in on a cold evening and by the time we emerged from the cave two hours later, night had fallen and we lay back on the surface watching the river steaming beneath a starlit sky until an abrupt coughing noise from the bank reminded us that we might not be the only big animals around and we made a swift exit.

Diver's Log: Cave Day 6

Today we went back to Ginnie Springs for the final two dives. I can only suppose that complacency had set in after the progress of the past few days but we were already fully geared up and heading for the water when Roger noticed that the gas mixture in our doubles was a rich NITROX 38. This would give us a PO2 of 1.52 at the planned maximum depth of the dive (30m/100ft) and, as the dive was to be in a cave with a high current flow, our safety procedures required that our PO2 not exceed 1.4. It was a stupid basic error on our part to miss this and we were very embarrassed. So we had to vent some of the oxygen-rich gas from the cylinders then top them up with air.

Once we finally got into the water, everything went well. We passed through "Lips," "Keyhole" and "Cornflakes" along winding passages and up into the "Big Room" where we turned. It was a great dive that ended with us simulating an emergency whereby we had to find our way out of the cave with no lights AND no line. Thanks to the fast current this proved easier than we expected.

On the second dive we collected the jump reels we had laid on the first then faced a final gas sharing drill where Peter and I had to pass through "Lips," a very tight restriction where only one diver can pass at a time and even then your chest is on the floor and your cylinders are scraping the cave roof. I was the out-of-air diver and took a couple of slow, deep breaths before handing the long hose regulator back to Peter and then watched his fins disappear through the narrow fissure in the rock. I gave him a few seconds to turn then followed, exhaling slightly and making sure I was negotiating the widest possible part of the restriction so I did not get stuck. As I emerged I saw Peter's light in front of me and his arm with the regulator extended towards me – a very welcome sight!

Divers Log: Postscript

Then, after a few minutes of decompression, hanging onto a large log and buffeted by the water flowing out of the cave, the course was over but for a bit of final paperwork. I left Florida feeling that I had accomplished something significant and with my love for my chosen sport enhanced but it was not until I returned to the ocean a few days later that I realized the full extent of my achievements. Back in open water but armed with enhanced skills that had been developed and fine-tuned in the restricted environment of the cave, I found I was diving so far within my newly acquired capabilities that my comfort level was much greater than it had previously been, (even after 15 years as a diver,) and elements of my diving that I had previously needed to think about were now second nature, instinctive and automatic. Not only has this improved my performance as a diver, it means that I am now a better instructor as I can direct more of my attention towards my students. (Log Ends)

Comment

It is fascinating to see how the tone of these logs changes as the course progresses and as the new cave diver develops his skills and grows in confidence. In the first few days, he was simply asking himself, "Can I do this?" but by Day 4 he has obviously answered that question with a resounding "Yes!" and starts to really enjoy himself and revel in his mastery of highly sophisticated skills.

He does not say so but it seems clear that he has been bitten by the cave bug and that this is likely to be just the first of many dive trips spent exploring flooded subterranean passages. I should include a warning here for those of you who might be drawn to follow in his fin-steps. Cave diving is not just an immensely challenging extreme sport; it is also seriously addictive!

Become a Better Diver by

Challenging yourself

Glossary of Cave Diving Terms

Restriction – a place where the cave narrows significantly.

Thirds = Rule of Thirds – a way of planning your gas supply so that you use a third of it going in, a third coming out and leave a third in reserve for your team-mate if he has a gas supply failure at the furthest point of the dive.

Gas-matched refers to Gas Matching – a procedure that enables divers in a team to ensure they keep enough gas in reserve even when they have different breathing rates or are using cylinders of different sizes.

Pull and Glide – a finning technique designed to help you swim against a current and conserve as much energy as possible. You pull against the rock with the palms of your hands and fin kick to propel yourself from handhold to handhold, a little like a rock climber swinging from grip to grip. In limestone solution caves such as those in Central Florida you do not use your fingers to pull, as the limestone will tear them to shreds. In the beginning, no matter how many times student cave divers are told this, they forget and end up with slashed digits and missing fingerprints.

Silting – a careless and misplaced fin kick into the several metres of silt that has accumulated in these cave systems over eons can cause the visibility to drop from 30m to zero in seconds.

Primary Reel – your largest reel with the most line, which you tie off outside the cave and use to connect you to the permanent line in the cave, when there is one.

Jump Reel – a small reel and line that you carry to set in places where there is a gap in the permanent line in order to maintain a continuous line to your exit.

Search Reel – another small reel that you keep to help you find the main line in case you lose visual contact with it in poor visibility.

Gold Line – a name for the permanent line laid in popular caves. The line begins well inside the cave entrance so that casual explorers are not tempted to follow it.

Sink / Sinkhole – place where a collapse in the land has created a hole allowing access to the cave. In Mexico these are called cenotes.

Equipment

20. Running the Rule over Regulators

Once you have decided you are going to be a diver rather than just occasionally dive, then you should buy your own regulator. It makes sound economic sense and it means you will no longer be exposed to the vagaries of the dive centre's rental fleet.

If your diving will take you no deeper than 40m (132 ft), and you stay within no decompression limits and avoid difficult sea conditions any well-known manufacturer's regulator will suit you just fine; even the basic models are robust and reliable. However, spend a little more and the regulator will be easier to breathe from, look after you better if you find yourself working hard underwater and have features that will make it more comfortable to use.

This encouraging news does not apply to cheap second stage regulators that are marketed and sold specifically as octopus regulators. It is best to avoid anything that is badged in this way. These second stages are invariably of inferior quality and cannot be relied upon at depth, presumably under the bizarre misguided notion that a regulator that you will only need in an emergency does not need to be a good one!

The Basics

The first stage of a scuba regulator is the bit that is attached to the cylinder valve. It "regulates" the high-pressure air in the cylinder converting it to an intermediate pressure several atmospheres above ambient pressure, that is, the pressure of the water around you.

The second stage of a scuba regulator is the bit that goes in the diver's mouth. It is connected to the first stage by an intermediate pressure hose. When you breathe in, a valve in the second stage opens and, because the air in the intermediate pressure hose is at a higher pressure than the ambient pressure air in your lungs, air rushes in with minimal assistance from you.

When you breathe in, the resulting pressure drop in the hose opens a valve in the first stage, which allows the hose to be filled up again directly from the cylinder. The first stage valve closes as soon as the required intermediate pressure in the hose has been reached. When the first stage or second stage valves start to wear, they fail to seal completely and this usually produces a "free-flow," an unstoppable stream of air from the second stage.

The regulator first stage also allows you to connect a high-pressure hose so you can read the cylinder pressure on a gauge.

Yoke vs DIN?

As you saw in Chapter 3, "Trials and Tribulations," a DIN first stage fitting consists of a threaded core with its own O-ring which screws into the cylinder valve so that an interior o-ring seal is made.

The yoke or International first stage fits over a cylinder valve fitted with an O-ring. It is tightened front to back with a screw so that a seal is formed against the valve O-ring when the regulator is pressurized.

The advantages of the DIN design over the Yoke are that you the diver, not the dive centre/cylinder owner, are responsible for the quality of the O-ring that seals the regulator to the cylinder. The interior o-ring seal also means you can wave goodbye to those irritating streams of bubbles emanating from behind your head. With no yoke screw jutting out behind the valve it is very difficult for the regulator to become dislodged if you knock it, (the main reason why cave divers and wreck divers use DIN,) and finally, the DIN fitting allows you to use cylinders with a higher rated pressure.

The main advantage of the Yoke system is that it is much more common, especially in the USA and destinations where US divers are in the majority. However, dive centres are increasingly equipping their cylinders with DIN/Yoke convertible valves so that they can cater for both options.

First Stage Ports and Port Plugs

A regulator first stage has a variety of ports to accommodate high pressure and intermediate pressure hoses. The high-pressure ports and intermediate pressure ports are different sizes to prevent you mistakenly fitting an intermediate pressure hose to a high-pressure port. Often the port designated for your primary second stage, (the one that you use most of the time,) is larger than the other intermediate pressure ports to permit greater gas flow and reduce breathing resistance. This is a key feature to consider, particularly if your diving sometimes requires you to work hard at depth, as it will reduce your susceptibility to CO_2 poisoning, (see Chapter 28 "The Black Gases.")

There are different sizes of O-ringed plug fittings designed to seal the ports on a first stage. A first stage regulator comes from the manufacturer with all its plugs fitted, except, sometimes, the plug for the primary second stage hose. If the shop offers to put your new regulator system together for you, make sure they also give you the plugs they have removed. Extra plugs are expensive to buy and they are an integral part of the product. Keep them in your spares kit; they will come in useful, especially if you ever dive doubles and need to configure twin regulators or a regulator for a pony bottle.

Second Stages

When choosing a second stage, comfort is a quality that is often overlooked. A heavy second stage can cause a degree of jaw discomfort if you are diving for three to four hours a day. The trend is increasingly moving towards smaller models made from lighter materials, although one possible drawback of a smaller second stage regulator is that the exhaust tee is not sufficiently extended to ensure your exhaled air will bubble invisibly away along the side of your face. Some tiny models can direct your bubbles uncomfortably upwards in front of your mask when you are vertical in the water.

Second stages with the exhaust on the side are popular with some divers. The main advantages are that the hose can be routed from the first stage over either the right or left shoulder and a panicked diver sharing air cannot mistakenly put the regulator in his mouth upside down.

Two very useful accessories that will make any second stage regulator more comfortable are a swivel and an orthodontic mouthpiece. An intermediate pressure hose charged with air can exert tension on the regulator second stage, requiring you to clamp down on the mouthpiece to prevent it from leaving your mouth. Attaching a swivel between the intermediate pressure hose and the second stage allows the second stage to move much more freely, reducing the pressure on your jaw and enabling you to unclench your teeth!

An orthodontic mouthpiece can further enhance your comfort as, with use, it moulds to the shape of your jaw and allows the regulator to rest more easily in your mouth. The only disadvantage is that a customised mouthpiece might not be comfortable for a diver who comes to you to share air but it is likely that the issue of comfort will be the last thing on that diver's mind!

Alternate Second Stage Regulators

The commonly accepted practice is for a diver to have two regulator second stages attached by intermediate pressure hoses to one first stage. While you are diving, one of the second stages (your primary) is in your mouth and the other (your back-up) is secured in a place where you can easily reach it.

A back up second stage is useful if the one in your mouth becomes blocked or if it starts to free-flow to an extent that makes it difficult to breathe from. You should also switch to your back up if your primary second stage has a tear in the mouthpiece or diaphragm causing it to "breathe wet' or if the cable tie holding the mouthpiece onto the second stage breaks off.

If a fellow diver runs out of air then the fact that you have two second stage regulators allows you to give one to the out of air diver and share your air with him without losing access to your breathing supply.

Alternate Issues

There would seem little doubt, therefore, that carrying two second stage regulators is a good idea but this raises a number of issues concerning how to set the system up.

Which second stage should you breathe from normally?

Where should you keep the second stage you are not breathing from?

How do you make sure your back up second stage will save you if your primary fails?

Which second stage should you hand to an out-of-air diver?

How will the out-of-air diver know which one you want him to choose?

How long should the intermediate pressure hoses be?

The second stage regulator you plan to hand off to an out-of-air diver needs to be attached to a hose long enough for the diver to breathe from it while remaining at a sufficient distance so that you can control your buoyancy unencumbered and you can both ascend comfortably side by side. However, this hose should not be so long that you have difficulty storing it when it is not deployed to another diver.

The longer hose and the second stage on the end of it should be brightly coloured and easy to see because this is the one you want the out-of-air diver to notice and take in an emergency. You do not want him to take a regulator on a short hose because then you will be in the very uncomfortable and potentially disastrous position of having a very anxious person right in your face.

Both second stages MUST be good quality regulators. Spending just as much money on your back-up second stage as your primary may save a life and that life could be yours. If in doubt as to the quality of your current back-up second stage regulator, next time you are at depth, stop, switch to it and take a few breaths. If it feels just as good and breathes just as well as your primary then you have purchased wisely. If it breathes hard or wet or not at all, take it out, put your primary back in, say a silent prayer of thanks that you have never had to test its quality in a genuine emergency and make a mental note to buy a new one.

Wherever you keep it, the back-up regulator needs to be secured so that it will never come loose and snag on the reef or drag in the sand and so that you can reach it quickly and easily in an emergency.

You should also be able to release it and put it in your mouth with one hand. Always assume that the other hand will be busy controlling buoyancy or making sure the out-of-air diver does not swim for the surface with his teeth clenched around the second stage he has just taken from you.

A Common Solution that Does Not Work

The set up that most divers are taught to use consists of a good quality regulator on a short hose that they breathe from and a cheaper, lower quality octopus regulator, secured to the right side of the BCD at waist level via a slightly longer hose. This is conventionally held to be sufficient to provide an effective means of resolving an out of air emergency but in practice it is more likely to turn an emergency for one diver into a tragedy for two. The following scenario suggests how this can so easily happen.

When a diver runs out of air, his first instinct is to hold on to whatever breath he has left in his lungs and this causes him to float up. He therefore needs to swim downwards to his buddy in order to share air. From above, the octopus regulator attached at his buddy's waist is invisible. The only thing the diver can see is a yellow hose disappearing under his buddy's arm. When he finally reaches him, the diver is much too desperate to have the presence of mind to tap his buddy on the shoulder and calmly signal his requirements. Instead, he takes the source of air he can most immediately see and this is the one in his buddy's mouth. Once he has taken it, he quickly finds that the hose is so short that, in order to breathe from this regulator, he needs to be pressed right up against his buddy's right hand side and facing him, mask to mask. In this position the buddy finds it very hard to reach his octopus without pushing the diver away. A struggle takes place. Even if the buddy eventually does manage to persuade the out-of-air diver to take his octopus and, as is likely, it does not provide the sort of performance necessary to sustain a hard breathing diver at depth, it will be rejected and the struggle will resume, this time over the one well-functioning second stage. Disaster ensues.

A Solution that Works

A solution that works is an adaptation of the regulator set up that many technical divers use. The diver breathes from a brightly coloured second stage regulator attached to a brightly coloured hose. The hose is at least 1.5m (5 ft) long and wrapped over the diver's torso from the right waist over the left shoulder and back over the right shoulder in a half-turn. Any extra length of hose is tucked into the waistband of the BCD or harness.

The back up second stage regulator is identical to the primary but black and attached to a black hose to make it less visible than the primary. The hose is as short as possible while permitting the diver complete freedom of head movement when breathing from it. When not in use it is kept under the chin, attached to a length of surgical tubing looped around the divers neck.

This arrangement allows an out-of-air diver to clearly see the regulator he should take and to remove himself to a reasonable distance from the donor once he has taken it. The donor just needs to dip his chin and pop his back-up regulator into his mouth with either hand for both divers to be breathing comfortably and ready to begin a controlled ascent.

With just a little practice, a regulator set up like this is very easy to manage and can turn an out of air emergency from a potential disaster into a minor inconvenience. Note that when gearing up, the long hose regulator is the last thing to be set in place to ensure that it does not become trapped under the BCD, harness or a clipped off high pressure hose.

A Word on Inflator Hose Regulators

These are the regulator second stages that are attached to your inflator hose. The significant advantage of inflator hose regulators is that they streamline your gear configuration, giving you a smoother profile. This helps you swim more easily, conserve air better and generally be more comfortable in the water. Another advantage of this arrangement is that the regulator you pass over is your primary; therefore, both you and the out-of-air diver know that it is working perfectly.

However, there are some caveats. First, because your primary is the regulator you will hand off, it MUST have a hose at least 1.5m (5ft) long. Otherwise the out-of-air diver will be too close and will get in your way as you switch to your inflator hose regulator. Second, as you are likely to be under a little stress while you are sharing air, it is important that the inflator hose regulator breathes easily, even at depth.

Third, and most important, before you decide to adopt this configuration, you must try it out. Rent a system from your dive centre and take a friend to the pool or a shallow beach location to practice tandem swims, ascents and buoyancy control with you breathing from the inflator hose regulator and your friend on your primary. You may find you have to change your normal habits, particularly if you usually control your buoyancy with the inflator mechanism, as this is now in your mouth! If it does not present you with too much difficulty and you go ahead and purchase an inflator hose regulator, practice with it until your skills become natural and instinctive. A warning: many people find a tandem ascent using an inflator regulator a very hard skill to master!

Hoses

Look after your low pressure and high pressure hoses. Catastrophic failure is rare but when one has failed it is usually because it has been trapped and kinked while in transit; for instance when a cylinder has fallen. Replace immediately any hose that starts leaking along its length or from the metal crimp at the regulator or gauge end. Do not leave it bubbling away until it eventually fails during a dive. Beware of using hose covers and wraps; these can look attractive but tend to both encourage corrosion and conceal wear and tear.

When a high-pressure hose starts leaking at the point where it meets the pressure gauge or console, the problem is likely to be the double o-ringed swivel at the connection point. The O-rings are tiny and it is a good idea to keep a couple of spares in your save-a-dive kit.

Clips

Clip your pressure gauge or console off to a metal D ring on your BCD or harness with a brass or stainless steel clip. Plastic clips and plastic D rings will break. Instead of clipping the gauges to a waist level D ring which requires you to reach down to consult them, try using a chest mounted D ring instead, run the high-pressure hose under your arm and position the gauge face up so you just have to glance down to see it. Not only is this more comfortable, it will ensure you monitor the gauge more frequently.

Consider attaching a small brass or stainless steel clip to your primary second stage regulator too, so you can attach it to your BCD or harness and it does not dangle free when you have to remove your equipment in the water and hand it up into a small boat.

Regulators on Decompression Cylinders

If you ever dive with a decompression cylinder and the gas in the cylinder is not the same as the gas in your main cylinder, you must make sure you stow away the regulator in such a way that you cannot deploy it without making a conscious decision to do so, and you identify the regulator clearly so you know by sight AND by touch which regulator you are about to put in your mouth. Accidentally, breathing a high oxygen decompression or ascent gas at depth has been the cause of numerous fatalities.

Become a Better Diver by

Considering how your regulator is configured
Equipping yourself so you can effectively rescue someone who comes to you to share air
Practicing air-sharing procedures with your buddy

It Only Takes a Few Seconds

(With many thanks to Curt Bowen and Advanced Diver Magazine)

At every level of training divers plan, train and choose their equipment to make sure that they are prepared for and able to survive any eventuality. At the top of the list is something referred to as catastrophic air loss.

This might be caused by an equipment problem such as a defective O-ring, a free-flowing regulator, the failure of a cylinder burst disc or a blown hose. It could be the result of getting a hose caught and cut by a sharp piece of metal as they swim through a shipwreck or it may be caused by the yoke screw of a regulator first stage banging against an overhang or cavern ceiling and getting bent out of shape.

In early scuba diver training, where divers normally carry only one source of air, the solution to an incidence of catastrophic air loss is to swim to your buddy, begin air sharing and ascend on his air supply. As discussed at length in Chapter 6 "Solo Diving," this is fine as long as you and your buddy are properly equipped, prepared and trained.

Technical divers prefer to be equipped with multiple air sources and back up supplies to deal with the threat but few divers really know how much time they will have to react in the event of catastrophic air loss. In 2012, the folk at Advanced Diver Magazine decided to run tests and published the results.

The Tests

Four different equipment problems were simulated. Each test was carried out at a depth of 30m (100ft) using a full aluminium 12 litre (80 cubic foot) cylinder filled to 200 Bar (3000 psi.) The test timed how long it would take for the cylinder to empty completely.

Test 1: High Pressure Hose Failure

This was simulated by cutting the high-pressure hose on a regulator, attaching the regulator to a cylinder, taking the cylinder to depth then fully opening the cylinder valve. It was 22 minutes before the cylinder was empty. (Yes, perhaps surprisingly, 22 MINUTES not 22 seconds, because high pressure orifices are so tiny.)

Test 2: Low Pressure Hose Failure

This was simulated by cutting a low-pressure hose on the regulator, attaching the regulator to a cylinder, taking the cylinder to depth then fully opening the cylinder valve. This time the cylinder took only 1 minute 21 seconds to become completely empty.

Test 3: Valve Burst Disc Failure

This was simulated by removing the burst disc from a cylinder valve at depth. This time the cylinder was entirely drained in 1 minute 14 seconds.

Test 4: Free-Flowing Regulator

This was simulated by manually purging the second stage of a high performance regulator at depth. The cylinder took 2 minutes 35 seconds to empty itself.

Comments and Recommendations

Catastrophic air loss is thankfully rare but the tests clearly show that if any of these things were to happen, except a high-pressure hose rupture, there would be insufficient time for a diver at 30m (100ft) without an alternate air supply or a reliable buddy nearby to ascend to the surface at a safe speed.

The results suggest a few fairly obvious recommendations.

Keep all your equipment well maintained, change out o-rings and hoses at the first sign of wear and do not use a cylinder that has bubbles coming from anywhere on the valve or cylinder neck.

Always have an alternate air supply when diving in an overhead environment such as a wreck or cavern or the virtual overhead environment of required decompression stops.

Always have an alternate air supply when diving deeper than 20m (66ft) or so unless you are with a reliable buddy with whom you have practiced air-sharing ascents.

21. Taking Control of Your BCD

Because the letters BCD are commonly held to stand for Buoyancy Control Device, some are led to assume that a BCD is an appliance that somehow controls your buoyancy in the water. It would be wonderful if that were the case but sadly it is not true. No matter how technologically advanced your gear is, you are still the one responsible for controlling your buoyancy in the water.

Your BCD can definitely help but you are the one that needs to be in full control because this is a piece of equipment that can create as many problems as it solves. When diver accident statistics are released, BCD issues are often high on the list of contributory factors.

Controlling your BCD is a straightforward three-step process.

STEP 1: Buy the Right One

Most people wear BCDs that are too big for them, mainly because they try them on standing up. The fit of the harness around your arms and shoulders should be comfortable and allow plenty of movement but make sure it is not too loose. Put it on; do up all the straps, buckles and Velcro wraps then ask your buddy to lift up the shoulder sections. If his hands hover around your ears when he does that, then that is where the BCD is likely to be when you inflate it at the surface at the end of your dive. A BCD is something you should definitely try before you buy and the smart dive shops know this. Pick the size that you think fits best in the shop and take the next size smaller too. Dive with both of them. The smaller one is probably the one you will keep.

Think carefully about what you are buying a BCD for. The primary requirement of a BCD is that it provides enough buoyancy when fully inflated to float you comfortably at the surface. Everything else is a question of style and personal preference. Avoid anything bulky and complicated. Most of us are naturally buoyant anyway. We float on the surface and, especially if we use conventional aluminium cylinders, our dive gear makes us even more positively buoyant. We need to carry weight to help us descend and the greater a BCD's integral buoyancy, (the buoyancy it has when deflated,) the more extra weight you are going to have to carry to get it under the water with you. So minimal integral buoyancy is an important feature.

Consider both wrap-around and back mounted designs. BCDs with the air cell entirely on your back tend to be easier to vent effectively and leave your chest area comparatively uncluttered. BCDs with wrap-around air cells tend to come with more and larger storage pockets. They will also keep you in a head up posture at the surface whereas the back-mounted BCDs work best as surface flotation devices if you lean back slightly and use the cell as a mini-raft.

Beware of air cells that have nooks and crannies where air

could become trapped and, especially if your diving career path may take you to harsh or overhead environments consider a BCD with two layers of protection, such as a plastic air cell within a tough cordura lining.

A foldable backpack is useful if you dive frequently in remote places only accessible by small aircraft and need to keep your bag small and a solid moulded plastic carry strap is a key feature if you plan to do a lot of beach diving.

The more straps your BCD has, the better the fit and the easier it will be to control. Not everyone likes to wear a chest strap or crotch strap but they do prevent your BCD from moving around. Also, as I mentioned in Chapter 3, two cam straps instead of one will ensure that your cylinder never falls out in mid dive!

D rings are very useful but they need to be made of solid stainless steel, not plastic, (and certainly not silver painted plastic!) One on the waist strap over each hip, and another on each shoulder strap at nipple height is all you should need. Use the waist D rings to clip on a reel or other accessories rather than shoulder strap D rings, which tend to allow things to dangle below you as you swim if they are not also secured to your harness at a second point. If necessary, a side-slung decompression or back up cylinder can be carried using clips attached to the shoulder and waist D rings on one side.

Quick release weight pouches at the waist can be useful for spreading the lead around but using these to store all your weight can destabilise you. Again, when you are standing up in the dive shop the weights may be positioned perfectly. But where will they be when you are horizontal in the water? If they just end up sagging below you, it will be difficult for you to find a good balance while you swim.

If you choose a BCD with weight pouches, it is essential that they be securely attached. Paradoxically, maybe, it is also important that the weights are easy to remove in the event that you find yourself on the surface with a malfunctioning BCD and are unable to maintain sufficient positive buoyancy to keep your head above water. You must know how to detach them quickly and, equally importantly, must be psychologically prepared to ditch the weights and pouches without a second thought as to their replacement cost.

Some BCD's have small trim weight pouches on the cam straps. These are great for spreading the weight around, particularly if you are diving with an aluminium cylinder, as they are in just the right place to counteract the positive buoyancy of the cylinder. But keep a maximum of 2kgs (4 lbs) of weight in these pouches and only then if you know for sure that you can float easily on the surface with the trim weights installed and without your BCD inflated, as you will find it difficult to ditch them in an emergency.

A final cautionary note; when you buy your BCD, watch out for the common dive shop practice of pricing BCDs without the inflator hose then selling the inflator hose separately as an additional "extra." So make sure that a hose is included when comparing prices. (All BCDs arrive from the manufacturers with an inflator hose attached,) Even if you already have an inflator hose on your regulator, it is a good idea to keep a second in reserve in case the original starts bubbling or cracking.

STEP 2: Get Acquainted

In the diver accident statistics mentioned above, lack of familiarity with the equipment is a commonly cited problem. Learn where your BCD controls are and figure out how you will use them in different situations.

Spend time studying your BCD, turn it horizontally and vertically and visualize where the air sits in the BCD when you are in various positions underwater. It will always gravitate to whichever part of your BCD is closest to the surface. Ask yourself how you would need to turn your body to vent air. In a head down, legs up posture, the air will be close to your butt and most BCDs have a "tail dump" so you can release air in this position. Know instinctively if your tail dump is on the left or right.

This is especially useful if you are in a closed overhead environment such as a wreck or a cavern. Another venting technique in such circumstances would be to roll your right shoulder down so your left shoulder is uppermost and use the shoulder pull dump on top of your inflator hose.

The inflator hose is the most commonly used BCD dump, but, in most BCDs, the mechanism on the end of the corrugated section is not a pump. No matter how fiercely you depress the button, you will only be able to use it to vent your BCD if the air in the BCD is at the level of your left shoulder, and the hose outlet is held between your shoulder and the surface.

Apart from the fact that they can be very buoyant, another disadvantage of larger volume BCDs with contoured wrap-around air cells is their tendency to trap air. It is important that you know how to vent your BCD completely. Failure to master this skill can make it difficult for you to descend and lead you to overweight yourself. Most significantly, it places you at risk of an out of control ascent at the end of a dive.

A good indication that you are not venting your BCD completely on descent and carrying too much weight to compensate is your posture while swimming underwater. Ask your buddy. Are you nice and flat and horizontal when stationary or do you swim with your head up and feet down? If it is the latter, the chances are that it is the excess weight on your belt that is causing your legs to drag and the unnecessary volume of air in your BCD that is lifting your shoulders.

You have a low-pressure inflator hose attached to your inflator mechanism to enable you to add air to your BCD directly from the cylinder on your back. This is a convenient alternative to oral inflation but it is not completely risk-free. The valve in the end of the hose can stick open and cause your BCD to auto-inflate. Be aware that this can happen, rinse the inflator mechanism with fresh water after every ocean dive to prevent salt build up and corrosion and practice disconnecting the hose underwater so you know you can do it if you ever need to. Just ease the metal sleeve back and pull until it pops.

Other potential points of weakness are the over pressure relief valve on the inflator hose and the plastic fittings covering the various dump valves, which can develop cracks or come unscrewed. If these fail underwater, you will lose the whole threaded cover and spring assembly and the BCD will become incapable of holding air. This is a potentially serious development but easy to prevent if you add a quick test of the fittings to your pre-dive safety check.

If this ever does happen then just swim slowly to the surface and once you get there, ditch your weights to make yourself positively buoyant!

A great way to familiarize yourself with your BCD is to slip it off and practice using it and adjusting it while pushing it along in front of you as a swim platform. Try this in a pool or area of shallow confined water first, of course. You will find this is a great confidence boosting skill and it really puts you in control of your BCD rather than the other way round. It is also a technique that you will find valuable if you want to check the source of a hissing noise behind your head during a dive or need to fix a slipping cam-band.

STEP 3: Set It Up Properly

You also need to control the equipment attached to your BCD and the things you keep in the pockets. Your octopus and your gauges console must be secured so that they do not swing around below you as you swim and they must be immediately accessible. Avoid hose-clips; most are useless and just allow the objects on the end of the hoses to hang free.

An elegant solution for your gauges is to attach a stainless steel or brass snap with cable ties and clip it to a chest D Ring on your BCD, (NOT the pull-ring at the end of your BCD shoulder adjustment strap!) Then just swivel the console around so it is facing upwards and all you have to do to check it is just glance down. See the previous chapter for an extended debate on options for your alternate second stage.

Conduct a regular inventory of your BCD pockets and the accessories you carry. Only take what you need and make sure the things you take on almost every dive, such as your SMB and dive light, are stowed away in a pocket or attached to your BCD harness. The rules are: one unsecured item per closed pocket and when you secure something to your harness attach it with two clips so that if one clip breaks you do not lose it.

Become a Better Diver by

Buying the right BCD
Learning its features
Taking control!

22. Dive Computers - Faith or Science?

Sometimes it feels as if decompression is a question of faith rather than science. It can be very confusing when you look at the different decompression tables used by various diver training organisations and see how greatly the no decompression times vary.

During a dive, when you compare the readings on your dive computer with others, you find that they too can differ considerably. You then do a little research on the Internet and find that there is a whole alphabet soup of decompression algorithms, none of them the same as another, each of which has devoted adherents.

This all creates uncertainty and leads divers to question what is safe, particularly as, when most of them first learned to dive they were given the impression that there was only one set of decompression tables and that these were inviolate and universally trusted.

It is perhaps understandable that instructors and training agencies will usually only introduce students to one set of decompression procedures, instead of presenting them with a range of alternatives and arming them with the knowledge to make their own decisions. It is only human for people to be drawn to promises of certainty. People like to be told that if they follow a particular course of action they will be safe.

Safe Diving

If you interpret "safe" as meaning "free of risk" then no dive computer, decompression table or decompression software can ever be considered "safe." Their various calculations and predictions are based on different theories on how gases and the human body behave. Although there are commonly accepted assumptions, the phenomenon of decompression sickness is not completely understood.

Unfortunately, the situation is unlikely to get clearer. The procedures sport divers use today are based largely upon more than a century of research into diver safety by the navies of the world and the commercial diving industry. However, with these organisations increasingly using remotely operated vehicles instead of human beings, they will no longer be spending so much money or time on the study of diving physiology. Nor is the sport-diving industry sufficiently well organised or wealthy to support significant scientific research or extensive validation programmes.

In fact, the picture may instead become further muddied as long-term scientific research is replaced by untested new theories posted on the Internet, a flat platform that can make them appear to have the same validity as long-established, tried and proven concepts and exacerbate the confusion.

Technical Influence

On a positive note, there has been much valuable progress in the practical application of decompression tables over the past two decades, as the advent of technical diving has led to a flurry of interest in alternative procedures. As more divers have acquired real world experience of dives beyond the usual recreational limits, they have found that simply extrapolating the standard methods typically used by sport divers is not always effective.

The result has been a number of innovations that are filtering into mainstream sport diving such as the practice of slowing an ascent with stops at intermediate depths and breathing from a gas with a lower inert gas content (and higher oxygen content) than the bottom gas to accelerate elimination of inert gas from the tissues, (see Chapter 11 "Ten Things that Technical Diving Teaches Us.") Mainstream manufacturers now offer multi-gas dive computers designed specifically for decompression diving with algorithms that incorporate deep intermediate stops.

More Good News

The good news is that the research and experimentation carried out over the past century have resulted in dive computers that are ideal for our current needs. Although there may appear to be substantial choice, the majority of models on the market are manufactured by a handful of companies who have dominated the industry for decades. The similarity in the screen configuration will help you tell which ones belong to the same "family." They may produce different readings for the same dive because they are based on different mathematical models, features may vary widely and some are more or less conservative than others, but they all operate within commonly accepted limits and no matter which model you choose, you can be sure that you will not be buying an inherently bad device.

How to Choose a Dive Computer

All dive computers measure pressure and time. They reinterpret the pressure as depth on the display screen and factor the measurements into a preset mathematical model to give you decompression information. Some computers also factor water temperature into the model and others allow you to enter other data such as age and dive conditions so that the computer can take these factors into account when delivering its decompression advice.

Dive computers will never be as sophisticated as the hardware you are used to deploying at home or at the office. They will always lag behind the leading edge of the Information Technology world because we divers are but a small niche market. However, there are already a number of companies who are using redundant technology from earlier generations of more mainstream devices such as mobile phones to create models with colour LCD screens, high-capacity memory boards, more accurate pressure transducers and rechargeable lithium ion batteries so the industry is not that far back.

Wrist vs Console?

You may have noticed that most dive professionals wear their dive computer on their wrist.

A strong argument in favour of doing this is that most of us wear a wristwatch and are in the habit of looking at our wrist when we want to know the time. We will therefore be more likely to look at our dive computer more frequently if we wear it in the same place.

One disadvantage of a wrist unit is that it is possible for you to jump in the water without it, although the likelihood of doing this is reduced if you make a habit of always keeping it attached to a D ring on your BCD when it is not in use.

Of course the best way of making sure you take it with you is if you never take it off and that is one of the major advantages of using a computer that doubles as your wristwatch. The other significant benefits are that not only will you be accustomed to looking at it; you will also be much more in tune with how it works and know how to find specific information on the display instinctively. Familiarity is important, especially in an emergency situation when you need to understand quickly what your computer is telling you. Divemasters often encounter experienced divers who turn up to dive having been out of the water for a while and cannot remember how to programme their dive computers.

Another disadvantage of wristwatch computers is screen size. The larger the screen the clearer the graphics can be. This is a major point in favour of console units. You are also much less likely to forget your console computer on the boat when you jump in, as it is a permanent fixture on your regulator.

To help you remember to keep an eye on it and to prevent it from getting damaged, if you choose a console computer make sure you clip it off to a chest mounted D ring and position it so that you can read it just by glancing down.

Air Integration

The primary argument in favour of integrating measurement of your air supply is that your computer can give you a prediction of time remaining at depth taking into account your decompression status, breathing rate and residual air supply.

The cylinder contents information can be transmitted via the high-pressure hose or via an electronic sender plugged directly into your regulator first stage and mated with a wrist unit or a miniature device inserted in the frame of a specially constructed dive mask.

The benefit of using a sender is that you can do away with one hose to give you a tidier configuration and this also removes the high-pressure hose as a potential equipment failure point.

However, the major problem with dive computers in general is exacerbated in the case of air-integrated units. Dive computers are battery-powered electronic instruments and batteries can fail. They are much more likely to fail when the device is in use. When a non-air-integrated computer fails on a dive you lose information on the dive to date and your decompression prediction. When an air integrated computer fails you lose everything!

What to Do When Your Computer Fails?

The best way to insure yourself against computer failure is to do what many professionals do and carry a second computer tucked into a pouch or a neoprene sleeve on your harness. This just needs to be a basic model that is always set to air, and the advantage of this over other options is that it enables you to continue the dive uninterrupted. However, if you have been relying on your main computer to monitor your air supply, you no longer know how much air you have left so once it fails your only option is to abort the dive.

A second option is to carry a set of decompression tables and refer to these, as long as they are the right tables for the dive and the gas you are breathing, you have an independent timing device in addition to your failed computer, and you have an independent depth recording device in addition to your failed computer.

A diver's watch and analogue depth gauge can take care of the last two requirements but you need to remember to reset the bezel on your watch and the maximum depth needle on the depth gauge before each dive for these to be useful in an emergency. A simpler alternative would be a digital bottom timer.

If the dive on which the computer failed is one of a series, do an extra long safety stop and an extended surface interval afterwards.

Decompression Tables

With the advent of computers, the practice of carrying a set of decompression tables on a dive, previously mandatory, has faded into disuse. Hard copy tables made a brief return to the scene during the early days of technical diving but now that reliable multi-gas computers are available they are now once again in danger of becoming something of an anachronism.

However, they can still have a role to play. If you understand decompression tables, your dive computer becomes your servant instead of your master and a set of tables, kept folded and slotted away unobtrusively in your BCD, can provide you with a useful reference in the event that your computer starts giving you implausible readings, as occasionally happens.

Another situation where it can be useful to have back up tables to refer to is when you are diving NITROX and have a NITROX computer that, like many, does not hold the programmed mix in its memory after the dive has finished. So, for those occasions when you forget to reprogramme the computer before the next dive and only notice as you descend that it has returned to its default settings, it is very handy to have a set of NITROX tables with you.

Decompression Software

A consequence of the simultaneous development of technical diving and the Internet is the profusion of decompression software programmes available for download. Most are designed for planning technical dives.

They can be fascinating to play with but it is wise to proceed with caution. Read widely about decompression theory before using the software for anything but entertainment. Playing with software is no substitute for diver training and any dive plans you generate should always be checked against proven tables or other software to see if they are plausible.

Remember too that any software can contain bugs and just because the programme comes up with a decompression profile does not mean it is safe for human beings.

Computers cannot get decompression illness but you can!

Become a Better Diver by

Recognising that our knowledge of decompression science is incomplete
Using computers conservatively and diving within both their limits and yours
Not dismissing the continued value of hard copy deco tables

The Best Dive Computer

The best dive computer is the one you know well, use on every dive and can understand intuitively. But if you are in the market for a new model, these are some of the key functions and features you might want to look for.

A well-tried and tested decompression algorithm.

A clear, uncluttered, easy to read dive screen.

A strong back-light and vibrant colours.

Intuitive internal navigation through different screens.

A presentation that matches your preference concerning graphics versus digits.

User programmability with dive parameters such as anticipated workload and personal data such as age.

A rechargeable battery.

Risk level options so you can choose the degree of conservatism.

A gauge mode option for free diving.

The ability to track decompression with multiple gases, including mixtures that include helium.

"Cloud based" dive log storage.

23. Look Behind You – Cylinders and Valves

This chapter deals with some of the less glamorous and under-appreciated elements of a diver's gear and if you have glanced at the title and thought, "this looks boring!" just wait a moment before you move on to the sexier aspects of our sport.

Your scuba cylinder holds the air that keeps you alive underwater and the cylinder valve is a key link in the process of moving this air to your lungs and keeping the supply going throughout your dive. They are vital elements of your life support equipment yet they are often taken for granted, misunderstood and frequently abused. It is time to give cylinders and valves their due billing.

Valve Handling

The valve on your scuba cylinder has a handle with a plastic knob attached. You turn the knob anti-clockwise to open it and close it by turning the knob clockwise.

This information may seem too basic in a book written for

advanced divers but the main reason I mention it here is to draw attention to an important basic skill that should be taught more widely. Provided with the knowledge of which way to turn the valve to open it, you can now visualize how you would do this if you ever found yourself entering the water with your air switched off. Professionals see divers in this predicament all too frequently and it happens to us too, more often than we care to admit!

I mentioned the drill earlier in Chapter 3 "Trials and Tribulations" but it is important so I make no apologies for repeating it here. It should be memorized and practiced until it becomes instinctive.

Reach down with your left hand, grip the base of the cylinder and push it up. Then reach behind your head with your right hand, grip the valve knob tightly and turn the knob in the direction away from your head (anti-clockwise.) The valve will open as soon as you start turning and you will immediately have air to breathe.

Not only in an emergency, but at all times, when opening and closing the valve, you only need to use your fingers and thumb. You do not need to grasp the knob in your palm and clench your fist. If you close it too tightly you can damage the valve.

After opening the valve all the way, leave it fully open. As I said before, it is one of scuba diving's notorious anachronisms that after opening a valve you should turn it back a quarter-turn or half-turn. A number of reasons have been put forward for why this should have been necessary at the dawn of the scuba diving era but it certainly has not been necessary for the past thirty years. However, the practice clings on still.

It is not only unnecessary; it is a bad idea, primarily because it introduces confusion over the status of the valve. If the knob will move both ways you do not immediately know whether it is nearly fully open or nearly closed and to descend with a valve that is only partially open can lead to breathing difficulties later as the cylinder pressure drops during the dive.

How Valves Work

Valves have a long fitting that matches the threads in the neck of the cylinder. They are screwed in carefully using a small amount of lubricant to avoid damaging the threads until the large O-ring at the top of the fitting is completely concealed within the cylinder neck. Then a final twist of a large wrench ensures a secure seal.

Internationally, as you might expect, there are a variety of different sized valve and cylinder threads. It is evidently important to make sure that the two match each other. Inconveniently, the differences are sometimes only slight. If a valve will not thread effortlessly and tightly into a cylinder the likelihood is that either the valve and cylinder threads are different or damaged.

The air flows out from the cylinder into the valve via a 5cms (2") long, narrow metal pipe screwed into the threaded end of the valve. This is known as a dip tube or anti-debris tube and it is there to make it very hard for anything inside the cylinder, such as flakes of corroded metal, to enter the valve and block it, when the cylinder is inverted. Sometimes you may pick up a cylinder and hear something rattling around inside; this is probably a dip tube that has worked itself loose. Do not dive with the cylinder until it has been repaired.

Most valves also have an over-pressure plug, concealing a thin disc that is designed to burst if the cylinder should become over-pressurized to a degree that might otherwise cause the valve threads to fail. For instance, if a full cylinder is left in the back of a car on a hot day, the heat can cause the pressure to increase considerably. When this disc bursts, the escaping air makes a frightening noise but both the cylinder and valve remain undamaged and intact.

Valve Care

Treat cylinder valves with the same sort of care you give to your regulator. They are made of brass and are not strong enough to sustain a heavy blow. This is one good reason why new divers are always taught not to leave a cylinder standing unsupported and to make sure that a cylinder cannot roll around in transit. Damage to a valve usually results in a bent handle or broken threads, either of which will cause the valve to leak.

If you pick up a cylinder from the airfill station and find that it is not completely full, a leaky valve may be to blame. Spray the valve and the top of the cylinder with a weak soapy solution to identify the source of the leak. If you see bubbles coming from the tank neck, the problem is either a worn O-ring or broken threads. If the bubbles are coming from the valve knob then either the handle o-rings or Teflon seat need replacing or the valve has taken a blow and become distorted.

Before attaching a regulator to a cylinder valve, open the valve briefly to allow a spurt of high-pressure air to clear any debris or water that might have fallen into the outlet hole while the cylinder has been stored.

By the way, another little historical hangover: you may hear a standard cylinder valve referred to by old-timers and their disciples as a K valve. This has nothing to do with its shape; it refs to the designation code for a valve in an early US Divers sales catalogue. Item J in the same catalogue was a more advanced valve with a lever activated reserve device designed to let a diver know when the cylinder pressure was low. This was before we had submersible pressure gauges, of course. As soon as they appeared on the market, valves with reserve devices became redundant: they are no longer manufactured.

Valve Types

DIN vs Yoke

I discussed this issue in Chapter 20 "Running the Rule over Regulators" but will run through it again here as the terms DIN and yoke/international refer to cylinder valves as well as regulator first stages.

The DIN system consists of a regulator with a threaded core that has its own O-ring and screws directly into the cylinder valve so that an interior o-ring seal is made. It is more commonly seen in Europe and the Mediterranean, but it is the choice of technical divers all over the world.

The yoke or international set-up is much more popular internationally. This is where the regulator fits over the cylinder valve and is tightened front to back with a screw so that a seal is formed against the exterior valve O-ring when the regulator is pressurized.

The yoke design may be more widely used but the DIN system has a number of significant safety advantages. First, the diver, not the cylinder owner, is responsible for the quality of the o-ring that seals the regulator to the tank. Second, the interior o-ring provides a much more secure seal. Third, and most important, in an overhead environment, the yoke/A-clamp screw jutting out behind the valve can easily get knocked. This in turn can cause the soft brass fitting to become dislodged from the valve. No wonder cave divers and wreck divers always use DIN!

Convertible Valves

These are valves which have a threaded insert fitted with an O ring on both ends. The Insert can be retained for use with a yoke/A-clamp regulator or removed to allow the valve to accommodate a DIN fitting.

Modular Valves

These are valves with a port opposite the knob that can accommodate a manifold bar for diving with doubles, or a second outlet to create an H valve configuration, see below. They come in right hand or left hand versions. Some manufacturers offer modular valves where the knob and the manifold port can be interchanged to make them right or left-handed.

H Valves and Y Valves

These are single valves with dual outlets that can accommodate two first stage regulators and are named after their shape. If one regulator starts to free-flow, you can reach back, close the valve knob controlling airflow from the cylinder to the malfunctioning regulator and still breathe using the other regulator. These valves therefore offer greater protection from regulator malfunction than a standard single outlet valve but, despite this safety advantage, they have not become widely popular.

Cylinders

The majority of cylinders used in recreational diving are tall, thin aluminium cylinders known in Europe and elsewhere as

12s and in the USA as 80s. In fact, the water volume of these cylinders is 11.1 litres not 12 and when full they contain 77.4 cu ft not 80!

Although these have become the industry standard cylinders, they are not necessarily the best option. You may have noticed that, given the choice, instructors and dive guides will opt for non-standard cylinders. This is because an aluminium 12/80 cylinder is heavy (14.2kg/31.4 lbs), uncomfortable for many people to wear due its length (66.2 cms/ 26.1") and becomes positively buoyant during a dive as its contents are used up (+2kg/+4.4 lbs in sea water when empty.) This can create problems when you return to the shallows at the end of a dive if you are unprepared.

Dive centres are primarily businesses and the main reason they choose this style of cylinder is that it is manufactured in huge quantities and is the cheapest option on the market. Aluminium cylinders are also more resilient to mistreatment than steel cylinders.

If you want to buy your own cylinders, there are better alternatives. For instance, if you find you always come up from a dive with 70 bar (1000 psi) remaining in a standard cylinder, you might be a lot more comfortable with an aluminium 9-litre (63 cu ft) cylinder. These are lighter (12.1 kg/26.7 lbs), shorter (55.5 cms/21.9") and become less positively buoyant when empty (+1.2kg/+2.6lbs.)

Steel cylinders are a more expensive option but they last longer, they are smaller and lighter than aluminium cylinders of equivalent volume and they are more negatively buoyant, which means you can remove some of the weight on your belt. Be aware, however, that the transition can take a little time to get used to if you are used to diving with an aluminium cylinder and steel cylinders need careful maintenance as corrosion inside and out can shorten their life considerably, (see the section on Looking After Cylinders below.)

Pressure vs Volume

Most scuba cylinders and their valves are designed for use with air pressures of 207 or 232 bar. This is their rated, service or working pressure and is marked on the shoulder of the cylinder. The most common working pressures marked on US cylinders are 3000 psi and 3300 psi respectively. One bar is the equivalent of 14.7 psi. This is also the atmospheric pressure at sea level. Another way of referring to 1 bar is 1 atmosphere absolute or 1 ata.

We use pressure gauges to measure the contents of our scuba cylinders and we always refer to our air supply in pressure terms. However, this is misleading as the volume of air represented by a pressure reading can vary greatly depending on the size of the cylinder.

For example, if you have 1500 psi in an 80 cu ft cylinder, you have 38.7 cu ft. of air. If you have 1500 psi remaining in a 30 cu ft decompression cylinder, however, all you have left to breathe is 15 cu ft.

In metric terms, if you have 100 bar remaining in an 11-litre cylinder, you have 1100 litres left but, in a 3-litre decompression cylinder, 100 bar represents only 300 litres.

The pressure is the same in both cases but the reading is only really useful if you know the volume of your cylinder, and, of course, your air consumption, i.e. the rate at which you breathe.

Diving with Doubles

If you find you need a larger air supply for the diving you want to do then a set of small doubles is often a better and safer option than a huge single cylinder. Doubles offer you a better equilibrium underwater and, whatever valve configuration you choose (below), they give you extra security against valve or regulator failure.

This is particularly important if your dive plan requires decompression stops as, once you have a decompression obligation, escape to the surface is no longer an available option in the event of equipment malfunction.

The extra security afforded by enjoying the increased air supply that diving with two cylinders provides must be balanced against extra weight to carry out of the water, greater mass to move through the water and the need for specific equipment to hold the two cylinders securely and give you adequate positive buoyancy at the surface.

Divers and manufacturers have come up with a number of methods to try to permit the attachment of double cylinders to standard jacket style BCDs but none of these offer a secure and stable option, no matter how many D rings are added or whether the name is changed to include the designation "tek" or "X."

The technical diving community has adopted a standard configuration for carrying double cylinders. This involves a back-mounted wing and harness system that bolts on to a double set of aluminium or stainless steel cylinder bands. The bands are best fitted over sections of rubber inner tube to prevent them from biting into the cylinders and to avoid corrosion from the coincidence of dissimilar metals.

If the concept of using double cylinders appeals, get some practice using the new equipment under supervision and learn a few tips and tricks by taking a course in planned decompression diving, which most training agencies offer for divers thinking of embarking on technical diving.

Valves for Doubles

Divers use a variety of valve configuration options with double cylinders.

Some choose to keep the two cylinders independent of each other. This is the easiest and cheapest option and offers a degree of protection from equipment failure in that, if a regulator starts to free-flow uncontrollably, they can close the valve to one cylinder and breathe from the other. However, this does mean that they lose access to all the air in the first cylinder.

Other disadvantages of using independent cylinders include the need to switch regulators from time to time in order to equalize the air supply remaining in both cylinders. Also, if you use right-handed valves on both cylinders it is very difficult to manipulate the valve knob on the left-hand cylinder.

A common alternative is to connect the two cylinders via a manifold bar, using a left handed valve on the cylinder on the left. The internal design of this assembly is such that you can breathe the air from both cylinders via a regulator attached to either cylinder valve. This gives you access from either regulator to what is effectively a single air supply with twice the capacity of each independent cylinder.

In the event of an uncontrollable regulator free-flow the cylinder valve to which the faulty regulator is attached can be closed, removing the threat posed by the free-flow while still allowing the air in both cylinders to be used via the good regulator attached to the other cylinder valve.

However, if either cylinder valve were to fail, it would be impossible to prevent the air in both cylinders from escaping, so, to combat this, many divers use a manifold with a valve knob placed mid-way along the bar, that can be opened to connect the two cylinders or closed to isolate one cylinder from the other.

This is called an isolation manifold. It offers the greatest security from the threat of equipment failure, but the third valve knob does mean there is now another piece of apparatus that can malfunction.

An important note on manifold bars: they are connected to the cylinder valves by threaded inserts with O-ring seals.   The manifold may look like a carrying handle for the heavy double cylinders, but it should never be used as such as the fittings can warp, the threads can break and the O-ring seal can be broken.

Mixing (Up) the Gases

Some divers advocate a practice whereby they dive independent double cylinders with different gases in each cylinder, for instance NITROX 32 in one for the deeper portion of the dive and NITROX 50 in the other for the ascent and decompression stops. They know that they must not breathe the wrong gas at the wrong stage of the dive as they risk either oxygen toxicity or decompression sickness so they come up with various ways of marking their regulators so they know which one is attached to which cylinder. However, they can never be absolutely sure, as they can never actually see the connection or the gas contents label on the cylinder.

Technical divers shun this practice, which was proven to be

unsafe in the early days of the sport when it was held responsible for a number of fatalities. There is no reason at all why it should be any safer now. When wearing doubles for planned decompression diving, the safest practice is to carry the same gas in both cylinders and a decompression gas in a separate cylinder mounted to your side where you can read the label, see exactly which regulator is connected to the valve and be sure which gas it is you are breathing, (see Smaller Cylinders below.)

Side-Mount Diving

Another way of diving with two cylinders is to wear one to each side rather than on your back using a specially designed harness and something often affectionately known as a "butt plate." The practice of configuring cylinders in this way is called side mounting.

There are several advantages of a side-mount configuration.

The cylinders are carried independently of each other and are attached to the diver in the water or near to the water. This makes pre- and post dive preparation easier on the diver's back and knees, which is especially useful for those with back problems.

It offers the diver a narrow, streamlined profile. In fact it was first devised by Florida cave divers who wanted to get through restrictions with low ceilings that did not permit a diver with back-mounted cylinders to pass. In a shipwreck, there is reduced risk of entanglement with overhead cables if you are diving sidemount.

The side-mount diver's gas supply is fully redundant and carried in completely separate systems, each with a first and second stage plus a pressure gauge. This offers similar gas management options to a set of independent doubles but the valves and first stages are within full sight at the diver's side rather than behind and out of sight.

The harness and cylinder attachment kits are light and take up little room in your baggage. They can also be used with cylinders of any size.

If this sounds interesting, a workshop with a qualified instructor is a great way to learn the technique and to find out the best ways to assemble the gear and configure your regulator hoses.

Looking After Cylinders

In order to make more sales, manufacturers use bright paint finishes to enhance the cylinders' visual appeal and offer rubber boots and plastic nets to protect the cylinder from damage.

While dings and scratches are certainly best avoided, the true enemy of the scuba cylinder is salt-water corrosion. Unfortunately, as we often find when we strip boots and nets from cylinders during the annual inspection process, boots and nets tend to aggravate corrosion by preventing the cylinder from being rinsed effectively and trapping salt water next to the metal. If you use a net or a boot, you must be meticulous about removing them and rinsing them frequently.

A similar problem occurs with elaborate paint finishes. When the coating becomes scratched or torn, seawater can penetrate insidiously between paint and metal. Often the first sign that this has happened is the appearance of a raised patch of bubbling paint. By this time the corrosion has already taken hold and the only solution is to strip that beautiful finish that persuaded you to buy the cylinder in the first place.

Internal corrosion is an even bigger problem as this can form unseen between inspections and develop to a point where the cylinder wall can become dangerously weak.

The interior of a scuba cylinder should always be dry. Compressors are designed to remove water from the air as they process it. From the beginning divers are told never to breathe a cylinder dry. Therefore internal corrosion should be a rare phenomenon.

However, professionals will tell you that it is far from unusual and that sometimes we open a cylinder up for inspection and find a pool of water in the base. Surprisingly this is not seawater, although it is slightly salty, which suggests that the problem lies with something that has become an industry habit, the practice of filling cylinders in water baths.

The faster you fill a cylinder with high-pressure air, the quicker you finish the job but the more heat you generate. When the cylinder subsequently cools the pressure drops, so you need to top the cylinder up again, which takes time. So rather than slow down the process and generate less heat, many busy dive centres fill the cylinders in a tank of water, which conducts some of the heat away.

The problem with this solution is that, although fresh water is used in the tank, dried salt on used cylinders dissolves into it to form a brackish mixture. This then splashes up onto the fill whips and cylinder valves and when the high-pressure air is released from the whips into cylinders droplets of salty water are carried into the darkness of the cylinder where they can begin their corrosive work undetected.

The advice, therefore, is, if you have your own cylinders; get them filled at a place where they do it slowly and in the dry.

By the way, if, after a dive, you use the high-pressure air from your cylinder to dry off your regulator first stage, be careful. You may well be achieving your aim of blowing some of the salt water away but, unless you first replace the little ball or pyramid that sits between the yoke screw and the first stage filter, you may be forcing droplets of corrosive, salty water into you regulator first stage too.

Cylinder Markings and Labelling

Many divers are unaware of the purpose and significance of the marks stamped into the shoulder of cylinders and the labels attached.

Protocols vary internationally but there are four main reasons for identifying cylinders.

1. So that staff at dive centres and fill stations can see at a glance a cylinder's age, rated pressure and inspection status. Because the large majority of cylinder explosions occur during the filling process, they need to be sure that the cylinder is safe to fill, that it has been inspected and tested according to the established practice and that both cylinder and valve are compatible with the intended gas content, fill pressure and filling procedure.

2. So that a diver knows that the cylinder they are breathing from contains the correct gas for the dive. Having said this, no matter what is shown on a cylinder contents label or tag, never believe what it says until you have analysed the gas personally. It may sound extreme but this caveat also applies to air cylinders filled in stations that also provide mixed gas fills. Busy professionals make mistakes, you are the one who will be breathing from the cylinder underwater and unfortunately all gases taste the same.

3. So that other members of the dive team can act as a second pair of eyes and see both the contents of the gas in the cylinder as well as the maximum depth at which it can be used. The label showing this information therefore needs to be large and prominently displayed.

4. So that, in the event of a vehicle accident while cylinders are being transported, emergency services have a visual indication of the potential hazard from the gas contained in a cylinder. If they cannot read the label or see the markings, they will always assume the worst, i.e. that the cylinder is fully charged with the highest risk gas.

Smaller Cylinders

A number of terms are used to describe smaller cylinders that divers often carry in addition to their main supply. There is often much confusion over which is which so here is a brief guide.

A pony cylinder contains a reserve air supply, is attached by brackets to the cylinder on your back and has its own regulator. This gives you a genuine alternate source of air and removes the need for an octopus second stage on your primary regulator. A good choice for deep no-decompression stop diving would be a 2 or 3 litre (13 or 20 cu ft) cylinder.

A decompression cylinder is usually carried clipped onto the diver's harness so that it hangs to the side and under the arm, (see Mixing (Up) Gases above.) It contains a gas with a higher level of oxygen than your main air/gas supply and is carried so you can switch to it as you ascend and shorten your required decompression time. The correct and safe use of decompression cylinders and their application and configuration all require training in planned decompression diving.

A stage cylinder describes a cylinder carried by a cave or wreck diver with a view to removing it and placing it securely either near the entrance or, on long penetrations at a planned point along the route, so they do not have to carry it through the narrow confines of the cave or wreck and can pick it up on their return. This is only a viable strategy if it is 100% certain that you will exit the same way you entered.

Spare Air is the trade name given to a tiny 0.42 litre / 3 cu ft cylinder with a dedicated mouthpiece that is easily clipped on to a BCD and can be handed off to an out-of-air diver or used to ascend safely if the user suffers a catastrophic failure of his main air supply during a no-decompression dive. It can be filled to a pressure of 200 bar (3000 psi) and topped up from a scuba cylinder. If a diver remains calm, it will probably give him enough air for a steady 10m (33 ft) per minute ascent to the surface from 30m (100ft), certainly better than nothing but not really a practical alternative to a pony cylinder and less useful to an out-of-air diver, (who is highly unlikely to be calm,) than a regulator on a long hose attached to your main air supply.

Become a Better Diver by

Considering alternative valve and cylinder options
Learning how cylinders are marked and labelled in your country
Keeping your cylinders and valves well maintained and corrosion-free

24. Surface Safety

A "Divers Lost at Sea!" headline screaming from the front page strikes at deep-seated human fears. We know this terror well; every day, somewhere in the world divers surface to find that they have drifted away and the boat they jumped off is out of sight. As you may be all too aware, a knot forms in the stomach, a burst of adrenaline courses through the body and a single thought occupies the mind; "I hope they can find me!"

As you will know if you have ever stood on a boat and looked out to sea searching for the fin of a dolphin or the fluke of a whale, the shifting water patterns created by the combination of wind, waves, tides and the sun's reflection can make it very hard to see an object at the surface: and from even a short distance, a diver's head is a pretty small object!

Be Prepared

Of course diving with reputable, well-equipped, safety-conscious operators with eagle-eyed experienced crew who know the area well is the first step towards ensuring your recovery and good dive centres working in areas where high current flow is possible will provide divers with surface marker buoys (SMBs) as part of the service. They will also make sure that all boats have a radio and anticipate engine failure by having either twin motors or a back up "kicker" that will propel the boat faster than the current it may be chasing!

However, of course, you should not just rely on the professionalism of your dive operator. If you have drifted away, you need to be able to give them as much help as you can to find you as quickly as possible.

This is another area where sport divers can learn from technical divers. As I mention a number of times elsewhere in this book, one of the basic tenets of technical diving is to anticipate what might go wrong and assess "the What Ifs."

Because of the long time that they spend in the water decompressing from deep dives and because many popular, deep shipwrecks are located far off-shore, often in areas of high and unpredictable current flow, technical divers have always been highly conscious of the risk of being lost at sea.

They combat the risk by carrying self-rescue and advanced signalling gear on every dive as a standard part of their kit. Many of these items could be easily secured to regular sport diving equipment without unnecessary encumbrance and just having them available would reduce the potential ill effects of being left at the surface for an extended period of time and significantly enhance the prospects of your being rescued. It is always tempting to spread out rescue gear among a team to reduce the number of items carried by each member. Resist this temptation. There is always the chance that you and your buddies can become separated at the surface so each individual must be self-sufficient.

Get into the habit of carrying these things on every dive, make it part of your pre-dive ritual to check that they are there and in working condition. Keep them in zippered pockets, one item per pocket, or attach them securely to your BCD in such a way that they don't dangle away from you as you swim and are easy to find when you need them. The first five items are essential!

A Surface Marker Buoy (SMB)

Carry an SMB on every dive. Choose long and thin rather than short and fat and go for either fluorescent yellow or fluorescent orange for maximum visibility, although one commercial diving survey reported that the easiest colour to pick out at sea was bright pink! Some models have white reflective tape sewn on the top; this is a really useful addition, as a flash of sunlight will draw a watcher's attention. Attach 6m (20 ft) of line to the bottom of the SMB so you can deploy it from your safety stop and give the boat crew advance notice of where you are. Or use a reel and line if you want to do as technical divers do and send your SMB up from depth to use the line as an emergency ascent platform. Deploying an SMB under water is something you will need to practice a few times but it is an important skill to possess: see guidelines at the end of this chapter.

Technical divers carry two SMBs but if you are diving as part of a team, then it is sufficient to have one each. Only put up one SMB per team at a time. Line takes on a life of its own in water and if two lines are in close proximity to each other they will often become entangled. Advice on deploying your SMB follows this chapter.

A Mirror

A piece of unbreakable mirrored card, (the stuff they use in aircraft bathrooms), makes an excellent signalling device over long distances and can be used to attract the attention of someone on a boat or in the air. Point the mirror in their direction and move it from side to side to catch the sun and create a flash. A CD or DVD will do the job just fine too!

A Dive Light

Take a light with you on every dive, not only night dives. It can make a great signalling device in low light conditions. A group of British divers adrift in the Red Sea a couple of years ago were not found until night-time when rescuers spotted their lights. Some small dive lights have a flashing function, which makes you even more visible. You can also buy purpose built small electronic flashing strobes that you strap on to the shoulder of your BCD. These have a long battery life and function automatically so they continue to flash even if you fall asleep or are unconscious.

Your light can be combined with your SMB at night to create a highly visible "light sabre."

A Noisemaker

Many divers carry a whistle, although these are not very effective except over short distances and even then only if the wind is in your favour. A power horn attached to your BCD inflator hose is more effective but test it from time to time to make sure it still works because they do not last forever and hold it as far away from your ear as possible when you let it off!

A Hood

Hoods are a good idea, not only because they help you retain body heat during a long dive. They can also be valuable in protecting the head and neck from the sun if you are floating at the surface for a long time. White reflective flashes on the hood will achieve the same signalling effect as a mirror.

Some of the following suggestions may seem a little extreme but are worthy of consideration if you are diving in circumstances where you have assessed that the risk of being lost at sea is greater than normal, perhaps when you are far from the mainland in areas of high current flow such as Cocos Island in Costa Rica or the Galapagos.

A Surface Survival Kit

For long decompression dives in the open ocean, technical divers always carry a kit containing the following items. They are often best stored in a double O-ring sealed pressure and water resistant canister in a zippered pouch secured to the rear of the harness: -

Sunscreen – because the sun can harm you even if you are on the surface for a comparatively short time. Choose a small plastic tube with a high SPF and a long shelf life.

Aircraft dye – a small tube containing powder which, when deployed, creates a slick of red dye at the surface so that a searching aircraft can follow your trail as you drift

A 3m (10 ft) length of parachute cord – to link the members of the dive team together at the surface and make sure they do not drift apart. By staying together you present a larger object for searchers to see, especially from the air.

EPIRBs (Electronic Position Indicating Radio Beacons)

A portable EPIRB may seem to be an unnecessarily expensive and high tech solution and it must be stored in a fairly large canister which makes it awkward to carry, but EPIRBs are increasingly being used by divers exploring wrecks that are far off-shore in areas where strong currents and heavy waves are common. By activating an EPIRB on standard wavebands a searching aircraft or vessel can easily track you and direct rescuers.

Signal Flares

These are very effective, easily deployed and visible over miles. However, they also need to be carried in a canister and have a use-by date so check them frequently. Do not allow them to sit in the canister unused and ignored. They will degrade over time.

Something to Drink

Dehydration is probably the most serious issue that you face if you are left drifting at sea for an extended period so, it is not an exaggeration to say that having a ready supply of something thirst-quenching to drink could save your life. A cheap solution is to pop a soft drink pouch, (Caprisun or a similar brand), into your BCD pocket each time you dive. A more technical approach to the problem would be to secure a small plastic Camelbak flexible water container to your harness or BCD and tuck it under your left shoulder. Route the drinking tube so that it curls around the back of your neck and comes up under your chin. Clean the pack out frequently as it is an ideal breeding ground for bacteria.

Become a Better Diver by

Planning for surface emergencies
Equipping yourself adequately

How to Deploy an SMB

Step 1. Get it Ready

Well before you arrive at your safety stop depth, take out your SMB and unclip your reel.

Attach the end of the line to the SMB and unfurl the SMB so that it drifts away from you. Keep hold of the reel.

Look at it carefully; make sure neither the SMB nor the line are snagged on you or your dive gear.

Pull the SMB back towards you.

Unlock the reel.

Step 2. Choose an Inflation Option

Option 1

Tilt your head, raise the open bottom of the SMB up above the exhaust of your regulator second stage and exhale into the bag, gently at first. (Be careful that the line does not get snagged as you do this.)

Option 2

Take your octopus, hold it under the open bottom of the surface marker and press the purge button gently and briefly.

Watch Out! If you purge too hard or if the regulator starts to free flow your SMB will fly out of control.

Option 3

Take your BCD inflator hose, hold it under the open bottom of the SMB and press both the inflate and dump buttons simultaneously.

Watch out! Make sure you press BOTH buttons so you don't inflate your BCD instead.

Step 3. Send it Up

Only put a little puff of air into the SMB at first, just enough to make it stand up.

Check where the line is at all times so it does not catch on you or your equipment.

Position yourself in the water underneath the SMB and the line and look up at it. Make sure you are not under a boat or platform.

Make yourself a little negatively buoyant.

Add one or two more little puffs of air until you feel the SMB wants to get going.

Add a final larger puff of air and then release it.

Keep hold of the end of the line.

Watch the SMB and the line as it rises.

When the SMB is at the surface pull the line tight so it stands up straight.

Check your depth, then do your stop keeping the line tight and looking up to make sure everything is OK on the surface.

25. The Concept of Configuration

An important step towards becoming a better diver is to acquire the habit of constantly reviewing the way in which your equipment is set up. As I mentioned earlier in Chapter 11, in the technical diving community this process is known as configuration. It can be defined as a never-ending quest for perfection!

Thinking carefully about how you put your equipment together makes you both a safer diver and a better team player. Because you have considered exactly how to store or where to place every piece of equipment you carry, you will be better able to use it in an emergency.

The Basics

No two divers have exactly the same requirements or preferences but good configurations do share a number of basic attributes. Here is a guide to getting started.

Your first task is to make sure you look good! Your profile should be clean and streamlined, not when you stand admiring yourself in front of your bedroom mirror but when you are horizontal in the water! Tape down or tuck away any loose straps. Nothing should be hanging down below you. This is not simply for aesthetic reasons. It helps prevent you getting caught up on a reef or wreck and the less interruption there is to the smooth flow of water over your body, the easier it is to swim against a current, allowing you to conserve both air and energy.

Accessories

These are the same reasons why each accessory you carry should be stowed away rather than just left to dangle down from your BCD. Everything must be secured so that it stays in place and is there when you need it but not hidden away so well that it is difficult to find and deploy.

There are a couple of crucial rules to follow. If you use pockets, only put one loose thing in each because if you have several items loose in the same pocket and pull one out, everything else will come out with it. Pockets with clips inside are a good idea. If you are attaching equipment to D rings, make sure each piece is held on by two points so that if one attachment point breaks it does not fall off and disappear into the depths.

Think carefully about what equipment you really need to carry. Look critically at each item, examine its purpose and consider its usefulness. The fact that you own something is not sufficient justification for carrying it on every dive. However, if a piece of gear is so important that its failure or loss would threaten your safety, make sure you have two of them. An obvious example is a back up torch on a night dive. Be wary of taking this concept too far. Carrying back-ups for non-essential equipment can over-burden you.

If you are sure you do not need something, leave it behind. This decision is not always straightforward. For example: you would not usually take a snorkel with you when diving in an overhead environment, but if the dive was on a wreck and involved a long surface swim out from the shore and back, then yes, it would be a good idea to take a snorkel so you can keep every breath of your air supply for the dive itself. Obviously, you would not keep the snorkel attached to the side of your mask during the dive but you could tuck it away in your BCD, (there are folding snorkels specifically designed for this purpose,) or strap it to your harness.

Hoses

Give a lot of thought to the length and placement of your alternate air source and high-pressure hose. Chapter 20 "Running the Rule over Regulators" discusses a number of options but the key point to note here is that there is no standard hose length, although many dive stores might like to pretend there is. Obviously, a large person needs longer hoses than a small person so assess what length you need and purchase accordingly. There is no need to accept discomfort or inconvenience by just taking what comes out of the box. Various lengths of corrugated inflator hose and low-pressure inflator hose are available too.

An Open Mind is the Best Accessory

You will have noticed that the aim of this chapter is not to preach the benefits of any particular configuration. As I said earlier, no two people are exactly the same. So, while it is an excellent idea to look at how other people configure their equipment, beware of just blindly copying your diving heroes or succumbing to peer pressure to conform to other divers' preferences.

Have confidence in your own solutions. If something works well for you, then that is all that really matters. When choosing your own path, however, by all means be inventive but avoid the temptation to get carried away and look for complex solutions. Keep everything as simple as possible.

Even when you feel you have arrived at a configuration you are pleased with, maintain an open mind. Always be prepared to adapt your style if you see something that you think might work better.

If you are part of a team, your configuration should ideally be compatible with the people you dive with. This does not mean that all of you need to carry exactly the same make and model of equipment but the thinking behind the way each diver's gear is set up should be similar.

Going Through Changes

Configuration is a process of evolution rather than revolution. Make changes one at a time and give yourself time to get used to each change before making the next. Do not embark on a testing dive before getting used to the changes you have made in relatively benign conditions.

Only keep the changes you are completely happy with. If anything feels awkward or uncomfortable, do not persist with it. It is surprising how easily a minor irritation can nag away at you subconsciously during a dive and raise your stress levels.

A Summary of Adjectives

So to summarise: a good equipment configuration is simple, comfortable and convenient, streamlined and appropriate, safe, user-friendly, sufficient but not excessive, individual, versatile and team compatible. It may sound like an impossible mission but the goal is well worth pursuing.

Become a Better Diver by

Giving careful thought to how you set up your equipment
Never abandoning the quest for perfection

26. Accessorize Wisely

We all have tools and accessories that we thought we would use but have just ended up lying in our gear bag unused and unloved. This chapter is a guide to the bits and pieces that you can buy in the certain knowledge that they will not suffer the same fate. It also suggests the qualities, functions and features you should be looking for when you are shopping.

I would make two initial points about buying dive equipment in general. First, in most cases you get what you pay for. Particularly when considering things that you might need to use in an emergency, it is not an exaggeration to say that you compromise on price at the potential cost of your safety. Second, when deciding what equipment to buy, a good place to start is to look at what your instructor uses.

There is one caveat to add to this second point. Equipment manufacturers and dive centres know that instructors, divemasters and guides are important opinion formers and will offer them attractive discounts and "key-man" pricing to try and get them to use particular brands. Some dive centres require that their staff only wear the equipment they sell. So, be aware that your instructor may not have chosen his equipment because he thinks it is the best, there may be financial considerations or he may just be wearing it because he wants to keep his job! However, this warning notwithstanding, it is still a good move to look at what the professionals use – after all this is what they wear to work every day!

Communication Devices

Before you think of investing in an underwater communications device of any sort, consider what you will use it for. If, as is commonly the case, you want it in order to keep in touch with your diving partner then you might want to review your buddy procedures first, (see Chapter 6 "Solo Diving.") If you and your buddy are not diving on the same page then no communication device, however complex, is going to resolve the issue satisfactorily. If, on the other hand, you cannot bear to spend an hour underwater without giving your buddy the benefit of your advice and opinions, make sure that your buddy is happy with this too. One of the joys of diving for many people is that it offers a temporary escape from the stresses of the surface world and gives you time to commune with your soul, away from the intrusion of others.

For messages too complex for hand signals, however, it is useful to carry a multi page slate or waterproof paper notebook, with a pencil attached and a back up hidden away in a pouch. Renewable pencils are a great idea, they are all plastic so there is no metal to corrode and if a lead breaks there is always another one behind it. Technical divers use ergonomically curved wrist slates to write down dive plans and make notes during the dive. These slates usually have slots so you can pass your computer wrist strap through and they have the additional advantage of being hands-free.

The erasable magic slates much beloved of some dive guides are effective communication devices but they are quite bulky, which makes them hard to tuck away when you are not using them.

Submersible Marker Buoys (SMBs)

An SMB is an essential piece of equipment on most dives. See Chapter 24 "Surface Safety" for the key features and benefits to look for.

Reels

A reel is a very handy addition to your gear bag. You can use one with your SMB to create your own ascent platform, you can run a line out to find your way to and from a descent line in poor visibility and, when wreck and cave diving, you will always need one to deploy a line into the overhead environment from outside your point of entry so you can find your way back if the visibility deteriorates.

Reels need to be simple, solid, tough and durable. Avoid anything that has a thin plastic case even if it has metal fittings, as the casing will crack under duress at the point of contact with the metal. Look at the brands cave and wreck divers use. When diving within typical sport diving limits, choose a smaller one with around 30m (100ft) of line, but before you use it, run the line out, measure it yourself and mark the actual length of line in indelible ink on the casing. It is not a nice surprise to send up an SMB from 30m (100ft) only to discover you only have 25m (83ft) of line on the reel! Secure the reel to your BCD or harness by two snaps to prevent it dangling. One should be attached to the casing and the other to the end of the line. The additional advantage of this second snap is that you can use it to connect the line quickly to your SMB.

Clips and Snaps

You use clips to keep your gauges in the right place and make sure you don't lose your accessories. Most dive centres have a display featuring a variety of contorted plastic devices, which are fragile and, in many cases, don't do what they are supposed to do. Hose clips just allow the hose to slip through and many of the accessory clips look fine when you are vertical but, once you are horizontal in the water, they simply act as extensions allowing the attached equipment to dangle even further below you than it normally would.

My recommendation is that you walk straight past this display and head for your neighbourhood hardware store. Stock up on brass or stainless steel piston or bolt snaps in different sizes and buy a pack of small zip or cable ties. Keep spares in your Save-a-Dive kit. The brass snaps are the best choice as they are cheap and less likely to corrode than the less economical stainless steel ones but they do have rough edges so, if you have fragile fingers or are a concert pianist, go for marine quality stainless steel snaps that are more expensive but smooth. Attaching these to your gauges and accessories with the cable ties, (at least two, in case one breaks,) keeps them close and allows you to move them around from D ring to D ring on your harness or BCD.

Dive Lights

The best dive lights are cylindrical, made of metal, have rechargeable batteries and are expensive. Buy a small light that is easy to stow away in your BCD or on your harness and that you can take with you on every dive, to peer into holes or under ledges or to signal in low light conditions. This can also be your back up light for night dives.

For your primary light on night dives pick a heavier, more powerful model with a minimum of 75 minutes burn time on a full charge. Cave and wreck divers use lights that have separate battery packs attached to a hand held lamp-head by an insulated cable, which offer them greater power and longer burn times.

It can be hard to navigate your way through the jargon surrounding dive lights but, when making your choice, remember that reliable battery technology and manufacturing quality are more important than massive light output.

Knives

I am ashamed to say that when I owned a retail store we used to sell a LOT of enormous Crocodile Dundee style dive knives; blades like the one Nick Nolte has strapped to his calf when he saves Jackie Bissett from the giant moray in The Deep.

In reality, few people actually need a knife like this; the main reason you carry a cutting tool these days is to deal with the entanglement hazard posed by fishing nets or line and a set of cheap disposable surgical shears or a razor-edged line cutter will do the job nicely.

Surgical shears are cheap, they can cut through brass coins and they make easy work of nylon line. Moreover, there is no chance of you stabbing yourself or puncturing your BCD with them as you flail around. The line cutter is also commonly known as a Z-knife, and it is specifically designed to cut line efficiently. Use oil on the blades to protect them from corrosion and ensure they retain their edge.

If you feel that you have to have a "proper knife," then keep it tucked away on your torso where it can be easily reached when you need it. When choosing a knife, note that titanium does not corrode but it is relatively soft and for this reason the screws securing the blade in the handle will be made of stainless steel, which does rust, so titanium knives still need to be cared for. Titanium also does not hold an edge as well as other metals or alloys.

Jon-Lines

Technical divers use a jon-line to deal with situations where they need to perform safety or decompression stops on an anchor line in rough water where the line is moving violently and making it difficult to maintain a constant depth. You can use a small reel and line but it can be complicated to control in difficult conditions.

A jon line fit for the purpose is a better choice. They come in a number of styles and are typically composed of a simple piece of webbing, rope or line, one end of which is clipped to or looped around the anchor line and the other held by the diver or attached to his harness. Using a jon line smoothes out the movements of the anchor line allowing the diver to float serenely without drifting away. It takes a little practice to learn to use one well but once you master the skill a jon-line is an effective tool. Consult your local technical instructor for practical tips and guidance.

Mirrors

I mentioned in the "Surface Safety" chapter that a mirror can serve as an effective daytime signalling device if you are lost at sea. It can also be a very useful tool to identify the source and severity of any hissing sound emanating from behind your head. Keep it secured to your harness under a strip of neoprene or taped to the inside of a BCD pocket.

Pointers

A short length of stainless steel rod known variously as a pointer, muck stick or critter stick can be of great benefit to both you and the marine environment by helping you maintain your buoyancy and your distance when you are close to the seabed or a reef wall. You just wedge the pointer against an empty piece of rock or sand and balance on it. It enables you to get close and create only minimal disturbance. You can also use the rod to point out the things you have found to other divers. Attach a clip to one end so you can tuck it away on your BCD when you are not using it.

Reef Hooks/Reef Anchors

These are clever devices that can keep you in place hovering above a reef when a current is running, enabling you comfortably to watch and photograph or film the action.

Become a Better Diver by

Acquiring the right accessories
Starting a Save – a – Dive kit

The Save-a-Dive Kit

In a number of chapters in this book I refer to a Save – a – Dive kit. This is a little box of spares and tools that all divers should carry in their gear bag to deploy and resolve an equipment-related emergency that might otherwise ruin a dive day. Here is a short list of a few of the essentials. Once you have included these, see what room you have for other things. Be careful not to let the kit become simply a last resting place for accumulated broken bits and pieces. Have a clear out once in a while.

Spare O rings of various sizes and a dental pick for removing them.

Zip ties (cable ties,) brass or stainless steel clips, surgical tubing and strips of neoprene to help secure gauges and accessories.

Duct tape and marker pen.

Din to Yoke converter and spare regulator dust cap.

Allen keys and TWO adjustable wrenches. You will need two to change out regulator hoses at the second stage end.

Mask scrub or artificial mask spit.

Spare mask strap, snorkel keeper and TWO fin straps. If one breaks the other one will break shortly afterwards!

Gases

27. The NITROX Revolution

It was a mixed group aboard the dive boat. Two of the couples were diving with NITROX 32; the third couple was diving on air. It was the second dive of the day and they were expecting to find most of the action at this site at a depth of 20m (66 ft) or so. The boat captain warned the air divers that they should pay particular attention to their computers as the NITROX divers would be able to spend significantly more time at depth without going into decompression and the air divers would probably find they needed to ascend long before the rest of the group.

Of course, the group found everything they were looking for, they all got carried away taking photographs of the cool animals and the air divers forgot that the warning and stayed with the group until everyone checked their gauges and started to ascend, when they noticed to their horror that they had accumulated a huge decompression burden. Fortunately, as the team had stayed together, the NITROX divers were able to stay with the air divers and help them out with gas sharing during their extended stops and everyone was fine.

Back on the boat the NITROX divers suggested helpfully that the air divers take a NITROX course, to which they replied that they already had NITROX qualifications, they had just chosen to use air for the trip. They did not explain why and the NITROX divers were too flabbergasted to ask.

In the Beginning

NITROX is the collective name given to gas mixtures for scuba diving that contain more oxygen and less nitrogen than air. It is not new. Scientists and researchers from the USA's National Oceanic and Atmospheric Administration (NOAA) had been using NITROX for many years to extend no decompression bottom times and improve decompression safety before one of NOAA's senior diving officers, Dick Rutkowski, left the service in 1985. As his retirement project, he decided to establish the International Association of NITROX Divers (IAND) so that, for the first time, sport divers could be trained in the use of NITROX. The manual and procedures Rutkowski introduced have become the industry standards. Indeed, the main reason why NITROX 32 (32% oxygen/68% nitrogen) and NITROX 36 (36% oxygen/64% nitrogen) are the most commonly used mixes in sport diving is that these were the scientists' usual gases of choice and known as NOAA I and NOAA II respectively.

The Network Grows

Divers were naturally drawn to the advantages that NITROX offered. The reduced percentage of nitrogen in their breathing gas meant longer dives, safer dives and less post dive fatigue and the risks posed by the additional oxygen content could easily be avolded.

Enlightened dive centres began blending NITROX mixes and the network grew quickly. In the intervening decades NITROX has gone from being a cool and mysterious new buzzword to become a universally accepted part of recreational scuba diving.

All the training agencies now offer programs, either theory only or with a couple of dives included, and most divers take a NITROX course early on in their diving lives. NITROX is widely available in dive centres, resorts and live-aboard dive vessels all over the world and, indeed, it is difficult to buy a dive computer today that does not have NITROX capability.

A Revolution Stalled

Technical divers and professionals benefit from using NITROX on almost every dive, yet, as the story at the beginning of this chapter demonstrates, many sport divers who have been educated in the benefits of NITROX, carry a NITROX qualification card and own a NITROX capable computer still choose to dive air even though it is not actually the ideal gas mixture for scuba diving at any depth. Down to a depth of 40m (132ft) NITROX is a much better choice as it offers extended no-decompression time at depth and/or reduced risk of decompression sickness as well as reduced fatigue at the end of the dive day. For deeper dives, TRIMIX has huge advantages over air, as I explain later in Chapter 30, "The Folly of Deep Air and the Joy of Mix."

Why should this be the case? If NITROX is so good, (and it is,) why doesn't everyone now use it all the time?

Teaching Issues

Is the way we teach NITROX diving at fault? Training agencies and instructors now offer pure theory courses that enable the student to obtain NITROX diver certification without actually doing any NITROX dives. It may seem strange that divers would purchase a diving course that does not involve getting wet but it is a popular choice. However, it does mean that many people have a NITROX certification card but have no supervised real time experience of diving with it.

Perhaps it is not surprising therefore that when they come to do some diving subsequently, the thought of choosing NITROX rather than air as their breathing gas does not occur to them as it has only been presented as an academic exercise. There has been no practical reinforcement of the benefits and no real life experience to consolidate in their minds the simple procedure of analysing and labelling a mix prior to diving it.

Or do we make NITROX diving seem too complicated when we teach it? Do we over-emphasize the science? Do we intimidate divers by dwelling too greatly on consequences of an oxygen toxicity hit instead of concentrating on how easy it is to avoid getting one?

True, the course involves an element of gas physics and a little basic mathematics but the physiology taught in most NITROX courses can expand considerably most new divers' knowledge of what is happening to their bodies when they go underwater on scuba.

Depending on your aptitude or inclination, the equations and physics can be assimilated and used or filed away as useful reference material. Practically speaking, the day-to-day application of NITROX diving is straightforward.

Diving with NITROX

When a NITROX diver books his diving with a resort for the following day, he asks what the planned maximum depths are for each dive and then selects and books his NITROX mixes accordingly. Then, when he turns up on the dock the next morning, he notes the gas mix on the analyzer when the shop staff hook it up to the cylinder, makes sure that the mix corresponds to the sticker on the cylinder and signs for it in the gas log. If he is smart, he will also write on the sticker his name, the maximum depth to which he plans to use the gas and which dive of the day he will use it on, dive 1, dive 2 or dive 3, whichever it may be, so no-one gets the cylinders mixed up. This simple procedure takes two minutes or so and in return the diver earns a dive day with more bottom time, shorter surface intervals, reduced risk of decompression stress and less post-dive fatigue.

Misconceptions

Oxygen toxicity is a very real danger and an oxygen-induced convulsion underwater can prove fatal. It is important that the phenomenon is introduced during NITROX diver training as it is the basis for the Maximum Operating Depth (MOD) concept. However, the actual risk to the sport diver is widely misunderstood. A diver staying within the normal range of single cylinder, no-decompression sport diving and remaining shallower than the MOD for their NITROX mix will not suffer an oxygen toxicity hit. There has never been a recorded case of this happening. The dangers of oxygen are entirely related to the dose you consume and the limits are well researched, well tested, universally accepted and dependable. Further reassurance can be found in the fact that the oxygen toxicity limits that we follow were devised by NOAA and the US Navy for divers working at depth and generating higher than usual levels of carbon dioxide, which increases a diver's susceptibility to oxygen toxicity. Therefore a sport diver lazily cruising the reef taking the odd picture is well inside the risk curve.

There is also much confusion about using standard scuba equipment with NITROX and this stems from disagreement between various factions within the diving community in the early days of the NITROX revolution. Today, however, the entire industry has agreed that it is completely safe to use your usual regulator with a NITROX mix that does not contain more than 40% oxygen. Beyond marketing terminology, there is actually no such thing as a NITROX regulator. Technical divers using decompression gases containing more than 40% oxygen will use an oxygen regulator, which has been cleaned and built using materials and lubricants that are more resistant to oxygen.

Cost

It may be that the fact that a NITROX fill often costs a few dollars more than air may deter some people from choosing it, although many operations are now including NITROX in their standard diving rates and recovering their investment in the technology by selling NITROX courses. It is likely, in any event, that in future the concept of charging extra for NITROX may become as antiquated as charging for wireless Internet access!

Become a Better Diver by

Recognising that air is not the best gas for scuba diving at any depth
Taking advantage of the benefits of NITROX

28. The Black Gases

The cameraman was in trouble; he was confused, holding onto the rail of the shipwreck for stability and breathing fast, but nobody had noticed because he was the senior member of the team, so everyone thought he could take care of himself, and he was using a rebreather and therefore not generating any bubbles.

It was the rebreather that was at the root of his problems. He had made mistakes in setting it up beforehand and had been inadvertently inhaling a portion of his exhaled carbon dioxide (CO_2) throughout the dive. His symptoms were a result of the consequent build up of the gas in his bloodstream and he was suffering from CO_2 poisoning, or hypercapnia.

When someone finally came to help him, he was barely conscious and it was only with the help of three colleagues that he reached the surface alive.

CO_2 is one of two gases that can have an enormous impact on a diver's safety but are widely ignored and misunderstood. The other is Carbon Monoxide, discussed later in this chapter. I call these the black gases.

The issue of CO_2 has come to the fore in technical diving in recent years, mainly because it has been a contributory factor in many rebreather accidents.

However, it is important that open circuit divers appreciate that CO_2 poses a significant risk for them too. CO_2 build up can increase a diver's susceptibility to oxygen toxicity and narcosis and it is a key contributory factor to the one thing that, above all else, causes divers to come to harm – panic! It is something that all divers should be aware of but its significance is often understated in basic training texts, which generally only tell you that a CO_2 build-up can give you a headache!

The Effects of CO_2

CO_2 is a waste product of the metabolic process and is potentially toxic.

Normally, breathing regulates our CO_2 level. If there is too much, chemoreceptors in the brain identify the build up and induce us to increase our breathing rate to flush out the excess.

It is common for divers to develop high levels of CO_2. This is because when we are underwater our breathing reflex is depressed by the relatively high partial pressures of oxygen and nitrogen acting on our Central Nervous System. We therefore fail to eliminate enough of the CO_2 that our body is producing, especially when we are deep and exerting effort. This is called CO_2 retention. If respiratory reflexes are depressed to the point where a diver does not ventilate his lungs sufficiently, the level of CO_2 in the bloodstream rises as a consequence to the point where hypercapnia ensues.

This tendency to retain CO_2 is exacerbated by a number of factors that prevent a diver from exhaling efficiently. These include the extra resistance imposed by the diver's equipment, the increased density of the air we are breathing at depth and the water pressure on the chest. This last factor may be greater or less than the gas pressure inside the airways depending on where the regulator is in relation to the chest.

Even if the respiratory reflexes are working well, in the case of a diver working hard on a deep dive with a dense gas such as air these factors alone may prevent the diver from ventilating the lungs enough to get rid of the CO_2 the body is producing.

Rebreather diving introduces an additional hazard: the potential for failure of the CO_2 absorbent, which removes CO_2 from the inspired gas. If this happens then the diver will actually inhale CO_2 and breathing will therefore not be as efficient at removing it from the body.

As the textbooks say, hypercapnia can indeed cause headaches but it can also produce confusion, dizziness, disorientation, light-headedness and shortness of breath. Panic can swiftly ensue. Extreme hypercapnia can cause a diver to become completely incapable of rational response and lead to unconsciousness.

How to Prevent and Combat CO2 Poisoning

Working hard at depth, fighting a current or finning hard are prime recipes for CO_2 build up. It can often sneak up on you, particularly if you are focussed on a task that requires some physical effort, such as freeing an anchor.

The deeper you go and the denser your air becomes, the less effort you should expend and the less work you should do. Factor such considerations into your dive plans. Furthermore, look ahead, anticipate and be flexible enough to change the plan. For example, if you are deep and find yourself fighting a current, either change direction and go with the flow or ascend to a shallower depth so you are not dealing simultaneously with the twin challenges of depth and exercise. Similarly, if you find you are descending down current from your intended dive site and see that it would involve a hard swim to get back on track, far better to abort the dive and do it correctly next time.

If your diving sometimes involves long, hard swims at depth, always ensure you have a high quality regulator that gives you the least possible breathing resistance and that it is working well. The manufacturer's manual will have the figures for you to compare when you are shopping around. Consider using specialized equipment to help reduce your workload. A diver propulsion vehicle (DPV), for instance, can minimise the effort required to cover a long distance although you need to make sure you stay well within the limits of the unit's power supply. Carrying a non-functioning DPV in the water can add significantly to your workload!

The most important thing is to identify the dangers before you descend into a physiological spiral where your mental and physical capacities become impaired to the extent that you are unable to escape. Once you have fallen into the incident pit, the only way is down. Knowledge and awareness are the two weapons you have at your disposal to ensure you stay ahead of the game.

If you feel the onset of panic, the solution is to stop all effort and concentrate on taking long and full breaths, especially when exhaling, to recover your mental equilibrium. The chapters "Mental Preparation for Scuba Diving", "Detecting and Dealing with Stress" and "The Art of Conservation" explain the recommended procedures in detail.

CO2 Narcosis

Many divers report a strange sensation following a fast descent to depth. The symptoms include confusion, disorientation and vertigo. The feelings disappear after a while and they are often misinterpreted as nitrogen narcosis. In fact, the effects of narcosis are cumulative and develop with increased time and depth, as I explain in the next chapter, "Diving Under the Influence." It is far more likely in such instances that the symptoms are due to CO2 build up during the fast descent and that the feelings dissipate as the diver acquires a good breathing rhythm and expels the excess CO2.

Shallow Water Blackout

Although it is not directly caused by CO2, there is a connection so this is a good place to talk about the widely misunderstood phenomenon known as shallow water blackout, which typically strikes at amateur free divers and snorkelers. A technique many free divers practice to extend their time underwater is hyperventilation. They breathe in and out aggressively to reduce their carbon dioxide levels as much as possible. This causes the breathing reflex and onset of anxiety to be delayed while they are underwater. Then they dive. As they are swimming their bodies metabolize the oxygen and convert it into carbon dioxide and the longer they are down the more oxygen is metabolized.

Human beings can function normally at oxygen partial pressures of between 0.16 and 0.5. At partial pressures greater than 0.5 we are at risk from oxygen toxicity, at partial pressures below 0.16 the oxygen level is insufficient for us to maintain consciousness.

At the surface, the oxygen partial pressure in the air the free diver breathes is 0.21. When he arrives at 10m (33ft), generally speaking, the percentage of oxygen in the air in his lungs is still 21% but as he is now at an ambient pressure of 2 atmospheres and the pressure of the air in his lungs has doubled, the partial pressure of the oxygen in his lungs is 0.42.

This partial pressure then starts to drop and continues to fall as the oxygen is metabolized. If the diver stays at depth until the partial pressure drops to 0.28, he is fine, but this equates to a partial pressure of only 0.14 at the surface. So, as he ascends and his oxygen partial pressure drops with the reduction in ambient pressure, somewhere at a point close to the surface it will fall below 0.16, the diver will black out abruptly and, if he is not positively buoyant, he will sink back down to the depths.

So, to avoid becoming a victim of shallow water blackout, don't hyperventilate, don't free dive over-weighted and always free dive in a team, one person up on the surface watching while the other is down.

Carbon Monoxide

This gas is completely invisible and odourless, but potentially fatal if present in your scuba cylinder in even small quantities.

It is usually only through carelessness or neglect on the part of the dive operator that carbon monoxide can find its way into scuba cylinders as the most common source is an engine exhaust close to the compressor intake. This might be a permanent fixture such as the exhaust from the compressor engine itself or it could belong to the dive boat engine. The carbon monoxide could also come from a car with its engine running parked close to a poorly located compressor intake. So the best way to avoid the risk of carbon monoxide poisoning while diving is to select a professional outfit.

Analysers are now available which can be used to detect the

presence of carbon monoxide in a scuba cylinder. Otherwise, you probably will not know until you start feeling unwell during a dive.

The toxicity of carbon monoxide is poorly understood. It bonds with the hemoglobin in our bloodstream much better than oxygen, so excess carbon monoxide can lead to a reduction in carriage of oxygen to body tissues. However, at mild to moderate levels this can be compensated by an increase in blood flow so that although the blood contains less oxygen, oxygen delivery is maintained. Indeed, it seems that carbon monoxide has some other effect on cells within tissues (particularly the brain) that produces the toxic symptoms. The symptoms are headaches, irritability, dizziness and confusion. There is little chance of a diver at depth detecting the symptoms of carbon monoxide poisoning before they start to impair his judgement.

If you ever do feel ill under water, do not just struggle on bravely, abort the dive and ascend slowly but not alone in case you become seriously impaired. This is another of those times (see Chapter 6 "Solo Diving") when it might be nice to have a buddy around!

Become a Better Diver by

Understanding that CO2 is not just a threat to rebreather divers
Avoiding the risk of shallow water black out
Knowing the causes and dangers of carbon monoxide poisoning

29. Narcosis - Diving Under the Influence

When you teach deep decompression diving on air, you regularly see people in the grip of narcosis. A diver leading a group will keep going beyond the turn point of the dive, finning away along the reef wall, oblivious to the fact that he has left his companions behind. Another will glance at his computer and, ten seconds later, will look at it once more, then again ten seconds after that. A third will wait at the bottom of the line, staring fixedly at a branch of coral for a good two to three minutes instead of ascending, until roused from his reverie. Later, he will tell you that he thought it was a moray eel and that he was waiting for it to move.

Incidents such as these can be amusing but there is a serious side to narcosis. The diver who heads off into the blue without his buddies loses the support of the team. If he is in an overhead environment he risks getting lost. The diver who cannot remember what his computer was showing just a few seconds after looking at it is suffering from short term memory loss and this can reduce his ability to follow a dive plan. And the one who delayed his ascent on account of a non-existent eel was increasing his decompression burden for every extra second he remained at depth and risking running out of gas in the final stages of his ascent.

Narcosis is an integral part of scuba diving. The only way to avoid it is not to dive deep or to use helium based diving gases. If you want to dive deeper than 30m (100ft) and do not have access to helium, then you are just going to have to get used to it!

What Is Narcosis?

Air is an intoxicating cocktail. Many people will tell you they enjoy the "buzz" of going deep on air. This feeling is partly a response to their subconscious awareness that they are no longer in complete control of their surroundings and that, if something were to go wrong, they may not be thinking clearly enough to handle it: something like the thrill of riding a roller-coaster.

However the "buzz" is also due to "anaesthetic potential", a dangerous property of all gases. In the right quantity, any gas can knock you out. Some gases, like nitrous oxide (laughing gas) have long been known as excellent anaesthetics. The major constituent gas in air, nitrogen, has anaesthetic potential and, as you dive deeper and as the partial pressure of the gas increases, the depressant effect on your Central Nervous System becomes greater. Divers call it narcosis. Jacques Cousteau called it "l'ivresse des profondeurs", the drunkenness of the depths!

As Cousteau poetically suggested, the effect is similar to alcohol. And just as with alcohol, it is dose related; the degree to which you are affected depends on the quantity you consume. The effects of narcosis are progressive and increase with time and depth. At 30 m (100ft) a diver breathing air will experience symptoms such as mild euphoria and slow reactions: by the time he gets to 50 m (165 ft) his judgement will be significantly impaired.

The subjective symptoms differ from diver to diver and from dive to dive, but the objective effect is the same. Often, it manifests itself as overconfidence, fearlessness or over-relaxation, which is beneficial to a degree but in an emergency this can produce confusion and slow response-time. For instance, the diver who is deep on air when he finds that his regulator is free-flowing may, in his befuddled state, remain at depth while he tries to fix the problem instead of ascending immediately or swimming to a team member for assistance. Narcosis also affects the memory. When you ask people to tell you about their dives, the things they always remember first are the things they saw during the comparatively shallow portions of the dive.

"I Don't Get Narked"

You may often hear divers claiming that they do not suffer from narcosis. Yet again, the alcohol analogy applies. Someone who has had a couple of drinks will often be heard to say that they think they drive better when inebriated. Similarly a diver at depth will often feel more relaxed and comfortable, confident and capable than usual. In fact, as with the drunk driver, the deep diver is actually euphoric and perceptually impaired, has a tendency to be less cautious, will accomplish tasks less effectively, react to events more slowly and have an inaccurate sense of the passage of time.

Dealing with Narcosis

However, the good news is that to a certain extent you can train yourself to accommodate your impaired state. Again the alcohol analogy is useful. A man sitting at a bar, having had a few drinks already, will reach for his glass and knock it over to the general hilarity of all around him. He learns his lesson, however, and the next time he is in the same situation he recognises the danger of just reaching out, knowing that his perception is clouded by the alcohol in his system and that there is a good chance that if he just extends his hand casually he will knock the glass over again. So he concentrates fully on the task, slides his arm slowly across the bar until his fingers gently touch the bottom of the glass, then, closing his hand around it, he pulls the glass across the bar towards him slowly. He then tilts his head to drink from it instead of testing his hand-to-mouth co-ordination by lifting the glass unnecessarily.

Similarly, a diver who recognises intellectually that he is impaired at depth and who is familiar with the effects of the narcosis has taken the first steps towards being able to deal with it. The next key stage is to learn to concentrate on important issues such as time, depth and the tasks to be performed instead of getting carried away with euphoria and allowing it to cloud the mind.

It is important to concentrate on maintaining a tight focus, slowing down and exercising mental control over every movement. Moving slowly is especially important when trying to perform a task at depth. Success is far more likely if the action is performed in a rehearsed sequence of steps rather than in one continuous, flowing movement.

Professionals also use memory cues. Technical divers always carry slates to write out run times, decompression schedules and back up plans and instructors have checklists of the things they need to do during a training dive and make notes for debriefing the students later. They know from experience that they cannot entirely depend on memory.

This is also one of the main reasons why it is essential that you should spend time rehearsing emergency drills and self-rescue skills until they become instinctive. Developing automatic correct responses to emergencies is the best way to combat the narcosis-assisted confusion that will prevent you finding the right solution if you rely on your intellect alone.

Contributory Factors

A number of factors can exacerbate the diver's predisposition to narcosis. These include fatigue, alcohol, stress, cold and dark water. Anticipating and mitigating the effect of these additional factors is the key to dealing with them, for instance using a drysuit in cold water and minimising alcohol intake and getting a good night's sleep before a deep diving day.

Carbon Dioxide (CO2) Narcosis

Many divers report that they feel a high degree of narcosis on their initial descent to depth but that the feeling dissipates the longer the dive continues. These symptoms are not consistent with the findings that narcosis increases rather than decreases with depth and time. As I mentioned in the previous chapter "The Black Gases" the symptoms are far more likely to be a result of a fast descent leading to a build up of CO2 in the blood stream, which reduces as the diver commences a normal breathing pattern and relaxes.

Oxygen Narcosis

There have been a number of studies suggesting that oxygen is also narcotic although there are no conclusive data and scientific opinion is divided. Aside from academic interest, the debate would only be significant for sport divers if oxygen were proven not to be narcotic, in which case NITROX might be a useful tool in reducing narcosis. However, in the absence of such proof, we must assume that NITROX and air are equally narcotic and plan dives accordingly.

Become a Better Diver by

Recognising the symptoms of narcosis and
Adapting your behaviour to mitigate the dangers

30. The Folly of Deep Air and the Joy of Mix

Training agencies set depth limits for diving on air and the manuals warn divers that it's not safe to exceed these limits but don't go into the reasons in any great detail. This seems to encourage many people to interpret the warnings as just well meaning advice that might apply to beginners but that certainly doesn't apply to divers with their advanced skills and years of experience. So, while they may pass the warnings on faithfully to their students, when they dive for fun they do not practice what they preach and exceed the limits, often with tragic results.

In this chapter I explain exactly what it is that makes deep diving on air so dangerous. But it is not all doom and gloom: if deep diving is your "thing;" if you are consumed by deep ambitions, I also introduce you to technology and procedures which will allow you to dive deeper than you ever imagined possible, and in relative safety.

But first, the true story of an incident that took place in Guam a few years ago but that, sadly, is typical of the sort of thing that still happens today, week in, week out, everywhere people dive.

A Cautionary Tale

Picture the scene: conditions are perfect with flat seas and a clear blue sky. The atmosphere on the small boat is thick with testosterone and there is much whooping and hollering and backslapping as the six divers prepare their gear. The gauntlet has been thrown down. The challenge: to descend quickly down a reef wall to a depth of 90m (300 ft) on a single cylinder of air, collect a handful of sand and then come back to the surface. The two individuals accepting the challenge are both male, young, physically very fit, good swimmers and experienced recreational divers. It is an initiation ceremony; the other men on board have all completed the task previously and have earned their "wings". They are here today to cheer the new guys on.

The six divers enter the water together and all descend to 40 m (132 ft) where the four "veterans" stop and watch the other two continue on down. At first, all they can see are two streams of bubbles, and then the two streams become one. Then the bubbles stop. They wait, time passes and they wait a little longer. After 15 minutes with no sign of their missing buddies, concern turns into full-blown anxiety. They separate, a couple of the guys head for the surface to run a boat search for bubbles or bodies, the other two stay underwater, peering down into the blue desperately hoping for a miracle: to no avail, the two divers are never seen again.

Every year, a lot of people die diving deep on air. Many of the victims are expert divers, instructors, and instructor trainers; even respected authors of scuba-diving books! Yet the practice continues amid almost universal ignorance of a simple truth;

survival is not a question of your courage or your competence as a diver. The risks you take in diving deep on air are all bound up with human physiology itself and none of us can beat that.

What's the Issue?

You may be surprised to hear that the main problem with Deep Air Diving is not the "Deep" bit! Diving deep is fine, as long as you have the right experience, the right equipment, the right training and, most of all, the right gases.

The problem is the air and what happens to your body and your mind when you breathe air underwater.

As former Director of Diving at the US National Oceanic and Atmospheric Administration (NOAA) J. Morgan Wells famously said, "Mother Nature provided the planet Earth with a NITROX atmosphere known as air. She never said that air was the best breathing medium for divers."

What Are the Problems with Air?

First, it contains oxygen. As those of you who have taken NITROX Diver training know, the generally accepted maximum oxygen partial pressure (PPO2) for a diver in the water is 1.6 atmospheres absolute (ATA). And even this value is only for brief exposures during a non-working phase of the dive (such as decompression stops). For a working phase, 1.5 ATA is a more appropriate maximum, and in fact, should be reduced further as the dive lengthens. 1.5 ATA PPO2 is reached on air at around the 60m (200 ft) mark so we can say that diving deeper than this on air places the diver at significant risk of an oxygen toxicity event, (disabling uncontrollable convulsions leading to drowning.) The increased density of air at such a depth also means that all divers retain a considerable amount of carbon dioxide (CO_2) in their lungs and bloodstream and CO_2 build up pre-disposes a diver to oxygen toxicity. In view of all this, it is easy to understand why even 60m (200ft) is considered too deep to breathe air without incurring unacceptable risk and why the technical training agencies now set 51m (170ft) as the maximum, even for an experienced diver equipped with a full back-up air supply.

The second problem with air is that it is dense. The deeper we go, the more air we need to take in to fill our lungs. This air is thick and more difficult to breathe efficiently. When our brain perceives that we are finding it hard to breathe, it concludes that we have a problem and enters emergency mode.

The third problem also has everything to do with how our bodies are designed to respond to an emergency. When we breathe air at depth we can generate a lot of CO_2 and, as I described in "The Black Gases" chapter, reduced breathing efficiency at depth creates a build-up of CO_2 in our lungs and bloodstream. It is this build-up and the resultant increased acidity of the blood that triggers our automatic emergency response system, the final phase of which is panic, the diver's worst enemy. To get an idea of what happens, pause and hold your breath now. Continue to hold it until you sense the onset of anxiety and then breathe out and relax.

The anxiety you felt when you did this was not a conscious response. Intellectually, you knew that you were not threatened, that you could just breathe any time you wanted, but your nervous system did not know that and as more and more oxygen in your bloodstream was converted to CO_2 by the metabolic process, it detected this and deduced, as it is programmed to do, that something was wrong. It over-rode your intellect and you started to get anxious.

Underwater, a trained deep diver with a clear head will identify the process that is causing this onset of anxiety, cease all activity and take a series of deep full breaths from the diaphragm, (not the chest,) concentrating especially on long, slow, and full exhalations. This will eventually bring the CO_2 in his bloodstream down to a manageable level.   An untrained deep diver or a diver badly affected by narcosis will not identify the body chemistry that is leading to his anxiety and, thinking that he is suffering from air starvation, will desperately try to breathe in more than he breathes out. This of course will cause the CO_2 level to rise still further and cause his anxiety to turn into full-blown unreasoning panic. A common diver response to such a situation is to spit the regulator out and bolt for the surface holding their breath. If you think it could never happen to you, just try holding your breath again, this time for a little longer, and see how logical your thought processes are just before you take that desperate release breath!

Finally, as I described in detail in Chapter 29 "Diving Under the Influence," air is narcotic and generates a variety of symptoms that adversely affect a diver's ability to control his dive or respond to an emergency.

What's the Solution?

Until only a few years ago, sport divers were unaware of the full physiological implications of deep diving and had no access to gases other than air so you can argue that many of the tragedies were borne of ignorance. But today, there is no such excuse; all over the world, hundreds of successful recreational dives to 90m (300 ft) and beyond are completed every year. The key to diving to such depths safely is TRIMIX, known to technical divers simply as "Gas" or "'Mix."

Ah, the joy of Mix; the long awaited emancipation of the deep diver! For years we had been venturing to the depths with our minds befuddled and senses numbed by narcosis, with CO_2 induced anxiety hovering threateningly at the edge of our perception as our air became ever more dense with depth and with the risk of oxygen toxicity an ever-present danger. Then, in the early 1990s, we were finally liberated, released from tenebrous ignorance into the glorious light of awareness. Finally, we owned the tools and knowledge to permit us to carry out deep dives with a clear head, reduced risk and a light, easily breathable gas in our lungs. At last, we could see through the fog clouding our brains, accurately identify what we were looking at down there and surface with a clear memory of what we had seen,

What Is TRIMIX?

TRIMIX, as the Greek scholars among you might guess, is a mixture of three gases, oxygen, nitrogen and helium. Helium is a very light, non-toxic, minimally narcotic gas. By adding it to our breathing gas, we can reduce the percentage of oxygen and thus reduce the risk of oxygen toxicity; we can make the overall mixture less dense than air, making it easier for us to breathe; and we can reduce the percentage of narcotic gases in the mix which means we will be diving with a much clearer head. The main disadvantage of helium is that it is expensive.

In commercial diving and military circles, they have known for a long time that adding helium to breathing gas has huge physiological advantages for a diver working at depth. Although, rather than TRIMIX, the breathing gas of choice for their deep divers is a mixture of oxygen and helium only, known as HELIOX. They use no nitrogen at all and very high percentages of helium because their primary concern is to minimize narcosis in the working diver and the consideration of cost is secondary to getting the job done.

Sport divers are not so fortunate; we do not have the luxury of vast funds. But, then again, when we dive we are usually just sightseeing and are not engaged on work that requires intense concentration. So recreational TRIMIX divers tend to add only as much helium as they need to keep the amount of oxygen in their breathing mix within safe limits and to keep the level of narcosis manageable. It is also thought that a little nitrogen in the mix tends to offset the helium-induced nervous system problems.

The easiest way to create TRIMIX is to add helium to air to create a mix known as HELIAIR although there is a drawback to this simplistic approach in that, because the relative proportions of oxygen and nitrogen in air are fixed, it is impossible to create an ideal mix for any depth using HELIAIR. The best TRIMIX is made by applying a set of calculations to work out what percentage of oxygen and nitrogen you need to have in your breathing gas for the target dive depth and then making up the balance with helium.

Diving with TRIMIX

Successful TRIMIX diving involves far more than just changing the gas in the cylinders and plunging in. This new world offers previously undreamed-of possibilities but it has its own new set of rules that must be respected.

While the rewards of going to depths hitherto beyond the range of sport divers are substantial, this is not a level of diving to be taken lightly. There are trade-offs for the ability to go to extreme depths with reduced narcosis, reduced levels of CO_2, lower gas density and lower risk of oxygen toxicity that TRIMIX diving offers. As you will see in the brief outline below, you need to be prepared for longer decompression times, carefully controlled ascents and total dependence on gases with high oxygen content for decompression. Self-discipline, attention to detail and a great deal of in-water experience are just as essential to success in deep diving on helium-based gas as the gas itself. But the most important element is thorough training in procedures that have been developed over the years to reduce the risk of this extreme diving to the minimum possible level.

During the training, you learn how to plan dives, design your own set of gas mixes and work with decompression planning software. As well as TRIMIX, you use one or more NITROX mixes in separate cylinders attached to your BCD harness and slung under your arms for the descent and ascent phases of the dives.

For dives below 75m (250 ft), the oxygen percentage in the TRIMIX must be below 16% in order to prevent oxygen toxicity at depth. Therefore, as such a low level of oxygen cannot sustain life on the surface, you actually enter the water breathing from one of the side-slung NITROX mixes. You continue to breathe from it on your descent until you are well past the depth at which your TRIMIX becomes breathable. This NITROX is referred to as your "travel gas."

Once you have switched regulators and are breathing from your TRIMIX cylinders, you turn the valve of your travel gas off so that it is impossible to lose the contents at depth via a free-flowing regulator or blown O-ring and you tuck the regulator away tidily so that it doesn't get caught up on anything during the dive. You are going to need it later on your ascent, as your travel gas will also be your first decompression gas.

Decompression Gases

Why do you need decompression gases on TRIMIX dives? The

gas mix that keeps you alive at depth contains a lot of inert gas, (helium and nitrogen), and very little oxygen. To try to complete the dive safely on this mixture would require many hours of decompression and a vast amount of gas, far more than any diver could carry. So, as you ascend you need to stop breathing it and start breathing a gas with a higher oxygen content as soon as you can so your body can release the helium and nitrogen that has built up in your body tissues and bloodstream more efficiently and thereby reduce your decompression time to a manageable level. Most TRIMIX dives end with the diver breathing from a cylinder containing either pure Oxygen or a NITROX mix containing 80% oxygen on his final decompression stops.

Something that a TRIMIX diver needs to bear in mind at all times is that he is carrying three or more different gases, any of which will kill him if he puts the wrong regulator in his mouth at the wrong depth. Now, that is a good reason to make sure he has a clear head!

But with that clear head, he will see places on this planet that few have ever visited and achieve the sort of dives that were once considered impossible. To adapt Shakespeare's iambic pentameter a little, "to air is human.........to TRIMIX, divine"

Become a Better Diver by

Knowing why there are real limitations to using air at depth
Using helium based gases for deep diving

31. Rebreathers- Are They the Future?

Most of us are still diving with technology developed in the middle of the last century. The guys who invented the Aqualung in the 1940s, Jacques Cousteau and Emile Gagnan, would be flattered yet probably horrified that we have not progressed far beyond their invention.

In other areas of our lives we have embraced new technology and many adventure sports have seen huge changes. The canopies used by skydivers, for example, bear no resemblance to those used by their predecessors a generation ago and modern technology has given them previously unimaginable safety features. Yet in the scuba diving world, other than a little tinkering, there has been a strange reluctance to move forward.

As far as the equipment we use is concerned there has been one significant change over the past two decades and, although it remains a niche market at present, it may well be that the technology that our children use for diving will have its roots in today's recreational rebreathers.

Rebreathers offer huge advantages: gas supply is no longer a consideration on most dives, the no decompression dive time is enormous compared to standard open circuit scuba, and the environmental impact of a rebreather diver is also greatly reduced, given the absence of both noise and bubbles.

The Story So Far

Rebreathers are not new: the concept has been around since Italian Giovanni Borelli first considered the idea of an underwater breathing apparatus in the 17th century. The first mass-market sport diving units appeared in the mid 1990s when Drager introduced the Atlantis semi-closed rebreather, heralding the dawn of what was touted as a new era for recreational divers. However market demand did not match media interest. Practically, divers found that the benefits of semi-closed systems did not merit the increased complexity and cost. They found that the units gave a diver about the same extended duration as an open circuit set of double cylinders and that the much-touted silence was interrupted too frequently by the periodic release of a stream of bubbles from the exhaust valve.

On the other hand, in the past decade, fully closed circuit rebreathers have succeeded in dominating the world of technical diving, mainly because of their phenomenal advantages in gas economy. They bring the cost of helium-based mix diving down to manageable levels, and enable explorers to undertake dives that would be impossible on open circuit. Underwater filmmakers have also seized on the practical advantages offered by silent systems.

Most of the models they have been using have been built by specialist boutique manufacturers or by expert and enthusiastic individuals. While the technology may be relatively straightforward in concept (see below), these rebreathers require a diver to be meticulous in his preparation and constantly focussed during the dive. They are highly unforgiving and allow virtually no room for diver inattention. To date, the advantages of the units for divers who do not dive on helium-based gas mixtures have generally been outweighed by considerations of cost, complexity, restricted availability and the absence of mainstream industry support.

The Way Ahead

One other reason why rebreathers have not caught on in mainstream diving is that most of us want to relax when we dive and we are not inclined towards equipment where the science and preparation time get in the way of the fun. So for any replacement technology to be accepted by the majority of sport divers, it will need to have all the advantages of standard scuba. That means it will have to be readily available, convenient, simple to operate, easy to maintain and economical. In order to persuade users to change their habits, it will also have to cure many of the problems associated with standard scuba such as weight, discomfort, noise, environmental disturbance and limited in-water time.

The introduction in 2011 of a range of rebreather training courses by PADI, the world's largest diver training agency has encouraged major manufacturers to look more closely at rebreathers. Given the failure of the early semi-closed systems the industry has concluded that fully closed circuit systems may be the answer, so new sophisticated, user-friendly and relatively low-priced closed circuit rebreathers are now appearing. These are armed with electronic wizardry designed to help the user monitor and assess the system's status in the same way that modern cars simplify the driver interface.

How Do Rebreathers Work?

Rebreather science reflects human physiology. Human beings only use a small amount of the oxygen they inhale. The majority of the oxygen we breathe in is exhaled again, accompanied by a volume of carbon dioxide (CO_2) more or less equivalent to the amount of oxygen we have used up. The nitrogen and the small quantities of inert gas that we breathe in along with the oxygen are not used at all. This means that, as long as you can remove the CO_2 from exhaled gas and have a means to keep topping up the oxygen so that it remains at a level capable of sustaining life you can keep breathing the same gas supply over and over again.

There are three general classifications of rebreather: oxygen, semi-closed circuit and closed circuit. Oxygen rebreathers can only be used in shallow water and are of little relevance to sport divers, although they are widely used by the military. The other two types of rebreather system are of far greater interest.

Semi Closed Circuit Systems

A typical semi-closed rebreather works with a single pre-mixed cylinder of NITROX. An injector allows gas to pass from the cylinder into a bag, called a counterlung, from which the diver breathes via a mouthpiece fitted with twin hoses, one for inhalation, one for exhalation. When the diver breathes out into the mouthpiece, his exhaled gas passes through a canister containing soda lime, which removes the CO_2, and returns to the counterlung ready to be used again, or "rebreathed." The combination of counterlung, mouthpiece, soda lime canister and diver is called the breathing loop. A constant trickle of fresh gas from the cylinder makes sure the oxygen level in the loop remains breathable.

The diver's lungs are the engines that drive the process. If there is too much gas in the loop, then it is vented into the water via an exhaust valve. If there is not enough gas in the loop then an over-ride valve opens and adds a stream of fresh gas directly from the cylinder, bypassing the injector.

Just as with open circuit NITROX diving, the maximum operating depth for a dive on a semi-closed rebreather is based on the oxygen level of the gas supply in the cylinder. Your decompression is calculated using a mathematical equation which factors in the gas you are using, the injection rate and your metabolic rate.

Closed Circuit Systems

Fully closed–circuit rebreathers typically have two cylinders, one with oxygen and the other containing a gas to be mixed with the oxygen. This second gas is called the diluent and will either be air, TRIMIX or HELIOX, depending on the depth of the dive to be carried out.

The user presets the desired partial pressure of oxygen (PPO2) that he wishes to maintain during the dive and the rebreather injects little spurts of oxygen into the breathing loop from time to time to maintain the required PPO2. The rebreather's computers constantly adjust the level of the oxygen in the breathing mixture to ensure that the diver is always breathing the optimum gas for the depth he is at, thus extending no decompression times to the maximum or reducing deco stop times to the minimum.

The diluent gas is only added on descent to maintain the volume of the breathing loop so once a diver is at the maximum depth of the dive, unless he loses gas as a result of mask clearing or has lots of ups and downs, the only gas he uses is the oxygen that the unit adds to replace the oxygen he has metabolized. This is usually around one litre per minute so a 3litre/200 bar (30 cu ft/ 3000 psi) oxygen cylinder fitted to a closed circuit rebreather will provide enough gas for 12 hours at any depth. Gas supply is rarely the limiting factor for a rebreather dive!

Again the CO_2 produced by the diver's metabolic processes is removed as it passes through a soda lime canister. The soda lime is typically sodium hydroxide, which reacts with CO_2 to form chalk, water and heat. Not only does this reaction ensure that the gas you are re-breathing is free from CO_2 contamination, it also means that the gas is warm and moist, rather than cold and dry as it is when you breathe from open-circuit scuba. One of the little-known advantages of rebreather diving is that it does not dehydrate a diver as rapidly as when he is using open-circuit equipment. You may recall that dehydration is believed to be a significant factor in cases of "unexplained" decompression sickness.

A Different World

A fully closed circuit rebreather can give you quite astonishing performance. For instance, using air as the diluent gas and a preset PO_2 of 1.3 ATA, when you are at 30 m you will be breathing a NITROX 32 mixture. Underwater you generate almost no sound: the racket of open circuit bubbles is replaced by the gentle cacophony of the reef. You hear the natural noises of the sea, parrotfish munching on coral, shrimp crackling, dolphins calling, occasionally punctuated by a slight hiss from your rebreather as the solenoid opens to allow a tiny amount of oxygen into the loop to replace the gas you have metabolized. When you ascend, the rebreather will add oxygen to your mix, and the nitrogen level will drop as the breathing loop vents the expanding gas. Therefore at 20m you will be breathing NITROX 43, at 10m you will be on NITROX 65 and at 3m, you will be breathing almost 100% O2 for your final safety stop. A three-hour no-decompression dive is easy to achieve! It really is a different world.

What Are the Problems?

The major problems with closed circuit rebreathers are three-fold and all to do with gases and their effect upon us.

First, despite the extended no decompression times, rebreather diving carries the same risk of decompression sickness as open circuit scuba.

Second, as I explained above, the level of oxygen you are breathing on a closed circuit rebreather is controlled by the unit's electronics systems and can fluctuate considerably. Oxygen is essential for life but in too high or too low quantities it is poisonous. The first rule of rebreather diving is " Always know your PPO2." You must always monitor how much oxygen is in your breathing loop. Too much oxygen can cause hyperoxia, whereby the diver's central nervous system short circuits leading to underwater convulsions and, often, death by drowning. Too little oxygen, or hypoxia, causes the central nervous system to shut down completely and the diver blacks out.

Third, CO_2 presents possibly the greatest and most insidious danger to rebreather divers, who rely on the unit's soda lime canister to control the CO_2 level in their breathing gas. Too much CO_2 in the body, a condition known as hypercapnia, results in uncontrolled breathing, confusion and disorientation. Once present, hypercapnia is impossible to control and has contributed to a number of rebreather diver fatalities.

The Next Wave

Generally speaking, the new rebreather systems that are emerging are smaller and lighter so they are easier both to wear and transport.

Typically, they include some or all of the following features.

Cheap reliable pre-packed disposable CO_2 absorbent canisters.

CO_2 monitoring technology.

Oxygen level monitoring.

Real time decompression calculation.

Eye level status display pods.

Alarm driven switching to open circuit.

Electronic firmware updates via the Internet.

Catching the Wave

A standard comprehensive rebreather diver course lasts 4 or 5 days and includes several hundred minutes of dive time. Because there is no conformity in the functions and features of the systems available, each course is model specific, usually combining a module on the general aspects of rebreather diving with a module on the particular unit the diver has chosen to learn on. This means that a diver certification on one unit does not qualify you to dive a different model although some instructors and training agencies may give credit to divers moving from one system to another and relax course dive time requirements.

But this also means that, unless you have the money and time to do several courses and try out a number of options first, you really need to make an informed choice before embarking on a training course.

An important thing to remember is that, no matter how many dives you have under your weight-belt, the first time you don a rebreather you are a beginner all over again and, although the learning curve may be easier to negotiate this time around because of your previous underwater experience, nevertheless accept that it should be a long time before you will be able to do advanced dives on your rebreather safely.

A Closed Circuit Mindset

If you are the sort of person who only finds out when they surface that they have dived deeper than they planned; if you sometimes run low on air without noticing; if you ever jump in the water with your air turned off or forget to tighten your BCD cam strap so that your cylinder falls out, then rebreather diving may not be for you.

Similarly, if you are the type who sees or hears a leaky O-ring and continues to dive, planning to fix it later, or someone who, if they start feeling sick on a dive, just carries on regardless, then you too may want to think twice about switching to closed circuit. On open circuit scuba, all the above are minor inconveniences at worst but it is not an exaggeration to say that on a rebreather such lapses in dive discipline and inattention to detail can be fatal.

The smart rebreather diver respects his unit and maintains it meticulously. He knows that he must understand completely all the ways in which the rebreather can hurt him and that he has to develop the discipline to monitor himself, the unit and his gauges and screens constantly so that he can anticipate and deal with any problems that occur quickly before they become life threatening. And he must hone his skills to the level where his response to a potential emergency is instinctive and correct every time. Open circuit scuba is very forgiving; it is tolerant of the careless diver. The rebreather is a merciless mistress. She is exotic, exciting, and can do things for you that you never dreamed possible but you disrespect her or neglect her at your peril.

Another point to bear in mind is that it is misguided to think of learning to dive on a rebreather as a " specialty course ". By all means, do a course to see if rebreathers are indeed for you but once you decide that they are, use the rebreather for all your diving so your skills and emergency responses become and remain instinctive.

The Key to Universal Acceptance

Up to now it has been the case that anyone who wants to do a rebreather training course is required to buy their own unit. However, the majority of the world's open-circuit divers do not own their own scuba cylinders and if a diver has never bought a cylinder, it is unlikely they will buy a rebreather.

This reluctance to purchase is not a reflection of their commitment to the sport, it just means they prefer to rent because either they don't want to store and maintain cylinders, they live somewhere where they always have to fly to dive or they have calculated that it makes sound economic sense not to buy.

This means that for rebreathers truly to emerge from their niche and join the mainstream they must become universally accessible. The units need to be cheap enough and reliable enough to persuade dive centres and liveaboards to invest in the new technology and have it available for rent.

Simplified training procedures will also need to be introduced for people who just want to use their rebreather in fully automatic mode and within no decompression limits.

One day, and it is likely to be soon, someone, somewhere, will introduce a system that fulfils all the requirements listed in this chapter and captures the imagination as Cousteau did with the Aqualung. Then we will all be diving on ultra-silent machines that give us the maximum amount of dive time possible within physical and physiological limits, warn us when there is a problem and advise us exactly what to do to solve the problem. They will be light, comfortable, fuss-free, easy to set up and intuitive to understand and we will be able finally to consign the Aqualung to the museums.

Become a Better Diver by

Keeping abreast of developments in rebreather technology, training and availability

Choosing Your Rebreather

When deciding which rebreather to buy there are also practical and logistical factors beyond simply buying the system with the best features. Consider the following ten key questions. -

1. What is the rebreather's mass and weight relative to your body size?

2. What is the cost, including electronics and dive computer?

3. What training do you need and where it is available?

4. Is the manufacturer an established company with a good track record of business success?

5. What is the unit's safety history?

6. What do current users say about the rebreather in online forums?

7. Does the manufacturer have outlets nearby that can provide product maintenance support and parts?

8. Do you have rebreather diving friends?

9. What units do they use?

10. Are these rebreathers available to rent in the destinations you want to visit?

Travel

32. Great Diving and Where to Find It

How can you guarantee that you will get great diving when you travel? The popularity of dive destinations ebbs and flows. Reputations often rely more upon the marketing skills of the local operators than the quality of the experience on offer. The animals that originally put a place on the map can tire of the attention and move on or disappear for other reasons. Sadly divers are not the only sector of the population interested in knowing where large populations of fish can be found. Local fishermen are always keen observers of where divers gather.

Industry media outlets are always on the lookout for new destinations but are these necessarily better than the old places? Online forums and travel review sites are a good source of opinion but you never know how informed or experienced the reviewers are. Nobody has been everywhere and we are always inclined to be subjective in favour of locations and dive operators we know and love.

The list of sites presented here is the result of an admittedly highly random survey of dive professionals around the world. These are the places they have on their dream sheets, either because they have been there and want to go back or because they have friends working there and trust their opinion.

I have created a number of themes to classify the selections that featured most often and added a short elevator pitch for each. The idea is to give you a quick oversight of what each place has to offer to pique your interest. The rest is up to you and your search engine of choice.

Before you write in and tell me, I know I have omitted some great destinations but my hope is that these are well-enough known to have already come to your notice by other means.

Dream Destinations!

Best for Variety

1) The Galapagos Islands, Ecuador

Close encounters with unique creatures above and below the sea, big animals and lots of them, fascinating land tours, the holy grail for everyone interested in the natural world.

2) Bali, Indonesia

The island of the gods offers mola mola, mantas, tiny critters, wall dives, black sand muck diving, fast drifts and the world's most accessible large shipwreck.

3) The Republic of Palau, Western Pacific

World-class walls and drift dives, teeming with fish, wonderful corals, caverns, caves, blue holes, loads of shipwrecks and a jellyfish lake.

Best for Big Animals

1) Yaeyama Islands (Iriomote, Ishigaki and Yonaguni), Southern Japan

These islands in Japan's southern tropical waters offer mantas, hammerheads and mysterious underwater ruins – or are they?

2) Tiger Beach, Bahamas

Clear blue water and white sand forms the backdrop to some phenomenal shark action, including tigers, lemons and hammerheads.

3) Revillagigedos Islands, Mexico (Socorro)

Off the tip of Mexico's Baja Peninsula: giant mantas, shark action, hammerhead cleaning stations, massive tuna, big schools, oh yes, and a population of humpback whales.

Best for Coral Reefs

1) Eastern Fields, Papua New Guinea

Open ocean diving on a huge submerged atoll in the Coral Sea: pelagic action above pristine, rarely visited reefs.

2) The Red Sea

The world's northernmost tropical sea with 2000 kilometres of coral reef: expect ultra-brilliant colours in clear blue water.

Best for Critters & Muck

1) Lembeh Straits, North Sulawesi, Indonesia

2) Ambon, Maluku, Indonesia

Of all the wonderful Indonesian muck diving locations, Ambon and Lembeh deserve equal top billing as the world's critter capitals: gentle, sheltered, conditions and a phenomenal variety of weird creatures in a relatively small area.

3) Milne Bay, Papua New Guinea

Has a strong claim to have been the birthplace of muck diving and was where the term was coined: incredible selection of strange critters but Milne Bay is much more than just muck.

4) Dauin, Negros, Philippines

A relatively recently discovered location: great muck diving on sandy slopes.

Best for Fish

1) Malpelo, Colombia

A huge rock 500 kilometres out into the ocean that is home to vast schools of fish, large and small, and a magnet for big ocean travellers.

2) Tubbataha, Philippines

In the middle of the Sulu Sea and only diveable from March to June, huge quantities of fish patrol the sheer walls of mountain peaks that only just break the surface.

3) Raja Ampat, Indonesia

The area with the greatest species diversity on the planet.

Best for Wrecks

1) Truk Lagoon, Chuuk, Federated States of Micronesia

A Japanese fleet sunk in World War Two, mostly merchant

ships. Shallow wrecks festooned in corals, deep wrecks full of artefacts, easily accessible diving once you have managed to get there: clear, warm water, lagoon-like conditions.

2) Scapa Flow, Scotland, UK

The scuppered World War One German fleet: dozens of shipwrecks all in diveable depths: cool water with unexpectedly good visibility.

3) Bikini Atoll, Marshall Islands

The ships that were sent to the bottom of the lagoon during the Able and Baker atomic bomb tests in 1946: battleships, submarines and, of course, the aircraft carrier Saratoga. The island is only intermittently accessible to sport divers.

4) North Carolina, USA

North Carolina's Outer Banks, the Graveyard of the Atlantic, are the last resting place of hundreds of ships which have come to grief there over the centuries: during World War Two the area was known as Torpedo Junction due to the activities of German U boats, several of which lie on the sea bed. This is also a great place to find Megalodon teeth.

Best for Caves

1) Florida, USA

The home of the largest cave diving community in the USA and the crucible of the technical diving revolution: a great place to learn to cave dive.

2) Quintana Roo, Yucatan Peninsula, Mexico

Warm water caving, beautiful underwater formations: another

excellent training location.

3) The Lot Valley, France

World-class, easily accessible sump diving for qualified cave divers.

Best for Ice Diving

1) White Sea, Russia

Beluga whales and northern lights beyond the Arctic Circle.

2) Lake Baikal, Siberia, Russia

Russia's Galapagos, the oldest, deepest lake on the planet, a huge, unique eco system that freezes solid in the early months of the year and is home to strange life-forms and the world's only fresh water seals.

Best for Cool Water Diving

1) Catalina, California, USA

Prolific marine life in and around the giant kelp forests with stunning visibility, especially during the cooler months.

2) Newfoundland, Canada

An area where Arctic currents encounter the Gulf Stream and where, in Spring and Summer, a plankton feast attracts a variety of whales and the rare narwhal: plenty of shipwrecks in great condition too!

3) Poor Knights Islands, Tutukaka, Northland, New Zealand

In and around the Poor Knights, only an hour off New Zealand's north east coast, a confluence of warm current and cooler sea creates a microclimate where a wide variety of fish from both tropical and temperate waters co-exist.

Best Major Events

1) Sardine Run – Indian Ocean, South Africa

In one of nature's most impressive circuses, sharks, whales, dolphins and seabirds chase and feed on millions upon millions of sardines as they make their way up South Africa's east coast in an annual migration that usually takes place between May and July.

2) Mantas "Cyclone" Feeding – Hanifaru, Baa Atoll, Maldives

Manta rays by the hundred bump into each other as well as cruising whale sharks as they compete for krill trapped by a confluence of tide and current in a tiny bay off this remote island in the Maldives. This happens at times between May and November with August and September the best months to witness the action. Local regulations may restrict you to snorkelling there so brush up on your free diving before you go.

Best for Fun!

Puerto Galera, Philippines

Warm, calm and clear water and an excellent variety of top dive sites close to the beach resorts and dusk-to-dawn nightlife.

Best New Frontier

Cendrawasih Bay, Indonesia

Remote and accessible only by island hopping your way across Eastern Indonesia, the attractions are pristine hard corals, shipwrecks and local fishermen hand-feeding "pet" whale sharks!

Become a Better Diver by

Experiencing new destinations and different types of diving

33. Life on Liveaboards

All divers go through periods in their lives when work or life takes them away from regular diving opportunities at home and their annual underwater time is restricted to vacations.

When this is the case, they understandably want to take full advantage of their limited leisure time and get as much diving as they can for their money in the time available. Live-aboard dive vessels provide the perfect solution.

In the last few years, even in times of economic downturn, this is an area of the industry that has been growing fast and the range of boat options and experiences available is expanding all the time.

Advantages and Disadvantages

The advantages are more diving in remote locations that offer more marine life and less environmental damage. There are new kindred spirits to meet, no phone or Internet and no absolute beginners. The disadvantages include restricted food options (usually), extremely limited nightlife, no escape route if the new friends you have found are not to your taste, no phone or Internet (yes, I know) and the possibility of seasickness.

What Is it Like?

You wake up early. Often you will have been sailing between sites during the night and the changing note of the engine and the fact that the boat is no longer moving will rouse you from your slumber. You throw on some shorts and a t-shirt and head for the galley for a small "first breakfast," a snack and some juice to wake you up and give you energy for the first dive of the day.

You greet your companions; a typical liveaboard carries between 8 and 16 divers. You will find as the trip goes on, the number of takers for the early morning dives will drop as the attraction of another couple of hours in bed becomes harder to resist. A similar phenomenon applies in the case of night dives but then sunset and Happy Hour are the competing distractions!

Your equipment is already set up and ready to go. You showed the crew how you like it set up on Day One and they are quick learners. During the trip, your dive gear lives on the dive deck in the space allocated to you and the crew takes care of all the pre dive preparations. There is hanging room for wetsuits though you will be diving so frequently your suit will never get really dry.

Depending on the boat procedures, you either fully gear up on deck or partly on deck and partly in the dive tender. There is usually a great deal of flexibility to allow for physical limitations or personal preference.

A full breakfast follows the first dive and from there the day progresses in a sequence of rest – dive – eat – rest – dive - eat until you fall into bed and are rocked to sleep by the sea.

Every boat will have sunbathing spots and shaded reading areas on deck. A liveaboard trip offers a great opportunity to perfect your relaxation techniques. There will be a communal lounge with drinks and snacks throughout the day and where you may be able to find a Scrabble game going on or someone running through their photos from the last dive. If you want privacy, you can retreat to your cabin, which will usually be a shared twin room with bunks or single beds, although the accommodation on newer boutique liveaboards can be positively palatial! If you are travelling alone you may find yourself sharing with a stranger. Many divers thrown together like this end up becoming life-long buddies.

There are showers on deck and in the cabins but remember that you are on a boat so be sparing in your use of fresh water particularly the supply from the hot tap!

Useful Advice

The following advice has been compiled based on the results of a couple of informal surveys, one among liveaboard dive guides and cruise directors who see the common mistakes repeated every week and a second survey conducted among a group of experienced live-aboard divers who between them have got pretty much everything wrong over the years and learned from the experience!

Things to Do Before the Trip

If you do not have a regular aerobic exercise routine, start one or, better still, go to the beach or a local pool and get some laps in. Acclimatize yourself, spend time outside at the weekends and ideally get a little sun.

Buy travel insurance and diver insurance including repatriation and recompression cover

Go through your dive computer manual with your computer in hand and remind yourself how it works, how to program a NITROX mix and what the screen looks like in dive mode and deco mode.

Check your dive gear for mould and damage. Ask a local dive club if you can join a pool session and check everything for leaks. If you find a problem, get the equipment serviced and then try it out again after it is serviced and before you leave.

Good Questions to Ask the Operator

What is the voltage on board and what format are the electrical fittings?

Are multi-voltage battery chargers available?

Is there likely to be Internet access or a mobile phone signal?

Is there a satellite phone for emergency contact? What is the number?

What is the water temperature likely to be?

What is included in the cost of the trip?

What extras do I need to pay for?

Are there dive lights on board I can use? Is there a rental charge?

Is NITROX available? Is there an extra charge for NITROX fills?

Is there medical oxygen on board? (There had better be!)

What toiletries are provided in the cabins?

Are towels provided in the cabins and/or on the dive deck?

What is the food like? This is particularly important if you have dietary requirements.

Choosing Bags

It might be better to avoid using purpose built logo bags that scream, "I have expensive dive gear inside!" Choose relatively anonymous lightweight luggage, long enough to accommodate your fins and fat enough for your BCD and suit. Wheels and a strong frame are great but balance those advantages against the increased weight. Some cases, when empty, can use up a quarter of your international baggage allowance!

Hand carry small, expensive and difficult to replace items such as your computer or prescription mask. Of course, the usual travel advice about never packing essential medicines or papers in your checked baggage also applies. A small rucksack is a good choice for hand luggage as this can double as a daypack for any land excursions you might make.

It is a great idea to bring a dry bag and a net bag. You can find dry bags in yachting and boating stores. They can either keep dry things dry in a wet area or, if drying time is short at the end of a trip, you can use them to pack damp things inside so everything else in your case does not get wet too.

A net bag will help you keep your small stuff together in one place on the dive deck and allow it all to drain between dives.

What to Pack

The general consensus of opinion is that most people bring too much stuff on liveaboard trips. You never need to dress up and, although you will have storage space in your cabin, this can be limited. A frequently repeated adage is, "pack only half the clothes you think you will need."

However, despite this advice, human nature dictates that you are unlikely to get your packing right first time as you will be understandably tempted to plan for unlikely contingencies. So when you get home and unpack after your first liveaboard trip, make a note of the things you did not use or wear and leave them out next time!

Here is a list of essentials that you WILL need.

Several t-shirts and a couple of pairs of shorts or light trousers.

Some sarongs. These are light, low volume and perfect for hot days, cool evenings or just covering up.

Sweatshirt or light jacket for cool nights on board.

Multiple swimsuits.

Toiletries and prescription medicine.

Extra contact lenses / spare glasses.

A medical kit, (see end of this chapter.)

Sunscreen and after sun lotions.

Ear plugs and an eye shade.

A small water bottle to carry around.

Charging cables for phone, camera, iPod etc.

Plenty of batteries and be prepared to bring the ones you use home again for proper disposal.

Voltage converters and adapters as necessary.

Diver certification card, NITROX certification card and current logbook.

Snacks from home, if you cannot live without them.

Cards or other icebreaker games (Scrabble, Trivial Pursuit etc.)

Good books and DVDs for the inter-dive downtime.

We are increasingly seeing divers who bring all their entertainment needs for a trip on laptops, Kindles and iPads. These are great for minimizing weight and you can bring the contents of a small library/movie theatre. The disadvantage is that you cannot hand the books and movies around or leave them on board when you leave for future divers to enjoy.

Dive Gear

As well as your usual mask, fins, regulator, BCD, computer and thermal protection, bring a back up computer to carry on all dives, so it has an accurate record of your inert gas loading if your primary computer fails. You will be a long way from the nearest dive store and while a good liveaboard will carry a selection of spares, it is best to be self-sufficient where the important things are concerned. So bring a spare mask strap, a regulator mouthpiece and two spare fin straps. (They often both snap at the same time.) And bring a snorkel, even if you do not normally wear one while diving. You may need it for dugong, dolphin or whale shark encounters!

What NOT to Bring

There is no need to bring shoes; apart from the ones you wear to travel. Everyone goes barefoot on board and you can use your dive booties for beach walking. Even if you are used to fixing your own gear, do not bother bringing your own tools. The boat crew will have everything you need. You can also leave your Fish Identification and Marine Life Reference books at home as most liveaboards have an extensive library of these. Some boats even supply lights for night diving to spare guests the burden of bringing their own.

Finally a few random pieces of sage advice from the experts. First, don't be afraid to sit a dive out once in a while and take a little time to enjoy the cruise. Second, no matter how miraculous your low air consumption rate is, there is no glory in being the last diver back on board as you risk losing out on both hot water and hot food. Last, if you can, plan to arrive a couple of days before your boat departs to acclimatize to the new time zone and allow your airline plenty of time to reunite you with any missing luggage.

Become a Better Diver by

Maximising your diving opportunities

A Liveaboard Medical Kit

On a liveaboard you will be a long way from the nearest pharmacy so carry a small personal medical kit. This should contain at least all of the following items.

Painkillers.

Anti-diarrheal tablets.

Anti-motion sickness patches/pills/wristbands. Many doctors recommend Touristil and if you are worried about the side effects of patches, cut them in half: they work just as well.

Band aids/plasters, both large and small in various shapes.

Ear Drops – use daily to prevent outer ear infections.

Antibiotic ointment for coral cuts.

Antifungal hydrocortisone cream for swimsuit rashes.

Anti-histamine tablets or cream for stings.

34. Behave Yourself - Diver Etiquette

In every sphere of human activity conventions arise which govern the behaviour of the participants. These may not always be set in stone or legally enforced; sometimes they just become established and generally accepted over time. Scuba diving is no exception. Here is a guide on how to behave underwater, on a dive boat and on the beach. There is also a section especially for photographers and the people who dive with them.

Animal Etiquette

The convention is look but do not touch! This does not just mean big animals like turtles, manta rays and whale sharks; it applies to the smaller animals too. In fact, you could argue, the smaller an animal is, the more vulnerable it is.

Some operators prohibit their divers from wearing gloves in an effort to discourage them from laying their hands on the reef and its occupants. There is much debate over whether a glove ban works and it is an issue that can arouse strong feelings. I believe that educating divers is more effective than imposing rules. I do not think that most of the people who wear gloves do so because they want to interfere with the marine life; nor that someone who is driven to disturb the animals is going to be dissuaded if they have to do it with bare hands. However, good etiquette also requires that if you want to dive with an operation, you abide by its rules. If they have a no-gloves rule and it upsets you too much, then choose another operator instead.

Captains, Instructors and Divemasters

These are the guys and girls who are paid to give you a good time, keep you safe and show you the cool things. They are the experts and the etiquette is to respect them as such. Sometimes you might disagree with their decisions; for example, last minute changes to the plan that conflict with your own goals for the day; and you may feel like arguing with them but often they can see the bigger picture and will explain this to you if you query them privately after the briefing. Usually, the pros really do know best, as the stories in this chapter illustrate. Of course, sometimes they will get it wrong but if they acted in good faith and their decisions were genuinely made in what they felt were your best interests then they should surely be allowed some leeway?

However, every walk of life has its bad guys and not all professionals are honourably motivated. Sometimes you may feel that the decisions taken by your hosts have been made specifically to save them time or money at your expense. Or you may feel that the discount that persuaded you to book with a particular outfit is being "earned back" by the operation cutting corners or selling you short on service. What do you do? Allow a few days for your objectivity to return and then write to the owner of the dive operation with a clear account of your complaints. If you do not get a reply or the response is unsatisfactory then go onto the diver forums and tell the world. It is important for the survival of the industry that high standards be maintained.

Here are a couple of stories that illustrate the sort of misunderstandings that can arise between dive professionals and their charges.

Misunderstanding #1 Kate's Courage

Kate was a divemaster in Hong Kong; it was a beautiful Sunday in early September and she was in charge of a dozen divers who had assembled at the dock for a day out on the boat. The sky was blue and the sea was calm. Everyone had turned up early and there was a buzz of excitement in the air.

However, Kate had been listening to the radio on the drive in and had heard that a storm was forecast later in the day. She knew from experience how quickly the weather could change in the South China Sea and she was concerned. She spoke with the captain and he told her he thought good conditions would hold at least through the day. All around, other dive boats had loaded their customers and were setting off.

Kate took a look at her group of divers. All were city folk and quite new to the sport. She gathered everyone round and explained regretfully and sympathetically that bad weather was on the way and she felt it would be better for everyone if they cancelled the trip.

The mood turned ugly fast. This was not news the divers had expected. After all, they could see other boats pulling out with happy divers on board. Some accused Kate of cancelling for no reason so that she could have a day off work; others called the dive centre owner and tried to convince him to over-rule her. He told them it was Kate's call.

Kate stuck to her decision and the divers eventually got back into their cars and departed, disappointed and annoyed. On their way back to the city the sky became dark and heavy drops of rain started bouncing off their windshields. Within an hour a fierce storm was battering Hong Kong. The dive boats that had gone out earlier rolled and pitched back to port through high seas, most with a cargo of very sick customers on board. Nobody dived in Hong Kong that day.

To their credit, some of the divers called the next day to apologize to Kate and thank her for sparing them from an unpleasant experience. But the apologies came too late to spare Kate the hurt of their accusations the previous day when all she was doing was trying to make sure they did not come to harm.

Misunderstanding #2: Technology vs. Experience

When hand-held GPS units first became available, a diver out on a liveaboard in the southern Philippines was playing with his new toy on deck as the boat set sail for port. Installing the co-ordinates he had taken at the start of the trip, he saw that the GPS indicated that the best direction home was a few degrees off the course the Captain had set. Wanting to get back as quickly as possible, he rushed up to the wheelhouse to enlighten the captain as to the benefits of modern technology. The captain was there as usual, leaning back on his tall wooden stool, his head against the bulkhead and his bare feet resting on the wheel, feeling every movement of the ship. He listened patiently then hopped off his stool and motioned the diver over to a chart where he politely showed him the peninsula of very solid land that they would have to sail over if they followed the course recommended by the GPS.

Tipping

The issue of when to tip and how much to tip causes a great deal of anxiety and although some dive operations try to establish a high tipping convention in their publicity materials, there is no established etiquette in the dive industry just as there is no world – wide agreement on the culture of tipping. Some nationalities tip heavily, some tip a little, some do not tip at all.

It is a fact that, no matter how attractive their lifestyle seems, dive industry employees work long hours and are not well paid. Neither do most dive operations add a service charge to the bill.

The best advice I can give is don't fret about doing the right thing or offending people. Neither should you concern yourself about what others in your group are doing. This should be a personal decision. When people ask me I usually tell them to tip dive industry employees the same sort of percentage they would expect to pay for good service in a restaurant in their home country, adding more if they feel the service has been extraordinary.

Hunting

There are laws and seasons governing spear fishing and hunting for food in most places: some are very strict, some surprisingly relaxed in these environmentally aware times. It is commonsense advice to make sure you know and abide by local laws but, beyond these, if you feel you have to shoot fish then the least you can do is follow the established etiquette.

Be sporting, free dive instead of using scuba when you spear fish.

Don't use a spear gun when other divers are nearby.

Don't hunt in areas where fish are used to interacting with divers.

Don't hunt in places where people feed fish to attract divers.

Don't spear fish at night using an artificial light source.

Take only what you can eat and eat what you take.

Lost Dive Gear

It is an established convention that an item of dive equipment found under water should be returned to its rightful owner. To benefit from this community-friendly piece of etiquette, make sure that you tape your email address or phone number to anything you think you might drop and if you come across something someone has lost make every effort to locate the owner. After all, what goes around comes around!

Dive Boat Etiquette

All dive boats and operations have different procedures and when you are diving with them the etiquette is to follow these. Listen and be flexible. If you dive with the operation frequently and want to do your own thing, there may be room for negotiation. If they won't compromise and it matters to you, vote with your feet and go elsewhere.

On day boats space is often very limited so pack with care, using a gear bag or small plastic crate that fit neatly under benches. Pack your scuba gear in reverse order of use; i.e. the things you need to get out first should be at the top. Stow your gear neatly out of the way and keep everything together both before and after the dive.

Bring everything you need but ONLY what you need. Keep your phone and cash in a dry bag in the dry area but keep your spares box with your scuba gear rather than in your dry bag, as there is every chance you will be in your wetsuit when your O-ring blows.

Keep out of designated dry areas if you are wet, even if you have a damp towel around you. On any boat, never leave a cylinder standing unsupported. They are heavy, metal objects and a falling cylinder can crush a toe, destroy a regulator second stage, crack a mask or demolish a dive computer as well as cause irrevocable damage to the valve.

For similar reasons, keep weight belts in a box or on the deck and out of the way; never put weights or a loaded belt on the bench beside you or anywhere else where the movement of the boat could cause them to fall.

The toilet on a boat is called the "head". This is not because it is where you should put your head if you feel seasick. The best place to hang your head is over the side of the boat, preferably the side where the wind will carry away the contents of your stomach when they appear. Your fellow travellers will appreciate it as will the crewmember whose responsibility it is to clean and unclog the head. The fish under the boat will be happy too at the unexpected delivery of manna from heaven.

Entry and Exit

When you are geared up and making for the exit the correct thing to do is move directly and with caution. You have a large object strapped to your back so it is a little more difficult to squeeze yourself through small spaces. Take extra care when standing up and sitting down; be aware that the person next to you might choose that exact moment to bend to strap on a fin and will not take kindly to encountering the swinging tail of your cylinder with the side of their head. I have seen countless near misses in my time, as well as many hits! Remember two basic rules: "look behind you" and "avoid sudden movements."

Once in the water, move away from the entry area to unite with your buddy so others can enter safely.

When returning to the boat, exercise ladder courtesy. Wait your turn, never hang below someone climbing the ladder in case they lose their grip, exit the water quickly then move away directly from the area above the ladder so others can follow you.

It is worth mentioning here, one particular aspect of etiquette that is rarely taught in dive courses. From time to time during a dive you will get kicked by a careless fin or batted by a flailing arm. The etiquette is to act as if nothing happened, while making a private note to keep a little further away from your assailant in future. You certainly shouldn't mention it once you are both back on the boat; they already feel bad for having caught you and, after all, as we said above, what goes around comes around and one day it will be you who inadvertently whacks one of your fellow divers in the head and you will be very pleased if they don't mention it!

Personal Etiquette

Keep it covered up! Diving involves changing clothing, which by definition can involve temporary nudity. One of the great things about our sport is that it brings together people from different backgrounds, walks of life and cultures, some of whom may not have a broad-minded attitude to public exposure or share your own high opinion of the beauty of your naked form. For the comfort of all, therefore, good etiquette requires discretion.

Stay humble; if you are a skilled diver and have a lot of experience, this will be recognised by those around you without you having to broadcast it. A professional can easily spot good divers by the way they set up their equipment, the way they observe and interact with others, the way they position themselves in the water and the high level of comfort they exhibit with all aspects of the diving environment. We may not show what we think but divers who feel the need to announce their exalted training level or high degree of experience loudly to everyone might as well be raising a large red flag saying, "I am potentially dangerous." Rest assured we will be watching them closely but not for the reasons they might wish.

A word here on post-dive snot or boogers – point it out to your buddy subtly with a smile. Fortunately, it is beyond the call of etiquette to offer to wipe it off.

Terminology Etiquette

In many areas of human interaction, a common bonding mechanism is the shared use of references, a code used by members of the group to identify each other and separate them from outsiders. In the military, this often manifests itself with the use of acronyms that are incomprehensible to the uninitiated. On the London criminal scene in the 19th century, the code they used eventually became known as Cockney Rhyming Slang.

In the early days of our sport, divers tended to do the same thing. A sign that you were not a real diver was to refer to flippers rather than fins or, in the UK, to refer to tanks rather than cylinders. These days the last thing we want to do as a community is alienate non-divers; we want to attract new people into the sport rather than make them feel outsiders. To spend even a few seconds of a diver training course requiring that the students use the correct terminology to show they belong is such a waste of time.

Underwater Photography Etiquette

I have often been called upon to deploy my legendary diplomatic skills to defuse potential flare-ups between photographers and non-photographers. The reasons behind the heated debates are always the same and, having been both photographer and buddy, I think I can see both sides of the argument so here is a quick guide to the major issues, presented in the hope that mutual understanding will promote greater harmony.

Different Folks

Here is the problem in a nutshell. Many divers don't care about taking pictures underwater nor do they have any idea of how much financial sacrifice it takes to buy an underwater camera system. For many other divers, taking pictures is the sole purpose of scuba diving. Their systems and their photographs are of such immense importance to them that they will not bother diving at all if they can't take their camera with them.

The Issues

Environment

Underwater photographers are often accused of callously causing damage to the seabed and the plants and animals that live there while they are manoeuvring to get a good angle for their pictures.

In their defence, most photographers do not deliberately set out to wreak havoc on the reef. However, burdened as they are with the destabilising potential of a camera and strobe system and with the technical limitations imposed by the behaviour of light underwater requiring them to get close to their subject, occasional accidents are hard to avoid. Furthermore, with their focus on what is going on in front of the lens, they are often oblivious to the peripheral impact of what they are doing. This can be misinterpreted as carelessness although if you see someone poised against the reef, camera in hand, do not assume that he has just landed there unthinkingly. He may have carefully chosen this particular spot specifically to avoid damaging anything and deserves the benefit of the doubt.

One could argue, however, that it is irresponsible of anyone to start carrying a big camera system with them before they have acquired sufficiently advanced buoyancy skills to give them instinctive positioning in the water. A phenomenon I refer to as subconscious brain/fin mimickery is to blame in many cases: the more the photographer thinks about his shot, the more his feet and legs start to wiggle around automatically and uselessly. An experienced diver is aware of the propensity of the legs to mimic brain activity and will focus attention on fin-consciousness and keeping his appendages still.

What is less excusable is the propensity of some photographers to manipulate their subjects into places where they can be seen more clearly, away from the environment that conceals them; an environment that they have chosen for their protection and which they have evolved to copy. This can render them highly vulnerable to predators. Touching marine life can also damage it or make it susceptible to disease.

Quite apart from offering us an uplifting experience, underwater photographs serve a valuable purpose by sharing the beauty and wonder of the creatures beneath the sea with those who cannot see them for themselves and who may thereby be more likely to support environmental causes.

But perhaps before photographers remove a delicate animal from its camouflage: before they wriggle themselves and their gear through a fragile ecosystem in pursuit of their quarry; they should ask themselves first if the end justifies the means and if the photograph is really THAT important!

Equipment

Cameras, housings and strobes are all delicate pieces of engineering and highly vulnerable to water so common sense suggests that you give the photographer and his gear plenty of space. A camera table is for camera related items only, don't put a drink down anywhere near a camera and remember that when you are wet after a dive, so is your hair. Craning your head over the shoulder of a photographer as he runs through his pictures post-dive can cause drops of sea water to fall onto delicate electronics.

Photographers need to take a certain amount of responsibility too and make sure they keep their precious and ultra-expensive equipment out of the way of the uninitiated. Remember they are divers; they are going to be excited when they come up from their dive and the security of your camera system is not going to be uppermost in their minds.

The best dive boats and resorts have camera only areas, even private rooms just for photographers.

Rinse Tanks

There is more conflict over the rinse tank than anywhere else on the dive boat, but this conflict is easy to avoid by following some simple rules.

Dive operations should use clear signs to indicate who and what each rinse tank is for.

Photographers must make sure that it is a camera ONLY rinse tank before they dunk their camera system in it. There is no point screaming afterwards.

The purpose of the camera rinse tank is not to store camera systems but to remove salt water as soon as possible after the dive. There are three key principles of rinse tank etiquette.

First, the fresh rinse tank water must be replaced frequently so that the increasing proportion of salt water to fresh created by repeated dunking does not cause the water to become brackish.

Second, camera systems should just be dipped into the tank, rinsed and withdrawn to a safe, stable location. They should not be just dumped and left in there while you change.

Third, keep camera systems apart. Murphy takes underwater pictures too and his rule dictates that when two systems are in close proximity, cords, cables and arms will become entwined and heavy metal trays will collide with fragile housing ports.

If you are not a photographer, make sure you know which tank is the camera rinse tank and never put anything else in there. The oft-exercised debates, such as whether or not chemical defog reacts aggressively with acrylic camera housing ports, are irrelevant. It is considerate and good diver etiquette to leave the camera rinse tank to cameras only and rinse everything else in another.

Some enlightened boutique liveaboards now offer the ultimate luxury, personal rinse tanks, one per diver!

Underwater

The generally accepted convention is that while a photographer is busy with a subject, it is his until he has finished with it. It is not done to intrude, either to take a peek at what he has got in his sights or to crack off a quick snap on your point-and-shoot.

However, photographers need to be considerate of others who might want to see the animal too, particularly if it is something unusual. When a group of folk has spent three days of liveaboard diving fruitlessly looking for a rhinopias, word is going to get around pretty quickly when a rhinopias is eventually spotted and there will be a bunch of divers circling around in a holding pattern waiting to land and take their turn with the star of the show.

Take your pictures and, if you want to come back to the animal, join the holding pattern and wait until everyone else is done.

Good etiquette dictates that a diver without a camera has just as much right as a photographer to see, watch and examine an animal. If a diver wants to savour the moment and burn the image of a rare creature into his brain rather than onto a digital card, that is his choice.

When they see a photographer in action, other divers should steer clear and be aware of how their positioning in the water might affect the shot he is striving so hard to perfect. Passing carelessly up current of a photographer can cause the debris of your passage to drift into his viewfinder. Swimming below a photographer working on a reef wall and exhaling will create a snowstorm of expanding and exploding bubbles all over his meticulously framed backdrop.

Risking It All

Photographers are often guilty of getting carried away by their trade to the extent that they forget to monitor their dive time, deco schedule and/or air supply adequately and end up either on a long deco, hogging the emergency cylinder, borrowing air from a fellow diver or worse risking decompression sickness by coming up early.

Of course, these outcomes are not the province of photographers alone but as well as risking harm to the culprit, they can all seriously inconvenience fellow divers, particularly in the worse case scenario of a decompression sickness hit on a live-aboard in a remote area which would require the boat to return to a port with a runway nearby and cause divers to miss a couple of days of expensive diving. None of which would be a problem, of course, in the case of a genuine accident but when the injury is self-inflicted, sympathy is understandably going to be muted.

Just because someone carries a camera, it does not mean that the laws of physics and the limitations of human physiology no longer apply. In fact, because photographers should be well aware that they may be distracted by the tasks in hand, all the more reason that they must anticipate the possible consequences. They should consider, for instance, a second dive computer attached to the camera housing within range of their peripheral vision and think about attaching a pony cylinder of NITROX to their primary cylinder.

Become a Better Diver by

Following the etiquette
Exercising a little respect and understanding

10 Tips for Diving with Photographers

1. Discuss the roles you are going to play and the division of responsibilities before the dive and make sure you agree.

2. See the safe completion of the dive and the acquisition of great photographs as joint achievements.

3. Remember that, as the guy with the camera will have his eye on the viewfinder most of the time, it is the non-picture-taking buddy who is mostly responsible for keeping the pair together.

4. However, good etiquette demands that the photographer indicate to his buddy that he has seen something and make sure the message has been received before stopping and settling down over a subject so that his buddy does not just swim off into the blue without him.

5. However reliable and devoted a buddy is, the photographer should take care not to fall into the trap of shifting the burden for staying within the dive plan onto his buddy's shoulders. A basic rule of scuba diving is that every diver's air supply and decompression schedule are his own responsibility.

6. While the photographer is busy, the buddy can keep within sight and try to find further targets. If they find something cool, they should wait and watch for the photographer to lift his head, then raise their arm to draw his attention. Move on, once the cool thing has been pointed out and acknowledged.

7. Photographers, assuming you are not merely set up for macro shooting, take a few photos of your buddy during the

dive and give them to him afterwards. Most of us don't have many pictures of ourselves underwater so we will always be very grateful.

8. Make sure you, as the buddy, are even more aware than normal of the effect your presence has on the environment around you. Suspended matter in the water column thrown up by a careless fin or hand movement can ruin the picture. Be aware of which way the current is running and where your bubbles will be going.

9. Not all photographer/buddy relationships will work well. It all comes down to empathy, mutually compatible diving behaviour and priorities and shared objectives but if a good relationship develops, it is a thing to be treasured.

10. You may have noticed that I haven't dealt with the issue of two photographers diving as a buddy team. The main reason I have not covered this, is because I believe it is an impossible thing. Photography is such an individual, single-minded pursuit that the likelihood of two photographers being able to stay together and work as a team while dedicating themselves to their respective goals is so remote that to try to suggest rules of etiquette would be futile!

35. Hidden Treasures - Muck Diving

You roll off the boat and dip your head below the surface to get a hint of the wonders that await you on this dive but it looks like you are in the wrong place. There are no glorious coral formations, there is no deep wall dropping below you into inky darkness. Instead the seabed seems grey and featureless and the visibility is reduced by the confluence of seawater and fresh water from a nearby river mouth. Here and there are scattered piles of debris, which must have been carried down from villages upstream.

Fortunately you trust your guides and sixty minutes later you ascend with your mind reeling and your camera's memory card full of pictures of some of the most incredible marine life you could ever have imagined.

You have just been on the equivalent of an underwater treasure hunt or, if you prefer, a game of hide and seek with some very clever opponents. This is muck diving!

The Genesis

While the first few generations of recreational scuba divers were marvelling at the beauty of coral reefs and hanging out in the blue watching for whale sharks and manta rays, a whole universe of amazing creatures were going about their business under the sea completely un-noticed.

How could they have remained undetected for so long? Well, first they were small, second, they had developed the art of concealment to a very high degree and third they lived in places that were not particularly pleasing to the eye. Primarily, however, they remained unseen because nobody was looking for them.

Then a few things happened to bring these little creatures into the limelight.

First, the big fish became fewer in number and harder to find. Second, divers became older and a little lazier and, third, there were significant advances in underwater macro-photography.

Most importantly a few enterprising individuals in Papua New Guinea, Indonesia and Malaysia started looking for marine life in unusual places where nobody had looked before and began to find some absolutely astonishing animals.

The era of muck diving had begun.

Where to Go

The best muck diving seems to be found in places where there is a shallow bay, a river mouth, human habitation, significant current movement outside the bay, shelter (in the form of a pier or jetty) and natural and human debris, such as rotting tree trunks and tin cans.

So far, the location that offers the best combination of these ingredients is Lembeh Straits on the northeastern tip of Sulawesi in Indonesia. Other locations discovered to date that also deserve honourable mention include a variety of sites right across northern Bali, Dumaguete in the Philippines, Pulau Mabul off the coast of Malaysian Borneo, Ambon and Alor in the Indonesian archipelago and Milne Bay in Papua New Guinea.

As it is such a hot trend, unsurprisingly, new muck-diving places are being discovered all the time.

How to Muck Dive

This is an underwater treasure hunt. You need to understand the behaviour of the animals you are seeking so you have an idea of where to look and what to look for. Move slowly and carefully, keeping yourself as near to the sand as possible without disturbing it. Look closely at everything and be patient: this is hard work! However, what can at first seem to be an impossible task becomes much easier with experience and the time you put in to learn your craft will reward you in wonderful ways. The thrill of discovery when you find something rare and exotic is hard to beat.

Be Careful

These are fragile animals and touching them can damage them. Removing them from their carefully chosen camouflage can also draw them to the attention of the very predators they are hiding from and, once you have taken your picture and departed in a puff of sand, you may leave them very vulnerable.

Be Considerate

Resist the temptation to pick the trash up from the seabed and take it home for green disposal. Your heart may be in the right place but the trash is likely to already have been recycled in the best possible way and may now be the home of a vulnerable creature who needs all the protection he can get on the black sand slope.

So curb your environmental instincts. Octopi in particular are the masters of converting discarded materials into mobile homes but they are not the only ones who need to find creative housing solutions. For small fish, a sheet of plastic can provide perfect protection from predators and an empty tin will serve as a romantic pied-a-terre for a pair of blennies.

Skills

The most important skill you can acquire as a muck diver is the art of remaining motionless in the water so as not to frighten the animal you are waiting for and so you do not disturb the often sandy, silty seabed and project debris into the water column, making the visibility even worse than it was and making good photographs even more difficult to come by.

Be aware of the movement of hands and fins, especially when you are excited as this is the time when your appendages are most likely to move of their own accord without purpose or conscious direction. As soon as the initial adrenalin rush of discovery has subsided a little, make it a habit to carry out a little review of where you are and what your legs and arms are doing before settling down to study or photograph your latest find.

Develop a fin kick that does not shift the water powerfully downwards. Florida cave divers, who are used to diving in situations where disturbing the layer of silt below them might be life threatening, have perfected a few specific techniques that muck divers would find extremely useful to copy.

A modified flutter kick moving the feet only, pivoting from the ankles and with the knees bent so your fins are above you. You cannot make fast progress with this technique but it ensures the water you displace when you flutter your fins remains within the water column rather than being directed forcefully downwards.

A modified frog kick, where you move your legs apart slowly then bring your fins together more quickly to provide forward propulsion. Again this should be done with the knees bent so the fin movement takes place above your body rather than behind it and so that the water displaced is directed horizontally behind you in the middle of the water column.

A reverse modified frog kick, as above but beginning with your legs together then moving them apart simultaneously in a single movement so the result is reverse rather than forward movement. This is an excellent technique to permit you to remove yourself from a tight corner without using your hands or needing to turn your body

Equipment

If you are keen to get next to the wildlife without disturbing it, get hold of an excellent tool that all the best dive guides and top spotters use and which I referred to earlier in Chapter 26 "Accessorize Wisely." This is a simple 30 cm pointer made out of stainless steel that you can either thrust into the sand for balance as you float looking for animals or deploy to gently guide a piece of intruding weed out of the frame of the photograph you are taking.

Most muck diving takes place in shallow water near the shore so keep all hoses and BCD fittings tucked in close to your body especially when you are horizontal. Ask your buddy to check your profile for you. You are going to be close to the seabed and you want to make sure you create as little disturbance as possible as you pass.

 Make sure you have a cutting tool accessible, surgical shears ideally, as there is likely to be fishing line around and with the poor visibility and your attention fixed on searching for the cool stuff you might inadvertently become entangled.

Always take a light with you; a critter that is hiding almost invisible to the naked eye can be much more obvious when you restore its true colours with your beam.

Think about getting a pair of short-bladed fins so you can manoeuvre more easily without disturbing the seabed.

What to Look For

You are looking for what muck divers commonly call "critters." The term "critter" is a common Americanism and derives from the word creature. The pointers mentioned in the previous section are often referred to as "critter sticks."

The stars of the muck diving firmament are rare fish with evocative and poetic names such as rhinopias, fingered dragonet, pegasus sea moth, flying gurnard and clown frogfish; fascinating invertebrates such as blue ring and mimic octopus and flamboyant cuttlefish and tiny and brightly coloured shrimps, slugs and crabs of all types.

How to Find Them?

There is no substitute for a sharp eye but you can increase your chances of early success by being aware of a few tips and tricks that the spotters use.

Look at every single feature closely and from a variety of angles. Every stone, piece of trash, pit and hole will conceal an animal even if you can't see it at first. Have patience and take your time.

Look ahead as well as beneath you so you see the octopus or eel that is poking his head out of a hole before he sees you, perceives your proximity as a threat and retreats below the sand.

Watch for movement as you pass. Something may have been spooked into burying itself. Move on, turn and wait; it will re-emerge in time.

Get as close as you can and examine everything closely. Two pieces of weed bobbing and weaving moving simultaneously but out of synchronisation with the waves might be Ambon scorpionfish. What looks like a detached piece of sponge next to a rock could be a baby hairy frogfish.

Learn where to look for specific creatures. For example, ornate ghost pipefish are often found concealed in the fronds of feather stars. Look for a frond that is not attached to the star. That will be the pipefish. Robust ghost pipefish, on the other hand, hide among sea grass. Look for the leaves moving in the current and look for a "leaf" that is not moving in rhythm with the others. Seahorses also hide among the sea grass

Cans, bottles, coconuts, juice cartons, pieces of bamboo and discarded clam shells are just a few of the things that the veined octopus (Octopus marginatus) may choose to adopt as its residence, (see next chapter.) If you find two separate halves of a coconut welded tightly together or a juice bag seemingly cemented to the top of a stick of bamboo, the octopus is inside. Retreat a couple of metres and wait to see if it will emerge.

Don't only look at the sand and the debris. Look closely at commonly found creatures that you would normally just swim by.

Sea cucumbers often host colourful emperor shrimps that live commensally with them as well as swimming crabs that live in the folds they make in the sea cucumber's flesh. Sea stars sometimes have harlequin shrimps feeding on them, while sea urchins are usually home to shrimps and baby fish that seek shelter between the spines. Zebra crabs live on fire urchins, small harlequin swimming crabs live on the trunk of tube anemones, below the fronds and porcelain crabs live between the fronds of sea pens

Just Scratching the Surface

Many of the creatures being discovered by muck divers are new to science and even where the animals were previously known we are observing new behaviour all the time. As I elaborate in the following chapter, it is exciting to imagine what surprises remain to be discovered by someone with patience, a sharp eye and a pointer.

Become a Better Diver by

Getting mucky!

36. Marine Life Diversity & Behaviour

If you think that you are scuba diving at a time when everything is known about life in coastal seas, think again. We are just starting out on the journey of discovery; the oceans are vast and marine life immensely varied.

When professionals gather we will talk of the diving day and compare notes on customers and water conditions but a topic of discussion that will occupy us for hours is what we have seen and how it was behaving? Every day, there is always something new to talk about.

Few of us have anything other than a hobbyist's academic knowledge of fish and animal behaviour. However, while we may not be qualified to understand and comment authoritatively on what we see from a scientific perspective, we do have enormous practical knowledge and no one in the world spends as much time in the water as we do!

Recent Beginnings

For hundreds of years all marine biologists could do was peer motionlessly through a glass or puzzle over dead creatures dredged from the depths. The baby boomers born in the USA and Europe around the middle of the last century were the first people ever to go under water for fun. Before that, everyone who had dived was doing a job and had neither the time nor inclination to take any notice of what was happening around him. Nor, before Cousteau and Gagnan came up with the idea of the aqualung, did anyone have the opportunity to move around very far, mostly tethered as they were to the surface.

Generally speaking, what we know of marine life comes from short submarine excursions into the depths over exceedingly small areas, deep-sea collections obtained by dragging the seabed and exploration along shallow coastal areas

Even in the tiny fragments of ocean that we think we know well, dive sites that are visited day after day, new discoveries are being made all the time. For a long time, divers would swim past gorgonian fans without looking too closely at them until, a few years ago, a fan harvested for an aquarium was hauled into a boat and a small piece dropped off and started wriggling around on the deck. Inspection revealed that it was a tiny seahorse. The news travelled fast through the diving community, guides started taking a closer look at gorgonians and sightings of pygmy seahorses, as they came to be known, started cropping up all over Indonesia, Malaysia. Papua New Guinea and the Philippines.

They had remained undiscovered for so long mainly because they are very small and no one had looked in the right place.

In deeper waters, the extent of just how little we know was demonstrated recently with the recent discovery of a new species of coelacanth on the walls of Manado in Indonesia, thousands of miles away from the only previously known population of this prehistoric fish on the other side of the Indian Ocean.

It is incredibly exciting to think that there is a great chance that when you go diving you may find something or observe behaviour that has never been documented by science. You can be on a journey of exploration even when you dive in a place where people go every day.

Even seasoned professional guides gape in astonishment when confronted with the contortions of the mimic octopus as it apparently imitates other sea creatures in an attempt to confuse potential predators and prey alike. Simply in the case of this one animal, new behaviour is being documented all the time. It appears that disguise is not the only weapon in a mimic's arsenal: I have seen one explode from the seabed into blue water to defend its territory and rise almost to the surface before sinking slowly back down to the sand.

The sea has a habit of laying on unexpected treats for frequent visitors. On December 4th, 2010 in the middle of an algae bloom dive guides on a black sand bay called Puri Jati in the north of Bali, Indonesia went out to their usual muck diving site to find the entire seabed covered with thousands upon thousands of small sea slugs, brown with tiny blue dots. They were there for two days and then they all disappeared and have not been seen since.

The Expert View

Most of us can merely observe; scientific expertise is required to place the behaviour in its true context. Puri Jati is well known for its population of the entertaining veined octopus that I referred to in Chapter 35 "Hidden Treasures." It is incredibly inventive and will scour the sand slopes searching for suitable things to use as a home. Empty sea shells and discarded coconut shells are common choices but, in the absence of a convenient residence fit for the purpose it will improvise with broken shards of shell, sections of coconut husk, chunks of bamboo, even palm fronds or tin foil fruit juice packets. Once it has gone to all the trouble to acquire suitable building materials, it is understandably reluctant to abandon them and is often to be found sauntering along the sea bed carrying its house under a couple of arms. It has even been seen using two half-coconut shells as wheels to propel itself down a slope, keeping a leg or two outside the "vehicle" for direction. For us such astonishing behaviour was just something we loved to show people, it took a group of Australian scientists a couple of years ago to identify it as the first time invertebrates had been recorded using tools!

Take a Moment

There is nothing more disillusioning for a dive guide than finally to manage to find that elusive, reclusive, superbly camouflaged creature that everyone has been searching for, only to have your divers all gather round for a few seconds, take a few pictures, then look up at you expectantly as if to say, "OK, seen that. What's next?" They have mentally ticked the animal off on their wish list and their thoughts have turned elsewhere. You want to tell them that this fish, this rhinopias, this mimic octopus, may be the only one they ever see and it is definitely the rarest, most exotic thing they will see on this dive so they might want to hang around a while and watch how it moves, watch how it works to conceal itself and observe it for a while. But, too late, your audience is gone, scouring the nether regions of a nearby sea cucumber for an emperor shrimp!

However, in the last few years, we have been noticing an increased interest in behaviour, coinciding with the popularity of muck diving, the ubiquity of cameras with video capability, the ease with which snippets of film can be posted on the Internet and the appearance of new marine life guides that describe and explain behaviour instead of just showing a parade of photographs. Divers are now not only asking to see specific animals, they want to see them interacting and exhibiting unique behaviour. They are timing their dive trips to coincide with certain events such as coral spawning. This is exciting for professionals although it does make our lives even more difficult. Finding the animals is hard enough: ensuring that our brief visit to their world coincides with a specific activity is much tougher. You can guess when the thresher sharks are going to be relatively shallow and just off the reef or even when the mantas are going to be over the cleaning stations; but knowing just when a jawfish is going to be hatching eggs in its mouth or when there is a chance that a pregnant pygmy sea horse is about to give birth demands an intimate knowledge of the environment or a great deal of luck.

Join In

So, how do you become a part of this journey of discovery? The first step is to take your time, move more slowly when you dive and open your eyes. Patience is a useful attribute. Do a little background research. Learn what to look for. Life in the sea is not always about survival techniques; it is much more complex than that. There are many examples of animals that live and work together. Some form exclusive life-long relationships; others form groups and even change sex from time to time to maintain the group. Some highly dissimilar animals combine in symbiotic relationships, to the benefit of either one or both and some will imitate the behaviour or appearance of another animal to gain advantage. Some fish seem obsessed with getting themselves cleaned constantly while others are happy to do nothing but provide a 24-hour valet service; and pretty much everything thinks about sex A LOT!

When you go on a dive trip, ask your guides to show you the things that they love to watch when they are diving for fun. They see animals indulging in exotic behaviour all the time and every professional has stories of things they see daily that are not in the books.

To end, here is one of mine. On a shallow reef in Guam's Apra harbour there is a large cable bobbin dumped on its side in 10m (33ft) of water. All around lies the sort of debris you might expect to find in a busy port, including a number of glass Coke bottles, some over 60 years old. If you pick up a Coke bottle from the reef and place it on the bobbin, a single damsel fish will rise from the reef and attack it, knock it over and continue to hurl himself against the glass until the bottle rolls off the bobbin back onto the sand. The scientific view is that this angry little fish is protecting a patch of algae, which damsels farm as a primary food source, but you can put anything else on the bobbin and the fish will completely ignore it. It just hates Coke!

Become a Better Diver by

Keeping your mind and eyes wide open

ABOUT THE AUTHOR

Simon Pridmore was born in England and brought up around the world. After spells as a teacher in Algeria and Oman, he joined the Royal Hong Kong Police in 1982. Ten years later he transferred to the Hong Kong Civil Service, an experience he credits with developing his writing skills. He left Hong Kong in 1997 to become a full-time dive professional and has never looked back.

Simon learned to dive in Oman in 1981. He trained with the Sultan's Armed Forces BSAC Dive Club and was drafted by the club to help teach classes almost immediately after graduation as a Class 3 diver because he was a "schoolie." Later he joined PADI as an Instructor then trained with Rob Cason at Fun Dive in Sydney, Australia to become one of the first IANTD Technical Instructor Trainers in Asia.

In 1995 Simon helped Rob in Phuket, Thailand run the first NITROX instructor trainer course in Asia. Later the same year, he and Paul Neilsen of Mandarin Divers in Hong Kong taught one of the first Advanced NITROX Instructor Courses in the region. The course was conducted simultaneously at La Laguna Beach Resort and Captain Greggs in Puerto Galera in the Philippines. Among the students was future world depth record holder John Bennett.

In 1996 Simon participated in the first sport rebreather training course in Asia, using ex-Australian Navy Dräger FGTs, and completed cave diver and TRIMIX Diver training with Tom Mount in Florida, USA. Then in 1997, after leaving Hong Kong, he established the first dedicated technical diver training centre in Southeast Asia at Professional Sports Divers in Guam, Micronesia and assisted Tom Mount in Thailand with the first TRIMIX Instructor Course in the region.

The same year, Simon dived with Capt. Billy Deans when he was contracted to carry out deep-water surveys using TRIMIX of the suspected wreck site of the sunken Spanish galleon Nuestra Senora del Pilar off the southern tip of Guam. In 2001, he was one of Kevin Gurr's Pilar Project team, which conducted what was, at the time, the most extensive dive operation ever attempted by sport divers exclusively on closed circuit rebreathers.

Between 1997 and 2003 Simon was licensee of the Micronesia franchise of IANTD, which included facilities in Palau, Truk, Kosrae, Majuro and Bikini. Then from 2003 to 2008 he owned and ran the IANTD franchise in the United Kingdom. While in the UK he also worked as Head of Sales, Marketing & Technical Support for Delta P Technology and Closed Circuit Research Ltd: manufacturers of the Ouroboros and Sentinel Closed Circuit Rebreathers and the VR range of dive computers.

Today Simon lives, writes and dives in Bali, Indonesia. As well as Scuba Confidential, he is the author of *Scuba Professional – Insights into Sport Diver Training & Operations* and *Scuba Fundamental – Start Diving the Right Way*. Together with Tim Rock, he has also published Diving & Snorkeling Guides to Bali and Raja Ampat & Northeast Indonesia. He writes regular columns for a variety of magazines and speaks at dive conferences all over the world.

ALSO BY SIMON PRIDMORE

Scuba Professional – Insights into Sport Diver Training & Operations (Sandsmedia / Createspace, 2015)

Scuba Professional is an excellent source of out-of-the-box ideas for instructors and dive operators. It is also an indispensable guide for those aspiring to join the dive industry. But it is not only for professionals. Serious divers who want to know what goes on behind the scenes will be fascinated by the topics addressed and the insights offered.

"There is quite simply nothing like this book: the ultimate backstage pass into the business of scuba." **Jill Heinerth Technical Instructor Trainer & Filmmaker**

"Terrific, really good! Simon captures the key characteristics of the diving instruction milieu with insight and clarity." **Associate Professor Simon Mitchell, Diving Physician**

"The closest thing we have to an 'insiders guide to the dive industry." **Peter Symes Publisher X-Ray Magazine**

Scuba Fundamental – Start Diving the Right Way (Sandsmedia /Createspace, 2016)

Do you know someone who is thinking of starting scuba diving? This book is for them. It is not your standard how-to scuba diving manual. It takes the philosophy of Scuba Confidential and Scuba Professional and applies it to the process of learning to dive. *Scuba Fundamental* is a unique, reliable and essential guide: one that beginners can trust completely and follow during the early stages of their diving life.

"Pitching a book at the correct level for divers-to-be is fraught with difficulty. Simon is a great dive writer, and I think he's finally cracked the problem." **Steve Weinmann – Editor, Diver Magazine (UK)**

"I wish I had had this book to read when I learned to dive. I remember being totally confused." **Robin Yao, Executive Editor, EZDIVE magazine**

"This is the book divers should give to friends when they say they want to learn to scuba dive." **Ian Thomas, Author and Scuba Instructor Trainer**

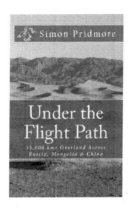

Under the Flight Path – 15,000 kms Overland Across Russia, Mongolia & China (Sandsmedia / Createspace 2017)

"A vivid, witty account of a couple's no-frills travel across Eurasia. An inspiration to real travellers - Yes! It's Possible! Do it! - but also an entertainment for those who prefer their armchairs." **John Man, author of Genghis Khan, Life, Death and Resurrection**

" Under the Flight Path is entertaining and informative, written in a lively, engaging style and the narrative flows beautifully." **Jackie Winter, author of Life in Tandem and Lipsticks and Library Books**

"Under the Flight Path is a special travel memoir that is a journey in itself. Warm, candid and funny." **Amy Johnstone, author and founder of Story**

"A fast-paced page-turner featuring Simon's special brand of humour, insight and knowledge of Russian and Asian culture and history. What a delight! **Tim Rock, Lonely Planet author**

**Diving & Snorkeling Guide to Bali (with Tim Rock)
(Doubleblue / Mantaray Publishing, USA 2016)**

**Diving & Snorkeling Guide to Raja Ampat & Northeast
Indonesia (with Tim Rock) (Doubleblue / Mantaray
Publishing, USA 2016)**

Printed in Great Britain
by Amazon